Soup Makes the Meal

Best wish

SOUP
makes the meal

150 Soul-Satisfying Recipes for Soups, Salads, and Breads

KEN HAEDRICH

THE HARVARD COMMON PRESS
·····
BOSTON, MASSACHUSETTS

THE HARVARD COMMON PRESS
535 ALBANY STREET
BOSTON, MASSACHUSETTS 02118

Printed in the United States of America

Printed on acid-free paper

Library of Congress Cataloging-in-Publication Data

Haedrich, Ken
    Soup makes the meal : 150 soul-satisfying recipes for soups, salads, and breads / Ken Haedrich.
        p. cm.
    Includes index.
    ISBN 1-55832-186-1 (hc : alk. paper) — ISBN 1-55832-187-X (pbk. : alk. paper)
    1. Soups. 2. Salads. 3. Bread. 4. Menus. I. Title.

TX757.H32 2001
641.8'13—dc21   2001024370

Special bulk-order discounts are available on this and other Harvard Common Press books. Companies and organizations may purchase books for premiums or resale, or may arrange a custom edition, by contacting the Marketing Director at the address above.

Cover and book design by Inkstone Design
Cover and interior illustrations by Melissa Sweet

10 9 8 7 6 5 4 3 2 1

Dedication

FOR BEV

You're the warmth in my soups

The leavening in my breads

The color in this salad bowl of life.

Contents

FRESH BEGINNINGS
*Springtime Soups from the
Pantry and Garden*

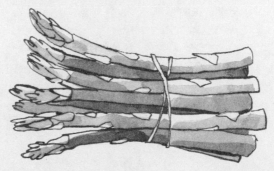

CONTENTS

WINTER HEARTY AND WHOLESOME
When Only Serious Soup Will Do

Acknowledgments

For whatever measure of success I've managed to attain as a writer, I have many people to thank, most notably the numerous fine editors and editorial assistants I've had the opportunity to work with over the years. They include:

Nancy Wall Hopkins, Nancy Byal, and Anna Anderson, my holy trinity of fine souls at *Better Homes and Gardens*: what a pleasure it has been.

Jill Melton at *Cooking Light*.

Kristine Kidd, Barbara Fairchild, Sarah Tenaglia, Anthony Head, Katie O'Kennedy, Victoria von Biel, and the late William Garry at *Bon Appétit*.

James Badham, formerly of *Bon Appétit*, now at *Islands* magazine.

Cindy Littlefield at *Family Fun*.

Georgia Orcutt at *Yankee*; Susan Peery, formerly of *Yankee*.

Sheila Buckmaster, Jayne Wise, and Jonathan Tourtellot at *National Geographic Traveler*.

Kathy Farrell Kingsley at *Vegetarian Times*.

Rochelle Palermo at *Cooking.com*.

Nissa Simon at *New Choices*.

In addition, I'd like to thank my agent, Meg Ruley, and Don Cleary at the Jane Rotrosen Agency for their usual fine work on my behalf.

My gratitude to Bruce Shaw, Pam Hoenig, Valerie Cimino, and the entire staff at Harvard Common Press for inviting me into the fold, keeping this book on track, and applying the polish that makes a good book a great one.

My children—Ben, Tess, Ali, and Sam—deserve a word of gratitude for their forthright appraisal of my cooking, and for not saying, "What, soup again?" (at least too often) while I worked on this book.

Thanks to my siblings and parents for everything you've done for me over the years.

And to Bev Moss, who helped and supported me in so many ways during the writing of this book.

Introduction

Those who know me well will tell you that one of my most oft-expressed cooking fantasies is to have a little café, just a handful of tables and some stools at the counter, and serve but one constantly changing menu day in and day out: soup, bread, and salad. It would, of course, be a friendly little place where the food is always good and reasonably priced, the conversation lively, a place my customers would feel at home and swap stories with their friends. I would be the cook, of course, but it wouldn't feel like work, since I'd be serving the foods I like best to people I care about.

The problem is, I've been having this fantasy for the last twenty years and I'm no closer to its reality than I was when I was a young man, which I no longer am. Life, family, and other dreams seem to have had their own way with me. Which, at this point, is probably all for the better: I'm past the point of wanting to spend twelve hours a day on my feet, in a hot kitchen.

The fact that you're holding this book, however, should indicate that I never did give up on the fantasy altogether; I simply did what anyone with a knack for words would have done, and translated it into print. No, that's not quite the same as putting a bowl of something hot and fragrant in front of someone and watching the pleasure that registers on their face once they've taken a slurp. But this is a good start, and the best way of sharing some of the wonderful soup, bread, and salad meals I've cooked up in my kitchen at home. Now the rest is up to you: find a recipe or menu that looks good, set aside a little time, and get ready to cook up something special. That's the one big advantage of inviting you into my kitchen via the printed page; you get to participate in the process. And I don't have to do the dishes.

I've given a lot of thought as to what I find so appealing about the idea of serving soup, bread, and salad together. And what I've decided—beyond the obvious inherent appeal these foods have for me—is this: I love the symmetry and balance of such a menu. It's a formula you can depend on, one—despite the ever-changing ways in which we approach mealtime—whose appeal remains sure and steady no matter which way the fickle winds of food fashion blow. We can rely on the formula in the same way, perhaps, that Neil Simon does when he sits down to write a play, knowing that he will do so in three acts. And just as Mr. Simon inserts characters and situations that suit the story, we can introduce recipes that fit our schedules, our circumstances, our budgets, and our appetites.

So, what you have here are fifty soup, bread, and salad menus that more or less take you through the entire cooking year. Among other things, these reflect a certain amount of seasonal opportunism, taking into account the availability of seasonal produce. I realize that the whole concept of seasonal eating is getting blurrier all the time, given the year-round availability of so much produce. Most of us can, for instance, make a fresh asparagus soup any time of year, not just in late spring when the local crop is arriving in the market. Be that as it may, there's still a prime time for much of what we eat and these menus are arranged in such a way to help alert you to those times. The difference between something that's merely fresh, and something that's fresh, local, and in season, often spells the difference between a good meal and an exceptional one.

Like most people today, I don't want to spend all my waking hours in the kitchen. Sure, there are some days I'm content to do simply that, but life seldom allows me the chance. Still, there are usually a couple of days a week, often on the weekends, when I want to serve something more than just another quick pasta dish, days when I want to cook for the sheer pleasure of it and then sit down to a fetching, delicious, family feast. Those are generally the days when I turn to one of my soup, bread, and salad meals.

Which brings us to the subject of breads. There's nothing I love more than a crusty yeast bread, and since yeast bread was my first love in the kitchen, I still make it as often as I can. I realize, however, that yeast bread takes a commitment of time that many people just can't make today. This would be a greater tragedy were it not for the fact that there are so many excellent nonyeast quick breads one can count on to deliver great taste with a minimum of effort and no kneading. Thus, the majority of the breads in this collection are the quick sort—biscuits, muffins, soda breads, cornbreads, and scones—that often take less than an hour to get into the oven and out. I should hasten to add—should you happen to be a dedicated yeast bread baker—that the yeast breads I have included here are spectacularly adaptable, and among them you will find breads that work beautifully with many of the soups in the book.

A Few Words About How to Use This Book

When you go to the clothing store and purchase an outfit, you buy a particular pair of pants, shirt, and sweater because you like the way they look together, right? And quite often they do more than just make a good match; they take on a life and personality all their own. Maybe it becomes a favorite church outfit, Friday outfit, night-on-the-town-with-friends outfit, or date outfit. Still, even if you like the way this one outfit works, you sometimes mix and match the items with other things in your wardrobe for other occasions, don't you? That's the way it is with these recipes and menus. The recipes in a given combination taste and look great together and they're joined by a common thread. But I sure as heck do a lot of mixing and matching of these recipes, and I hope you will, too.

In fact, I think it's a safe bet that there are many, many times when you will use this book à la carte, so to speak, picking and choosing something that looks good to you and matching it with something else from another menu. Please do. It makes perfect sense and, besides, I'd be the first to admit that there will always be a measure of arbitrariness to designing a menu. Just because this soup, that bread, and another salad add up to a wonderful meal in my book is no guarantee that they will for you.

I'm sorry sometimes that my little "soup kitchen" is never going to be a brick-and-mortar reality. But I'm very grateful you have this book in your hands so that you and I can share, if only in spirit and from afar, these favorite recipes. Here's hoping that this book—like the café of my fantasies—brings you pleasure in the kitchen, joy at the table, and fond meal-time memories for years to come.

Taking Stock

I'm of two minds when it comes to soup stock: on the one hand, there's nothing quite like your own. Homemade stock will always have better flavor than anything you get in a can or from a cube. On the other hand, since I live in the real world, too, I know that stock is no longer the by-product of our daily lives. Perhaps it once was, when we all lived on farms and country cooks were at the stove all day long, tossing choice morsels into the stockpot. Today, the country cook has been supplanted by the soccer mom, the corporate parent, the career office worker. We may be multitasking, but seldom is the task *du jour* a date with the stockpot.

So, first let's talk about an ideal world, where homemade stock is still possible. It really isn't difficult, nor labor intensive—just time consuming, though little of it is actual hands-on time. It's really weekend work, when you don't have to feel rushed about it. Then let's talk about the convenience items, like bouillon cubes and canned broth, that most of us, at least occasionally, find ourselves dependent on.

Making Homemade Stock

There are two kinds of soup stock: the kind you read about in cookbooks and the kind people really make. The former is always a work of art, a thing of beauty that's nuanced to within an inch of its life—meticulously measured, simmered, skimmed, clarified, and otherwise blessed.

Then one day you walk into a professional kitchen and you see what stock making is really all about. It's less a piece of precision choreography than it is a free-for-all, the stockpot representing a sort of bubbling, borderline compost heap into which nearly everything goes in quantities that defy rhyme or reason: vegetable scraps, meat trimmings, and leftovers. There's no recipe, and seemingly few rules, but in the final analysis they still make great stock.

My point, if I have one, is this: stock making for the home cook is not an art. It's hardly even a craft because you could almost teach a monkey to make stock—that's how simple it is to do. Are there rules and guidelines? Sure, a few, but nothing you wouldn't eventually figure out on your own if I didn't mention it here. And even if you broke the rules, winged it, added too much of something and not enough of something else, you'd probably be fine. Unless you break rule number one.

Rule number one has to do with the most important four-letter word in soup making: salt. In a nutshell, less is more, and more is probably going to be too much. Remember that as your stock concentrates, so does the salt. Add very little salt to the stockpot when you begin—no more than about $1/2$ to $3/4$ teaspoon. You can't do much about a stock that's been overly salted because, if you dilute the stock with water, you end up diluting the flavor.

The next rule is to wrap as many of your herbs and seasonings as you can in a bundle the French call a bouquet garni. There's a good reason for this. When you make meat-based stocks, impurities rise to the surface of the liquid in a foam, which you will need to skim off. Problem is, lots of other things will rise to the surface, too—namely herbs—and you will eventually skim them away if they're not contained. A bouquet garni keeps them all in one place. By the same token, vegetables for stock should be cut into large pieces too, or you'll find yourself constantly skimming around them.

More About Salt

I don't think I'm overstating the case by saying that salt is the single most important ingredient affecting the outcome of your soup. Salt gives definition to flavors that seem vague without it. It doesn't like to—and never should—grab the spotlight. Its purpose is to linger in the background, lending encouragement and bringing out the best in others.

Think of salt as something that you add in stages, not—like when you're mixing a bread—something that goes in all at once. In baking, you generally have no choice. In soup making, you do, so exercise that choice. In the first stage, you add roughly half to two thirds of the salt the soup will need; a certain amount of salt is a given. Beyond that, add it gradually, letting it dissolve and incorporate for several minutes. Then taste again before adding any more. Don't shake salt out of a shaker into the soup; the salt in the shaker will get damp and clumpy. Or—worse yet—pour it out of the box into a measuring spoon directly over the soup pot; a spill could have tragic results. Rather, keep it in a ramekin or other open container near the stove and add it in pinches big and small, always with dry fingers so it doesn't stick. This method makes it difficult to over salt a soup, essentially training the cook to use salt with the discretion it requires.

How to Make a Bouquet Garni

Just as a bouquet of flowers can fill a room with a lovely scent, a bouquet garni can impart a wonderfully subtle flavor to a potful of stock. Soup stock made without a bouquet garni isn't tragically flawed, it's just a little lacking, not quite what it could be—and unnecessarily so, since a bouquet garni is both simple to prepare and one of those little stock-making rituals you're sure to look forward to once you've learned how to do it.

To make a bouquet garni for chicken or beef stock, bundle together 5 or 6 full sprigs of parsley, 2 bay leaves, several sprigs of thyme, and a thick strip of lemon zest. Nest them in a rib of celery, tie them together with kitchen string, and add them to the stockpot. Peppercorns should go into a small cheesecloth bag, gathered together and tied. Use the same method to make a dried bouquet garni, if fresh herbs aren't handy. Simply mix equal parts—about 1 teaspoon each—dried parsley, thyme, and chopped bay leaves and tie them in a little cheesecloth bag. Add the bag at the beginning and remove it with the other solids when the stock is drained.

Once your stock begins to boil, turn down the heat and simmer very gently. You want the liquid to reduce gradually, by roughly half, over the course of several hours. Don't stir the pot or the resulting stock will be cloudier than it will be clear. And don't ask me why.

Stock is strained by placing a colander over another pot or bowl and carefully emptying the contents of the stockpot through it. Remove the colander after 15 minutes of drip-drying. Let the stock cool to room temperature, then refrigerate it. The next day, skim off and discard the fat that will have hardened on top of the stock and store. The stock can be refrigerated for a couple of days, but, if there's any doubt about when you will use it, pour it into plastic freezer containers and freeze right away; it will keep frozen for up to 1 month.

Basic Chicken Stock

4 to 5 pounds chicken parts
(backs, wings, and scraps)

3 ribs celery

2 large carrots, peeled and halved
lengthwise

2 large onions, halved

1 large leek, white and light green parts,
halved lengthwise and rinsed well

1 large parsnip, peeled and halved
lengthwise

3 cloves garlic, peeled

1 bouquet garni (page 3)

5 black peppercorns, tied up in a
cheesecloth bag

5 quarts cold water

3/4 teaspoon salt

1. Put all the ingredients in a very large stockpot. There should be enough water to easily cover everything. Bring to a boil, skimming the foam from the surface of the stock with a large spoon. When the liquid reaches a rolling boil, turn down the heat and simmer the stock, uncovered, for 3 to 4 hours, skimming occasionally. The stock is cooking properly when bubbles break on the surface but the liquid is not boiling madly. Do not stir.

2. When the liquid is reduced by roughly half, remove the stock from the heat and strain it through a colander into a large bowl or another pot. Let the stock cool to room temperature, then refrigerate. The next day, skim the hardened fat from the surface of the stock and discard it. Pour the stock into plastic freezer containers and refrigerate for up to 2 days or freeze.

MAKES ABOUT 2 QUARTS

BASIC TURKEY STOCK: Prepare the chicken stock but substitute a turkey carcass, wings, and other turkey parts for the chicken parts. Add a sprig of sage and rosemary to the bouquet garni, if desired. Proceed as for the chicken stock.

BASIC BEEF STOCK: Prepare the chicken stock but substitute 4 pounds of beef bones for the chicken parts. Have your butcher split the bones to save you the trouble. Place the bones in a large roasting pan and brown them in a preheated 450 degree F oven for 30 minutes. This browning will give the stock a darker color and a deeper, more "roasted" flavor, and it will render out the fat. Transfer the bones only—not the fat that's cooked off them—to the stockpot, adding 2 halved and seeded tomatoes as well. Proceed as for the chicken stock.

Basic Vegetable Stock

Aside from the obvious difference that it contains no meat products, vegetable stock follows a slightly different routine. For one, the vegetables are first sautéed to quickly bring out the flavor. And the stock is simmered for a much shorter time. Include other vegetables at your discretion.

1½ tablespoons olive oil
2 medium-size leeks, white part only, halved lengthwise, rinsed well, and coarsely chopped
1 large onion, chopped
3 cloves garlic, bruised

2 ribs celery, chopped
2 large carrots, peeled and coarsely chopped
1 bouquet garni (page 3)
10 cups cold water
½ teaspoon salt

Heat the olive oil in a very large soup pot or stockpot over moderate heat. Add the leeks, onion, and garlic and cook, stirring, for 10 minutes. Add the remaining ingredients and bring to a boil. Reduce the heat slightly but continue to cook at an active simmer, uncovered, for about 30 minutes. Strain the stock through a colander into a large bowl. Let cool to room temperature, then refrigerate. Freeze the stock if not using within a day or two; it will keep for up to 1 month.

MAKES ABOUT 6 CUPS

Stock from Convenience Products

As I implied earlier, in an ideal world we would all make our own soup stock on a daily basis. We do not live in that world. In our real world, people have jobs, kids, and mortgages that are coming due. We might fit stock making in there somewhere, but the rest of the time we use convenience products that allow us to get soup on the table tonight for dinner.

Among these convenience items are canned broths, bouillon cubes, and granulated bouillon. The flavor of some of these products is quite good—full, smooth, and satisfying. Others are less so. I find that certain canned vegetable broths, especially on their own, hit a discordant note or two. Whatever sins these products are guilty of, however, they are often disguised or hidden in the final analysis.

Despite explicit admonishments on nearly all of these products warning us not to, I generally dilute them, both for reasons of economy and gastronomy. How much I dilute them depends on the nature and circumstances of my soup. If you're preparing, say, a soup with lots of strong flavors such as tomatoes, sausage, Italian herbs, and beans, you can dilute them more freely—in the case of a simpler soup, like chicken noodle, where the broth plays a larger part, less so. *As a rule of thumb, however, I generally add ¹/2 cup water for every 1 cup of prepared broth I use in a soup.*

Bouillon cubes and granulated bouillon are convenient and less expensive than some of the better prepared broths but their flavor tends to be less refined and saltier. But again, you can make excellent soup with these products. Most say to use 1 teaspoon or 1 bouillon cube for every 1 cup water used, but I usually use 1¹/2 cups water and get very good results.

If you're going to make soup often, it pays to experiment with different convenience products. Sample them plain (heated), see which ones appeal to your palate, and how much, if any, you should dilute them for making soup. Then stick with this routine so it becomes second nature in your soup making, and one less thing you have to think about.

FRESH BEGINNINGS

*Springtime Soups
from the Pantry and
Garden*

TONIC FOR A SPRING TUNE-UP

A Spring Tonic Soup
....
Wheat Germ Carrot-Raisin Muffins
....
Asparagus, New Potato, and Pasta Salad
....

Springtime is full of rituals. We clean out the garage, prepare the garden, dust off the exercise equipment we've neglected all winter. Our body goes through its own rituals, too, adjusting to more sunlight, a little less sleep. The seasonal change sometimes brings on a cleansing cold: for weeks we feel terrible, then gradually regain our health and strength, in the end to feel like a new person.

This combination is built around the flux of spring, a time of fresh new promises and new produce. For cranky colds and days when you're feeling less than perfect, there's a restorative tonic soup. When you aren't feeling your best, or are perhaps a little bit blue because spring is dragging its feet, you don't want to putter with a soup for hours on end; this soup knows that and it can be put together very quickly. And you'll feel much better after you've eaten it.

Springtime encourages healthy new eating habits, too; these wheat germ carrot muffins are one way to facilitate that. I love to bake with wheat germ because I like the nutty flavor. And since I'm not getting any younger, I do what I can to incorporate into my diet as many good-for-me foods as I can. For more on this, please read my headnote to the recipe.

The increased level of activity that comes with spring—riding bikes, running, gardening—can make for sharp appetites, of the sort you'd want to stoke with this spring-inspired pasta and potato salad. It's hearty enough that you could almost make a meal of it alone. But even if you do, come back another time for the soup and muffins because they should not be missed.

A Spring Tonic Soup

In her book *The Savory Way* (Bantam Books, 1990), Deborah Madison has a recipe for a spring tonic soup. I liked the idea so much I borrowed the name, though not the recipe. Hers is quite a bit more complex, including escarole, sorrel leaves, and nettles, whatever they are. You might call mine the abridged version. This is essentially the soup I've been making for years when my kids are sick and have to lay off the rich foods and eat something light, brothy, and restorative. Among other attributes, it has a great aroma and a steamy bowl placed before you clears the sinuses immediately. There's lots of garlic here, too, which we all know will help us live to be a hundred. But you don't have to be ill to enjoy the soup, just hungry. If you have leeks on hand, use a couple of them instead of the onion.

1½ tablespoons olive oil

1 large onion, finely chopped

1 large carrot, peeled and diced

1 large all-purpose potato, peeled and diced

1 parsnip, peeled and diced

4 cloves garlic, minced

5 cups vegetable stock

¼ to ½ teaspoon salt, to your taste

Handful fresh parsley leaves, chopped

Large handful spinach leaves (3 to 4 ounces), rinsed well and coarsely chopped

Freshly ground black pepper to taste

1. Heat the olive oil in a medium-size soup pot or large saucepan. Add the vegetables and garlic and cook, stirring occasionally, over moderate heat for 5 minutes. Add the stock and salt, then bring the soup to an active simmer.

2. Simmer the soup, partially covered, for 5 minutes. Stir in the parsley and spinach and season with pepper. Simmer the soup, partially covered, for 5 more minutes; check to see if it needs more salt or pepper. (Colds tend to dull the taste buds, so sick folk might need a little extra flavor punch to actually taste the soup.) Serve piping hot.

MAKES 4 TO 5 SERVINGS

Wheat Germ Carrot-Raisin Muffins

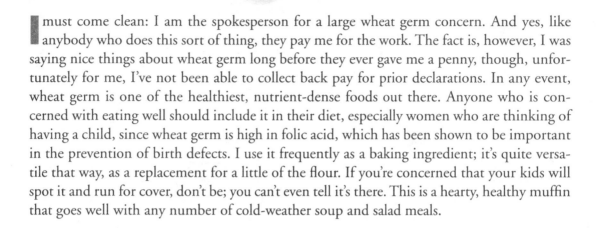

I must come clean: I am the spokesperson for a large wheat germ concern. And yes, like anybody who does this sort of thing, they pay me for the work. The fact is, however, I was saying nice things about wheat germ long before they ever gave me a penny, though, unfortunately for me, I've not been able to collect back pay for prior declarations. In any event, wheat germ is one of the healthiest, nutrient-dense foods out there. Anyone who is concerned with eating well should include it in their diet, especially women who are thinking of having a child, since wheat germ is high in folic acid, which has been shown to be important in the prevention of birth defects. I use it frequently as a baking ingredient; it's quite versatile that way, as a replacement for a little of the flour. If you're concerned that your kids will spot it and run for cover, don't be; you can't even tell it's there. This is a hearty, healthy muffin that goes well with any number of cold-weather soup and salad meals.

1 cup raisins or currants	1/4 cup finely chopped walnuts or
2 cups unbleached all-purpose flour	pecans
1 1/2 teaspoons baking powder	1 large egg
1/2 teaspoon baking soda	1 cup buttermilk
1/2 teaspoon salt	1/4 cup pure maple syrup
1/2 teaspoon ground cinnamon	1/4 cup sugar
1/2 teaspoon ground ginger	1/4 cup vegetable oil
1/4 cup toasted wheat germ	3/4 cup grated carrots

1. Cover the raisins or currants with warm water and set aside for 15 to 20 minutes. Near the end of soaking, preheat the oven to 400 degrees F. Grease 10 muffin cups; set aside.

2. Sift the flour, baking powder, baking soda, salt, and spices into a medium-size bowl. Mix in the wheat germ and nuts. Set aside.

3. Whisk the egg in a separate bowl. Whisk in the buttermilk, maple syrup, sugar, and oil. Make a well in the center of the dry ingredients and add the liquid. Stir gently until almost blended, then add the carrots and (drained) raisins or currants and stir just until blended. Divide the batter evenly between the cups.

4. Bake muffins until lightly browned, 20 to 22 minutes. When done, the muffins will be golden and should feel springy to the touch. Let cool in the pan, on a wire rack, for 2 or 3 minutes. Run a knife around the edge of the muffins, then turn them out and let cool on the rack. Serve warm from a cloth-covered basket.

MAKES 10 MUFFINS

Asparagus, New Potato, and Pasta Salad

The turmeric in this salad gives it a pale yellow blush that reminds me of the Easter season. My preference is to use only the asparagus tips here and save the stalks for the stockpot or some other use.

....

1 pound fresh asparagus

1¹⁄₂ pounds small red-skinned potatoes

3 tablespoons olive oil

3 tablespoons mayonnaise

2 tablespoons tarragon vinegar

1 tablespoon Dijon mustard

1 tablespoon chopped fresh parsley leaves

¹⁄₄ teaspoon sugar

Dash of cayenne pepper

Pinch of turmeric

Salt and freshly ground black pepper to taste

¹⁄₄ pound thin spaghetti, broken in half

3 hard-cooked eggs, peeled and chopped

....

1. Bring a large saucepan of salted water to a boil. Cut the asparagus stalks in half, saving the bottoms for another use. Cut the top portion of the stalks in half; set aside. Halve the potatoes if they are small, or cut them into bite-size chunks if they're larger.

2. When the water boils, add the potatoes and return the water to a boil. Let it boil for about 3 minutes, then add the asparagus. When the water returns to a boil, cook the vegetables until both are tender, another 5 to 7 minutes. Drain, then immediately spread the vegetables on a platter to cool. Fill the same saucepan with salted water and bring to a boil once again.

3. Meanwhile, whisk the olive oil, mayonnaise, vinegar, mustard, parsley, sugar, cayenne pepper, and turmeric together in a large bowl. Add the still-warm vegetables and toss well, seasoning with salt and black pepper. Set aside.

4. When the water comes to a boil, add the spaghetti. Cook the pasta, according to the package directions, until tender. Drain well, then immediately add to the vegetables and toss well. Let cool in the bowl, gently tossing once or twice.

5. When the salad has cooled, cover with plastic wrap and refrigerate if not serving promptly. To serve, transfer the salad to a serving dish and garnish the top with the chopped egg.

MAKES 5 TO 6 SERVINGS

MODEST MEANS, RICH RESULTS

Cabbage Paprikash Soup

....

Oatmeal Bannocks

....

Potato, Beet, and Pickle Salad

....

Money can buy a lot of things, including a good meal, but it would be a mistake to conclude that those of lesser means have historically enjoyed fewer good meals than the rest of us. Quite often, just the opposite is true. Is the fisherman's family—whose wife serves stew made from fish heads and scraps—any worse off than the politician's family who eats the fillets purchased from the fisherman? I think not.

This menu features a few of the foods that cooks of lesser means have traditionally cooked with, because either they were plentiful or cheap, or there was little else to choose from in the sparsely populated early spring pantry: cabbage, oatmeal, potatoes, and beets. Some think of them as peasant foods, but good cooks see right to the heart of the matter: good taste. And there's an added irony when you consider how reliably high in quality these items are. I can buy 10 pounds of potatoes for three dollars and not find a bad one in the batch.

Cabbage is a great addition to soup. When you sauté cabbage, as I do for this paprikash soup, its natural sweetness melts into the broth and gives it a complex, earthy flavor. Potatoes could go into the soup, but I serve them on the side instead, here with beets and chopped pickles dressed with mayonnaise and sour cream. It's a little rich, but perfect with the lean tomato acidity of the soup.

Bread is the bannocks, sometimes made with barley flour, sometimes with oats. They originated in Scotland, where wheat does not grow well. Imagine sort of an oatmeal scone with fewer of the refinements, and you'll have a good idea what a bannock is. They're one of the oldest recorded breads and peasant food extraordinaire.

Cabbage Paprikash Soup

Easy to make and economical, this is one of those winter standards you crave if you happen to live where the weather turns cold and wet in winter, as it surely does here in New England. (We have a saying in New Hampshire, "We've got eleven months of winter and one month of damn poor sleddin'," and there have been many years when there was more truth to that than I'd care to remember.) All soups have a particular feel in the mouth, a way of going down; this one has a sharp, cleansing feel, with a slight but distinctly sweet-tart tomato bite that tastes wonderful. It's a pretty soup, a sort of rusty paprika red that looks quite inviting with a dollop of sour cream and garnish of fresh parsley.

2 tablespoons unsalted butter	1 large carrot, peeled and grated
1 large onion, quartered and thinly sliced	2 tablespoons tomato paste
4 cups cored and thinly sliced cabbage	Juice of 1 lemon
Salt	2 to 3 teaspoons sugar, to your taste
2 cloves garlic, minced	Freshly ground black pepper to taste
1 tablespoon sweet paprika	Sour cream, for garnish
6 cups chicken or vegetable stock	Chopped fresh parsley leaves, for
½ cup canned chopped or crushed tomatoes	garnish

1. Melt the butter in a medium-size soup pot over moderate heat. Stir in the onion and cook, stirring, until translucent, 8 to 9 minutes. Add the cabbage, salt lightly, and cook until all the cabbage is wilted, about 10 minutes more. Stir in the garlic and paprika and cook, stirring often, for 1 minute. Add the stock, tomatoes, carrot, and tomato paste and season again with salt. Bring to a boil, then reduce the heat to moderately low and simmer gently, stirring occasionally, for 10 minutes.

2. Add about half each of the lemon juice and sugar; simmer briefly, then taste, adding more sugar and lemon juice to get a mellow but distinctly sweet-tart broth. Season with pepper. Serve piping hot, with the garnishes.

MAKES 6 SERVINGS

Oatmeal Bannocks

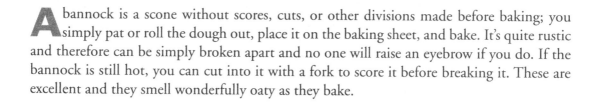

A bannock is a scone without scores, cuts, or other divisions made before baking; you simply pat or roll the dough out, place it on the baking sheet, and bake. It's quite rustic and therefore can be simply broken apart and no one will raise an eyebrow if you do. If the bannock is still hot, you can cut into it with a fork to score it before breaking it. These are excellent and they smell wonderfully oaty as they bake.

$\frac{1}{3}$ **cup rolled (old-fashioned, not instant or quick-cooking) oats, plus a few to sprinkle on the sheet and on top of the bannocks**

$1\frac{1}{3}$ **cups unbleached all-purpose flour**

$\frac{1}{3}$ **cup whole wheat flour**

$\frac{1}{3}$ **cup sugar, plus a little to sprinkle on top**

$2\frac{1}{2}$ **teaspoons baking powder**

$\frac{1}{2}$ **teaspoon salt**

$\frac{1}{4}$ **teaspoon ground cinnamon**

6 tablespoons ($\frac{3}{4}$ stick) cold unsalted butter, cut into $\frac{1}{4}$-inch pieces

$\frac{1}{2}$ **cup finely chopped walnuts**

$\frac{1}{2}$ **cup light cream or half-and-half, plus a little to brush on top**

1. Preheat the oven to 425 degrees F. Lightly grease a large baking sheet and sprinkle with a few oats. Set aside.

2. Mix oats, the flours, sugar, baking powder, salt, and cinnamon together in a large bowl. Add the butter and cut it into the dry ingredients with a pastry blender—or with your fingers—until the mixture resembles a fine meal. Mix in the walnuts.

3. Make a well in the center of the dry ingredients and add the cream all at once. Stir with a wooden spoon just until the dough coheres; let rest for 3 minutes.

4. With floured hands, knead the dough in the bowl 2 or 3 times. Turn out onto a lightly floured work surface and divide the dough in half. Put half of the dough on a large piece of wax paper or plastic wrap. Fold half of the paper or plastic over the dough, then pat the dough out into a circle just slightly thicker than $\frac{1}{2}$ inch. Remove the paper or plastic and transfer the dough to the prepared baking sheet. Repeat for the other half of the dough.

5. Brush about 1 tablespoon of cream or milk over each bannock. Sprinkle each one with oats and a little bit of sugar. Bake the bannocks until golden, 15 to 17 minutes. Transfer the bannocks to a wire rack and eat as soon as possible.

MAKES ABOUT 6 SERVINGS

Potato, Beet, and Pickle Salad

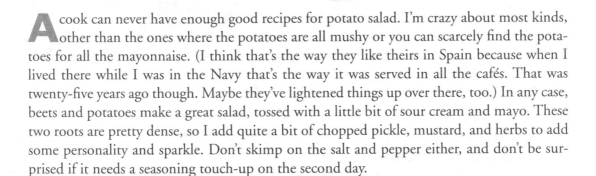

A cook can never have enough good recipes for potato salad. I'm crazy about most kinds, other than the ones where the potatoes are all mushy or you can scarcely find the potatoes for all the mayonnaise. (I think that's the way they like theirs in Spain because when I lived there while I was in the Navy that's the way it was served in all the cafés. That was twenty-five years ago though. Maybe they've lightened things up over there, too.) In any case, beets and potatoes make a great salad, tossed with a little bit of sour cream and mayo. These two roots are pretty dense, so I add quite a bit of chopped pickle, mustard, and herbs to add some personality and sparkle. Don't skimp on the salt and pepper either, and don't be surprised if it needs a seasoning touch-up on the second day.

5 or 6 medium-size beets, tops discarded
    and scrubbed
3 cups bite-size red-skinned potato
    chunks
Salt
2 tablespoons red wine vinegar
1¹⁄₂ cups diced dill pickles
1 rib celery, finely chopped
¹⁄₄ to ¹⁄₂ cup finely chopped red onion,
    to your taste

¹⁄₄ cup mayonnaise
¹⁄₄ cup sour cream
1¹⁄₂ tablespoons Dijon mustard
1¹⁄₂ tablespoons chopped fresh dill
1¹⁄₂ tablespoons chopped fresh parsley
    leaves
Freshly ground black pepper to taste

1. Put the beets in a large saucepan and cover with plenty of water. Bring to a boil, then continue to boil until the beets are tender at the center, 30 to 45 minutes; test with a paring knife or cake tester. Drain. When cool enough to handle, rub off the skins and cut the beets into ¹⁄₂-inch dice. Transfer to a large bowl.

2. While the beets cook, put the potatoes in a medium-size saucepan and cover with salted water. Bring to a boil and cook until just tender, 8 to 12 minutes. Drain, then spread in a shallow casserole and splash with the vinegar. Let cool to room temperature.

3. Add the pickles, celery, onion, and cooled potatoes (with any loose vinegar) to the beets. In a small bowl, blend together the remaining ingredients and pour this dressing over the vegetables. Toss well to coat evenly, seasoning with salt and pepper. Cover with plastic wrap and refrigerate if not serving right away.

MAKES 6 SERVINGS

WHEN LETTUCE MAKES THE SOUP, BEANS THE SALAD

Lettuce Soup

....

Crostini of Olive and Sun-Dried Tomato Spread

....

White Bean and Artichoke Heart Salad

....

It's funny how we develop food prejudices, and interesting what it takes to get past them. Take me and lettuce soup, for instance. For just about my entire adult cooking life, I had seen recipes for it here and there. And just as frequently I would skip right over them without a second glance. It didn't matter that these recipes appeared in reputable places. There was simply no appeal. As far as I was concerned, you ate lettuce in salads, period. It probably didn't help that my daughter Tess keeps bunnies. At one time she had about fifteen of them in a couple of bunny condos she and I built. Off the kitchen, in their little dining nook, was a big bowl of bunny water and next to it a spot where Tess would put their nightly salad of kitchen trimmings, the latter inevitably ending up floating around in the former by morning when we went out to feed them. To me, that was lettuce soup.

At least it was until I went to visit my friend Brother Victor (see page 79), a cookbook author himself. While I was at his monastery he prepared soup for us. On the stove was a big pot of simmering stock and vegetables; next to it was this mountain of greens, including watercress, sorrel, parsley, and enough lettuce to feed a Marine division. As we spoke about food and cooking and the monastic life, I watched as he shoved great handfuls of greens into the soup only to see them disappear into the broth. There was no measuring cup in sight. It reminded me of a road worker throwing huge leafy tree limbs into a chipper and seeing them reduced to almost nothing. Anyway, to get to the point, he pureed the soup, we ate it for dinner, and it was one of the best soups I've ever had. Which is how lettuce soup ended up here. Take it from me, this is worth trying.

I like to serve toasts with this soup; they just go well together. The toasts I've made here are covered with a Mediterranean spread of olives and sun-dried tomatoes. Since the flavor is fairly forward, and the soup more subtle, serve the soup first and then the toasts with the bean and artichoke heart salad. To keep the salad from becoming too much of a production, I use canned white kidney beans and artichoke hearts, but, if you prefer, you can substitute any other dried cooked white bean.

Lettuce Soup

This is most interesting and delicious when you use a variety of greens for a rounded flavor. A few sorrel leaves give it a pleasant tang; watercress makes it peppery. Don't be too concerned about exact quantities because it's hard to put too many greens in this soup. If anything, err on the side of too much. You can make this more or less rich by using milk, light cream, or heavy cream.

2 tablespoons olive oil

2 shallots, minced

1 clove garlic, minced

3 small heads Boston lettuce, washed

Handful fresh parsley leaves

Handful fresh watercress or sorrel leaves
  or both

5 to 6 cups chicken or vegetable
  stock, to your taste

Salt and freshly ground black
  pepper to taste

1/2 to 1 cup heavy cream, light
  cream, or milk, to your taste

1. Heat the olive oil in a large soup pot over moderate heat. Stir in the shallots, garlic, lettuce, parsley, and any other greens you're using. When the lettuce starts to wilt, cover the pot, and braise the greens, stirring occasionally, for 5 minutes.

2. Add the stock and season with salt and pepper. Bring to a simmer and let simmer for 5 minutes.

3. Using a large slotted spoon or skimmer, transfer the soup solids to a food processor, adding a little of the broth. Process the greens until there is just a bit of texture left to them.

4. Add the greens back to the soup along with the cream or milk. Heat the soup for several minutes, then serve.

MAKES 5 SERVINGS

How to Sweat a Soup (and Other Soup-Making Tips)

Nobody just plain cooks a soup. They sauté, simmer, sweat, and boil—among other choices—depending on the desired result. To some extent, these are relative terms—is that a gentle simmer or a very active one? So, in the hopes of making some sense of these choices, let's take a closer look.

SAUTÉ: This is the quickest way to take vegetables—such as onions, peppers, and celery—to the point where water or stock is added to the pot. When you sauté vegetables, you generally heat them in just enough fat to keep them from sticking to the pan, using just enough heat to cook them quickly but without scorching. If garlic is used, it is usually added near the end of the sauté so it loses its raw flavor but doesn't brown and turn bitter.

SWEAT: When you sweat vegetables, you use lower heat than you would for a sauté and the pan is often kept covered, creating a sauna-like effect. Sweating is effective if only a small quantity of onion is used; onions will taste sweeter if they're sautéed. Or, with a delicately flavored soup, sweating is preferable if you want to eliminate the possibility of the vegetables taking on even a slight scorched flavor. The advantage of sweating is that the extra moisture in the pan eliminates the need to putter over the pan and stir frequently while you're prepping the rest of the ingredients for your soup or dinner.

SIMMER: A simmer can be gentle, quite active, or somewhere in between. This is where soups are generally held for most of their stove time. A gentle simmer means there's very little surface activity, perhaps an occasional bubble or two rising to the surface. An active simmer is almost a slow, steady boil, but not quite.

BOIL: For the most part a no-no when you're making soup. Boiling often results in solids heading to the bottom of the pot where they are likely to stay, get stuck, and then burn. A low boil is sometimes okay for short periods, but the soup should be stirred frequently. It's fine, of course, to boil beans when they're precooking prior to going into soup. And I almost always bring soup to a near boil just before I serve it because that's the way I like it.

Crostini of Olive and Sun-Dried Tomato Spread

There's been a lot of interest in this sort of thing in recent years, and by that I mean good toasted bread spread with a little something and served as an appetizer. The topping often has what we think of as Mediterranean ingredients: olives, tomatoes, garlic, and Parmesan cheese; this one has all of them, processed into a thick spread that goes on the toast then goes back into the oven briefly. If you'd rather, I've also used feta cheese in this instead of the Parmesan and it tastes equally delicious.

10 sun-dried tomatoes
10 large pitted imported green olives
1 clove garlic, chopped
¼ cup olive oil
1 teaspoon fresh lemon juice
1 tablespoon chopped fresh basil leaves
    or 1 teaspoon dried

⅓ cup freshly grated Parmesan cheese
    or ½ cup crumbled feta cheese
6 thick slices Cuban Bread (page 24)
    or other good crusty store-bought
    sourdough or Italian bread

1. Put the sun-dried tomatoes in a medium-size bowl and pour enough boiling water over them to cover well. Set aside to rehydrate, 45 to 60 minutes. Drain and chop coarsely; set aside.

2. Put the tomatoes and everything else—other than the bread—in a food processor and process to a textured but fairly smooth puree, scraping down the sides as needed. Taste and correct seasonings. Transfer to a small bowl.

3. Toast the bread on both sides in the oven, toaster, toaster oven, or even on the grill, if you happen to be using it. Smooth some of the spread over each slice. Rewarm briefly in a hot oven—just a minute or so—and serve right away.

MAKES 6 SERVINGS

White Bean and Artichoke Heart Salad

Canned cannellini beans, I must tell you, are not my first choice for flavor and texture, but you can't beat them for convenience. That said, do substitute your own beans if you don't mind going to the trouble of cooking them, though trouble is hardly the word, since it's a simple matter to presoak, then boil them until they're tender.

One 19-ounce can cannellini (white kidney) beans

One 14-ounce can artichoke hearts

1 green bell pepper, seeded and cut into thin strips

1 rib celery, thinly sliced on the bias

1 small red onion, halved and thinly sliced

4 ounces provolone cheese, cut into cubes

1 to 2 tablespoons chopped fresh parsley leaves, to your taste

1 to 2 tablespoons chopped fresh basil leaves, to your taste

5 tablespoons olive oil

2 1/2 tablespoons red wine vinegar

1 clove garlic, minced

1 teaspoon tomato paste

Salt and freshly ground black pepper to taste

3 to 4 ounces baby spinach leaves, arugula, or mesclun salad mix

1. Drain and thoroughly rinse the cannellini beans in a colander. Transfer to a large bowl. Drain the artichoke hearts. Cut them into quarters and place them on paper towels, flat side down, to drain. Transfer to the bowl with the beans. Add the bell pepper, celery, onion, provolone, and herbs.

2. Whisk the olive oil, vinegar, garlic, and tomato paste together in a small bowl. Pour over the vegetable mixture and toss gently, seasoning with salt and pepper. Add the greens and toss again briefly. Arrange the salad on a serving platter. Cover with plastic wrap and refrigerate if not serving right away.

MAKES 6 SERVINGS

SPRINGTIME MEANS MUSSELS

Creamy Mussel Chowder

* * * * * * * * * * * * *

Cuban Bread

* * * * * * * * * * * * *

Asparagus Vinaigrette with Croutons and
Hard-Cooked Egg

* * * * * * * * * * * * *

A good creamy seafood chowder is a glorious thing, and the best ones are made at home. I say that only after years of living in and traveling throughout New England, and sampling a hundred or more variations in restaurants from Maine to Connecticut and everywhere in between. Sadly, the offerings are pretty predictable: high-end restaurants nearly always go overboard on the heavy cream and vermouth. They mistake richness for character and flavor. Low-end joints and the chain eateries serve tasteless bowls of pasty chowder thick enough to stand a spoon in. The better chowders seem to nearly always come from the mid-scale neighborhood places with reputations to uphold and enough faith in their chowder to charge five or six bucks for a bowl. A good chowder is worth it, the ingredients are not cheap and there's a fair amount of labor involved.

Still, I believe few boughten chowders are as good as the one you can make at home. This menu celebrates homemade seafood chowder—mussel, not clam. Mussels—at least the Maine ones you commonly find in the market—are tastiest in spring, usually April, because of the heavy plankton blooms which make them good and fat, and the high glycogen concentrations that make them sweet. (Not only have I tasted the difference, but I read this in an informative publication, *The Great Eastern Mussel Cookbook* by Cindy McIntyre and Terence Callery [Eriksson Publishers, 1995], a great primer on the subject.) I'm partial to mussels for their flavor, economy, and ease of preparation and handling. Their broth is the basis and foundation for this filling soup that I like to make on the weekend when I'm not feeling pressed for time. You should never rush the preparation of seafood chowder.

Which makes this a good match for Cuban bread, a shorthand version of French bread. This is a wonderfully inviting, crusty bread that seems to have fallen out of favor in recent years among serious home bakers, with the booming interest in slow-rising artisan-type breads that have more complexity of flavor and cachet. I'm a great fan of the latter but the charms of Cuban bread are far too many to ignore. I, for one, hope it stages a major comeback among home bread bakers.

Asparagus, on the other hand, will never have to stage a comeback of any sort. Everyone seems to love it, especially in springtime when the first new crop hits the market. If you've never tried it like this—cold, with vinaigrette and eggs—you're in for a real treat.

Creamy Mussel Chowder

Mussels are, by far, my favorite shellfish. When I want a special little treat all for myself (my kids are vegetarians), I steam up a couple of pounds of mussels in wine and dig in. So it should not surprise you that, despite New England's claim to clam chowder fame, I prefer a mussel chowder. Mussels are more tender, for one; chewing on clams has always felt more like exercise than pleasure to me. And the flavor is exquisite; clams have nothing over mussels. The texture of a good chowder should be full-bodied but never gummy, and I think you'll find this one just about perfect in that respect.

1½ cups dry white wine

1 medium-size onion, sliced

2 bay leaves

1 teaspoon chopped fresh thyme leaves
  or ½ teaspoon dried

4 pounds mussels, scrubbed and
  debearded (page 64), and those with
  broken shells discarded

2 large all-purpose or waxy potatoes,
  peeled and cut into ¼-inch dice

¼ teaspoon salt

3 tablespoons unsalted butter

1 rib celery, finely chopped

2 shallots, minced

3 tablespoons unbleached all-purpose
  flour

3½ cups half-and-half

Freshly ground black pepper to taste

¼ cup chopped fresh parsley leaves,
  for garnish

1. In a large, heavy, nonreactive pot, combine the wine, onion, bay leaves, and thyme and bring to a boil over high heat. Add the mussels and cover tightly. Reduce the heat to moderately high and cook, shaking the pot once or twice, until the mussels steam open, about 5 minutes.

2. Using a slotted spoon, transfer the mussels to a large bowl and let cool. Discard any cracked mussels or ones that haven't opened. Set aside 12 mussels in their shells, for garnish. Shuck the remaining mussels. Coarsely chop half of the shucked mussels. Combine the whole and chopped mussels and set aside. Strain the cooking liquid through cheesecloth and set aside.

3. In a medium-size saucepan, combine the potatoes with enough cold water to barely cover. Add the salt. Bring to a boil over high heat and cook the potatoes until just tender, about 10 minutes. Drain, reserving the potato cooking water.

4. In a medium-size nonreactive casserole, melt the butter over moderate heat. Add the celery and shallots and cook, stirring, until slightly softened but not browned, about 5 minutes. Sprinkle the flour over the vegetables and cook, stirring constantly, until lightly golden, about 2 minutes. Stir in the reserved mussel liquid and bring to a boil, stirring. Reduce the heat to low and stir in the half-and-half, potatoes, and potato cooking water. Stir until heated through. Add the shucked mussels and simmer gently for 8 to 10 minutes. Season with salt and pepper. Serve the chowder with 2 whole mussels in each bowl. Garnish with the parsley.

MAKES 6 SERVINGS

Cuban Bread

I would love to know how this bread got its name. I first came across it in James Beard's now classic *Beard on Bread* (Knopf, 1973), and I've seen it in other books, but never with a proper explanation of how it came to be called Cuban. In composition and execution, it is much closer to what we know as French bread. But it deviates from both French and most other breads in one significant way: the shaped loaves are put into a cold oven before they've had time to rise, the oven is turned on, and the second rising takes place more or less simultaneously with the baking. This abbreviated chronology produces some very good bread, not as complex in flavor and light of crumb as real French bread, but excellent nonetheless. And, bottom line, you have shaved a good 30 to 40 minutes off the total time needed to go from mixing bowl to finished bread. Not bad. My preference here is for a light wheaten loaf, thus the half cup of whole wheat flour. You can diddle with the proportion of unbleached to whole wheat flour if you like, or leave the whole wheat out entirely and just use unbleached, whatever is your preference. My guess is that once you've made this, you'll make it fairly often.

1^1/$_2$ cups warm water	3^1/$_2$ cups unbleached all-purpose flour
2^1/$_2$ teaspoons active dry yeast	1^1/$_2$ teaspoons salt
2 teaspoons sugar	1 tablespoon olive or vegetable oil
^{1}/$_2$ cup whole wheat flour	Cornmeal or semolina, for dusting

1. Pour the water into a large bowl. Sprinkle on the yeast and sugar; whisk once or twice and set aside for 2 or 3 minutes. Stir in the whole wheat flour and 2 cups of the unbleached flour. Beat vigorously with a wooden spoon or rubber spatula for 100 strokes. Cover with plastic wrap or a pan lid and set aside for 10 minutes.

2. Stir the salt and oil into the dough. Stir in enough of the remaining unbleached flour, about ^{1}/$_3$ cup at a time, to make a firm, kneadable dough. Let rest for 5 minutes.

3. Turn the dough out onto a floured work surface and knead with floured hands until the dough is smooth and elastic, about 10 minutes; use only enough flour on the work surface to keep the dough from sticking. Place the dough in an oiled bowl, rotating it to coat thoroughly with oil. Cover the bowl with plastic wrap and set aside in a warm spot until doubled in bulk, 45 to 60 minutes.

4. When the dough has doubled, punch it down and transfer to a lightly floured work surface. Knead for 1 minute, then divide the dough in half. Shape each half into a ball, cover loosely with plastic wrap, and let rest for 10 minutes. While you're waiting, lightly oil a large baking sheet and dust with cornmeal or semolina.

5. Working with one piece of dough at a time, flour lightly, then roll or pat the dough into an oblong 13 to 14 inches long. Brush the surface very lightly with water, then roll the dough up snugly, like a carpet. Tuck in the ends and turn them under, to make nice blunt ends. Transfer the dough to the prepared baking sheet, seam side down. Repeat for other half of the dough, leaving plenty of space between the loaves. Let rest for 10 minutes.

6. Very lightly brush the surface of the loaves with water. Using a sharp, serrated knife, make 3 long diagonal slashes about ^{1}/$_2$ inch deep on each loaf. Place the baking sheet in a cold oven on the center rack. Set the oven to 400 degrees F and bake until the tops are golden brown and the bottoms sound hollow when tapped with a finger, about 35 minutes. Transfer the loaves to a wire rack if not eating right away. This tastes best eaten warm.

MAKES 2 LOAVES

Asparagus Vinaigrette with Croutons and Hard-Cooked Egg

Sometimes all it takes is a few croutons to give a cold vegetable salad its credentials, and I think this recipe illustrates my point nicely. Everything is arranged on a large plate in rows, the asparagus is dressed, then all is tossed just before serving. If you want an extra touch, garnish with shards of fresh Parmesan.

2 slices good white bread, preferably rustic country bread

1 teaspoon olive oil, or more to your taste

1 clove garlic, minced

1½ pounds fresh asparagus

3 cold hard-cooked eggs, peeled and thinly sliced

Creamy Mustard Dressing (page 66)

Salt and freshly ground black pepper to taste

1. Preheat the oven to 325 degrees F. Cut the bread into large cubes and transfer to a large bowl. Drizzle with the olive oil. Add the garlic and toss well. Spread the cubes on a baking sheet and toast until dry and light golden brown, about 15 minutes.

2. Break off the lower, woody section of each asparagus spear and discard. Cut the upper section into 2 or 3 smaller sections. Drop the asparagus into a medium-size saucepan of lightly salted boiling water and cook until tender, 5 to 7 minutes; check one to be sure. Drain and set aside to cool. Transfer to a plate, cover with plastic wrap, and refrigerate.

3. When you are ready to serve the salad, arrange the asparagus in the center of a serving platter. Make a row of croutons and a row of egg slices on either side. Spoon plenty of vinaigrette over the asparagus. When you're ready to serve at the table, toss with two spoons, and season with salt and pepper.

MAKES 6 SERVINGS

DINER DREAMS

Chicken Noodle Soup
....

Apple Butter and Cheddar Cheese Crepes
....

Smokin' Chef's Salad
....

I grew up in New Jersey, where there are more good diners per mile than in any other state in the country. I was crazy about the diners of my teens. The service was always fast (if not particularly refined), the food reliably good and copious, and when I was cruisin' the highways with the likes of Bruce Springsteen—another Jersey boy—blaring on my radio of my Dad's '64 Impala, I knew where I could find the sort of good diner fare I've featured here: chicken noodle soup, chef's salad, and apple butter crepes.

Apple butter crepes? Well, not exactly. I had hoped to say apple pie, but how on earth does one squeeze an apple pie into the rather rigid confines of a soup, bread, and salad book? I'll tell you how: by expanding the definition of bread to include crepes. Why not? If a crepe is a sort of pancake, and a pancake a form of sweet bread, then it follows that a crepe is really a flat bread, correct?

Whether or not you agree, I think you'll find this is a menu worth trying. I've tinkered with standard-issue diner fare one other way: by giving the chef's salad a smoky profile, by way of barbecue sauce in the dressing. It works great. I roast the peppers, too, but unless you're up for it, just use raw peppers. As for those crepes, which I spread with apple butter and grated cheddar, serve them with the salad, soup, or by themselves. It all goes down even better when served with a little Springsteen.

Chicken Noodle Soup

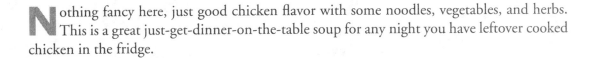

Nothing fancy here, just good chicken flavor with some noodles, vegetables, and herbs. This is a great just-get-dinner-on-the-table soup for any night you have leftover cooked chicken in the fridge.

1 tablespoon unsalted butter

1 medium-size onion, finely chopped

1 rib celery, finely chopped

1 medium-size carrot, peeled and diced

1 bay leaf

6 cups chicken stock

¼ to ½ teaspoon salt, to your taste

½ teaspoon dried oregano

½ teaspoon dried basil

Pinch or 2 of crumbled dried sage

2 ounces thin spaghetti, broken into small pieces

1 to 2 cups diced cooked chicken, to your taste

Freshly ground black pepper to taste

2 to 3 teaspoons tomato paste, to your taste

1. Melt the butter in a large saucepan or medium-size soup pot over moderate heat. Stir in the vegetables and bay leaf, then cover and sweat them, stirring occasionally, for 3 minutes.

2. Add the stock, salt, and herbs to the pot. Increase the heat and bring to a lively simmer, covered. Stir in the spaghetti and chicken, season with pepper, and return to an active simmer. Partially cover the pot and simmer until the spaghetti is tender, about 10 minutes, stirring in the tomato paste during the last few minutes. Serve piping hot.

MAKES 5 TO 6 SERVINGS

Apple Butter and Cheddar Cheese Crepes

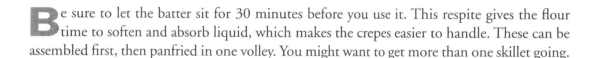

Be sure to let the batter sit for 30 minutes before you use it. This respite gives the flour time to soften and absorb liquid, which makes the crepes easier to handle. These can be assembled first, then panfried in one volley. You might want to get more than one skillet going.

CREPE BATTER

3 large eggs

1½ cups milk

1 cup plus 2 tablespoons unbleached all-purpose flour

1 tablespoon sugar

¼ teaspoon salt

1 tablespoon unsalted butter, melted

COOKING, FILLING, AND ASSEMBLY

Unsalted butter for the pan

¾ cup apple butter, plus extra for garnish

8 ounces extra-sharp cheddar cheese, grated

1. Put all of the batter ingredients in a blender or food processor and process until smooth. Remove the lid and scrape down the sides, in case there are dry spots; process again. Pour the batter into a large measuring cup or pitcher and let sit at room temperature for 30 minutes. You may also cover with plastic wrap and refrigerate the batter overnight.

2. When you're ready to cook the crepes, heat an 8- or 9-inch nonstick skillet over moderate heat. Rub a little butter in the pan with a paper towel.

3. Using about ¼ to ⅓ cup batter per crepe, pour or ladle the batter into the hot pan. Immediately tilt and twirl the pan in a circular motion to spread the batter and cover the bottom. It should take no more than 3 or 4 seconds to spread the batter. Cook the crepe on the first side for 45 to 50 seconds, then flip (see page 30) and cook on the second side about half as long.

4. Slide or invert the crepe out of the pan and onto a plate. Place a piece of plastic wrap over the crepe. Repeat for the remaining crepes, layering them between pieces of plastic wrap.

5. To assemble the crepes, smooth about 1 tablespoon of the apple butter over the surface of a crepe, leaving a ½-inch border around the perimeter. Sprinkle a little cheddar cheese over half of the crepe, then fold the noncheese half over the other half. Fold again, to make a quarter-circle wedge. Repeat for the remaining crepes.

6. To panfry the crepes, melt a little butter in a large skillet over moderate heat. Add several crepes, without crowding them, and fry for about 30 seconds. Flip and fry them on the second side. They should stay in the skillet just long enough to melt the cheese and brown the surface. Serve right away with dollops of apple butter on the side.

MAKES 12 CREPES, ABOUT 6 SERVINGS

Flipping Crepes

When I do a cooking demonstration and show this technique, everyone loves it. For some reason, people think this is a riot; I'm still not sure why. In any case, here's how it works. This is so much easier than using a spatula, you'll be amazed.

When you go to make the crepes, put a small bowl of iced water on your work counter; the water should actually have ice in it. Have a dry towel handy, too. Now, when you want to flip the crepe, loosen the far edge with a butter knife, pulling the edge up and toward you ever so slightly. Quickly—this should take all of 5 seconds—stick your fingers in the cold water for a moment, dry off your fingers, then gently grasp the crepe with two hands where you loosened it. In one motion, peel the crepe toward you and flip it over in the pan. No burned fingers, crepe intact. Remember: *peel* the crepe toward you. Inevitably, when I show someone how to do this, the first time they try they yank the crepe straight up and it rips to shreds.

Smokin' Chef's Salad

A chef's salad, when it rises above some of the conventions that make it feel like it's stuck in the 1950s or '60s, is really an excellent dish. Here I've given it a smoky makeover, adding roasted peppers and a creamy barbecue dressing. Gone too is the iceberg lettuce. In its original incarnation, iceberg leaves were oftentimes the "bowl" in which the salad reposed—a cute but dated idea. Instead, I use hearts of romaine and, if I have some around, I'll use a bit of mesclun mix or other greens. Everything is lined up nicely on a platter, then served with the dressing on the side. This salad involves a number of steps, but nothing complicated and you can save a little time if you use raw pepper strips instead of roasted.

SALAD

3 large green bell peppers

1 large head romaine lettuce

12 to 15 cherry tomatoes, to your taste, halved

1/2 to 3/4 pound thick-cut ham, to your taste, cut into strips

2 ripe avocados

6 hard-cooked eggs, peeled and quartered lengthwise

6 to 8 ounces smoked cheddar cheese, to your taste

CREAMY BARBECUE DRESSING

1/2 cup plain yogurt

1/2 cup mayonnaise

1/4 cup barbecue sauce, preferably not too sweet

1 teaspoon Dijon mustard

1/2 teaspoon Worcestershire sauce

2 tablespoons finely chopped fresh parsley leaves

1 clove garlic, minced

1. Using a grill or gas burner, roast the peppers by holding them directly over the flame with metal tongs until the entire surface is blistered and charred. Or, using a broiler, simply place peppers on a baking sheet on the top shelf of the oven. (In either case, you'll have to turn the peppers often to roast them evenly.) Put the hot peppers in a bowl and cover with plastic wrap for 15 to 20 minutes.

2. When the peppers are cool enough to handle, rub or scrape off the skins (with the back of a paring knife blade) and cut out the stems and seeds. Cut the peppers into strips and set them aside in a small bowl.

3. To assemble the salad, wash the lettuce and pat the leaves dry. Stack the leaves and cut into 1/2-inch-wide crosswise strips. Arrange the lettuce down the center of a large serving platter. On one side of the lettuce, make a row of cherry tomatoes, then a row of the pepper strips.

4. Make a row of the ham strips on the other side of the lettuce. Halve the avocados and remove the pit. Cut the flesh into large chunks. Spoon the avocado chunks in a row down the other side of the ham. Divide the quartered eggs evenly on both sides. Cut the cheddar into strips and scatter them around.

5. Blend all of the dressing ingredients together in a small bowl. Transfer to a serving bowl and pass the dressing at the table.

MAKES 6 SERVINGS

STALKING VICHYSSOISE

Asparagus Vichyssoise

· · · · · · · · · · · · · ·

Cornmeal Muffins with Bacon Bits and Pecans

· · · · · · · · · · · · · ·

*Cherry Tomato, Cantaloupe, and
Red Onion Salad*

· · · · · · · · · · · · · ·

Time was, you could make a solid impression as a cook if you knew how to make vichyssoise. It didn't matter that it was, and is, the simplest of cold pureed potato soups. In fact, you could even collect gourmet points just for *pronouncing* it correctly, as it often was not. There's a funny headnote in the revised edition of *The New York Times Cookbook* (Harper & Row, 1990) in which a rather testy Craig Claiborne chides readers that someone should start a campaign to instruct Americans that vichyssoise is not pronounced "veeshy-swah," but rather "veeshy-swahze."

What Mr. Claiborne would have thought of me calling a cold *asparagus* soup a vichyssoise, I can't say, though I can't imagine it would be printable. Thankfully, we're more relaxed about such gastronomic name-dropping nowadays. If it's a cold, creamy soup with at least *some* potatoes in it—the thinking goes—it's okay to trot out the name.

I think this version of asparagus vichyssoise is as much fun to eat as it is to pronounce. It's delicious, a soothing shade of green, and prettier still with a sprinkle of fresh dill on top. To show it off best, serve it in little chilled glasses and everyone will be delighted.

How about a warm muffin with that cold soup? These bacon corn muffins with toasted pecans are just right: full of flavor and savory bits, but not so fancy that they'll upstage the soup. Rounding out the palette of colors on this menu is a salad of cherry tomatoes, cantaloupe, and red onions. It doesn't take much imagination to figure out how great all of this looks and tastes together.

Asparagus Vichyssoise

I usually buy asparagus in 1-pound bunches, which is what this soup calls for, but if you grow it or happen to have extra on hand, do garnish the soup with cooled steamed asparagus tips. Then just use the rest of the stalks as I do here: the bottom half simmers with the broth, the top goes into the sauté mixture. This soup is a lovely shade of green, almost a light Easter green, which happens to be a great time of year to serve this because the first good asparagus is starting to come to market. (If you get a cold, damp Easter day—as we often get in New Hampshire—this tastes wonderful hot as well.) Served in chilled ramekins or glasses, it's an excellent starter course for summer entertaining.

1 pound fresh asparagus

4½ cups lightly salted chicken stock

3 tablespoons unsalted butter

1 large onion, chopped

2 ribs celery, chopped

1 large or 2 medium-size all-purpose
   potatoes, peeled and cut into ½-inch
   dice

Salt and freshly ground black pepper
   to taste

1 cup light cream

Chopped fresh dill or lemon thyme
   leaves (optional), for garnish

1. Cut the entire stack of asparagus in half with a chef's knife. Cut each bottom stalk into several pieces and put these bottoms in a large saucepan with the chicken stock. Bring to a simmer and continue to simmer, covered, for 20 minutes. Remove the asparagus with a slotted spoon. Transfer to a colander and place over a saucepan. Using a mug or other instrument, mash down on the stalks to extract as much liquid as possible. Discard the stalks.

2. Melt the butter in a large skillet over moderate heat. Add the onion and cook, stirring, for 5 minutes. Cut the asparagus tops into 1-inch pieces and add to the onion along with the celery and potato; season with salt and pepper. Cover the skillet and gently sweat the vegetables for 5 minutes over moderately low heat. Spoon ½ cup of the simmered stock into the skillet, cover tightly, and cook gently until the potato is tender, another 7 to 8 minutes. If the liquid evaporates, add more. Remove from the heat.

3. Scrape the vegetables into a food processor and process to a puree. Stir the puree back into the chicken stock along with the light cream. Simmer for 5 minutes, seasoning with salt and pepper as appropriate. Remove from the heat and transfer to a large bowl. Let cool to

A Potential Processor Problem

Maybe this has happened to you, though probably not more than once: you turn on a food processor full of hot soup to puree and it blows out the top and all over the place. This is no laughing matter because it can result in serious burns. So, please, when you puree hot soup, never fill the bowl more than about one-quarter full. You can add somewhat more if you're just pureeing the solids, which is the better way to go. I have a huge 6-inch-diameter skimmer-spoon I use for ladling solids out of soup and into the processor and it works beautifully. Another tip: when you do process hot soup, rather than just hitting the "on" button, pulse the machine very quickly several times to get the solids moving; this helps prevent blowouts as well. Another option is to buy one of those handy immersion blenders that you stick down inside the soup pot. I don't own one but I know some cooks who do, and it might be the best and safest solution of all.

room temperature. Cover with plastic wrap and refrigerate until chilled and ready to serve. Garnish each portion with chopped herbs, if desired.

VARIATION: For a richer version, use some or all heavy cream instead of light cream.

MAKES 5 TO 6 SERVINGS

Cornmeal Muffins
with Bacon Bits and Pecans

Bacon seems to have made nearly everyone's list of bad-for-you foods, but I still sneak a few strips for breakfast now and then when nobody is looking. (These things are never half as bad for you if no one is there looking on in horror.) While I'm at it, I sometimes cook up extra for these cornmeal muffins. One-half shrunken pound of crisp-cooked bacon doesn't look like much, but it's enough to add a smoky flavor that's only enhanced by the earthiness of the pecans. Pine nuts are good, too—giving the muffins an exotic, Southwestern profile—but they're pricey and I rarely have them on hand. Given bacon's bad-boy image, some might blanch at the suggestion, but for great flavor you can substitute a tablespoon of warm bacon fat for an equal measure of the oil or butter. Serve with apple jelly.

¼ to ½ pound bacon, to your taste	1 large egg
1½ cups unbleached all-purpose flour	1½ cups milk
1 cup fine-ground yellow cornmeal	¼ cup vegetable oil or unsalted butter,
2½ tablespoons sugar	melted
2½ teaspoons baking powder	¾ cup finely chopped pecans, toasted
¾ teaspoon salt	(page 218) or not

1. Grease a 12-cup muffin tin and preheat the oven to 400 degrees F.

2. Put the bacon in a hot large skillet and fry until it is crisp-cooked. Transfer to a paper towel-lined plate. When cool enough to handle, chop and set aside.

3. Sift the flour, cornmeal, sugar, baking powder, and salt together in a large mixing bowl. In a medium-size bowl, whisk the egg until frothy, then blend in the milk and oil or butter. Make a well in the center of the dry mixture and add the liquid all at once. Stir briefly, add the pecans and continue to stir just until blended.

4. Divide the batter evenly between the muffin cups. Bake on the center rack of the oven until the tops are lightly golden, about 20 minutes. Transfer the muffins to a wire rack or, if you're serving them immediately, put them in a cloth-lined basket and serve.

VARIATION: These are excellent with cheese. Add up to 1 cup grated smoked cheddar or Gouda or ½ cup crumbled blue cheese.

MAKES 12 MUFFINS

Cherry Tomato, Cantaloupe, and Red Onion Salad

These colors are gorgeous together, especially alongside the light asparagus-green soup. I like cherry tomatoes for off-season salads: their quality tends to be far superior to that of large tomatoes, any of their sins less apparent. The cantaloupe adds sweetness that the tomatoes often lack when they're not in season, and the onion brings a pleasant crunch and flavor to the whole. This isn't nearly as good with dried herbs, so do use fresh if at all possible.

½ large red onion

2 teaspoons sugar

1 lemon, cut in half

2 tablespoons fresh orange juice

½ small ripe cantaloupe or other small melon, seeds removed

12 to 15 cherry tomatoes, to your taste

Salt and freshly ground black pepper to taste

10 to 12 fresh mint leaves, to your taste

8 to 10 fresh basil leaves, to your taste

1 tablespoon olive oil (optional)

1. Slice the onion very thinly and transfer to a large serving bowl. Sprinkle on the sugar, juice from half of the lemon, and the orange juice. Cover with plastic wrap and refrigerate for 15 minutes.

2. Cut the melon into bite-size chunks and add to the onion. Halve the cherry tomatoes and add them as well. Salt lightly and pepper a bit more generously. Stack the herbs and slice into very thin strips; toss with the salad. Taste; if it seems to need a bit more sharpness, add more lemon juice or a splash of vinegar. Add the olive oil, if desired—it will add a tiny bit of body to the dressing—and toss again. Serve immediately.

MAKES 6 SERVINGS

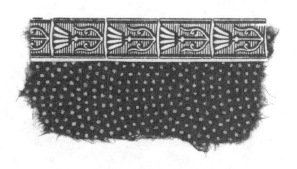

A TRIBUTE TO JAMES BEARD

Farm Country Vegetable Beef Soup

....

Wheaten Parker House Rolls

....

Marinated Cauliflower and Zucchini

....

James Beard, as you likely know, was the Dean of American Cooking. He has been honored and paid tribute by many organizations and persons far more important than myself, and fittingly so. Think of this, then, as a small birthday tribute—Beard was born on May 5, 1903—from one grateful cook who gleaned much of his inspiration and many of his early recipes from this formidable cook.

I'm fortunate in that I have several friends who worked closely with Beard for many years, so I have something of an insider's knowledge of him. But none of that has meant nearly as much to me as his writing on food, which was as engaging and opinionated as it gets. He loved to write about the places he'd been, the food he had eaten, the people with whom he had shared it. He loved American food, too. Back when the rest of us were smitten with French and other exotic cuisines, and looked down our noses at American food, he championed it. In the introduction to one of his books, he writes that "Food and eating habits have fascinated me throughout my life, and after sixty-five years I have come to the conclusion that perhaps American cookery is one of the most fascinating culinary subjects of all."

The menu here, then, is a compilation of recipes I learned to make through Beard's books: a meat and vegetable soup, a good American dinner roll, and marinated vegetables. Like Beard, they aren't fancy. Nor are they exact replicas of his recipes. After all, I've been making some of these for nearly thirty years now. So, of course, I've added some personal tweaks and touches. But the point is, his writing inspired me to try these recipes and I did, and that's the best kind of food writing there is.

Farm Country Vegetable Beef Soup

In his *James Beard's American Cookery*—which I have a 1972 copy of, published by Little, Brown—Beard titles my inspiration for this soup "A Hearty Main-Dish Soup," noting that it is typical of the soups served in the farm country "when stockpots were kept going on the back of the stove and when one's own garden provided vegetables in late summer and fall." Like many of the recipes he published, you got the idea that this soup was more of a blueprint than something written in stone, which has always been something I liked about his recipes. In that spirit, think of this list of vegetables as a suggestion and add whatever else you might like or have on hand. In Beard's original recipe, he doesn't even bother to sauté the vegetables; he just throws everything in the pot and brings it to a boil. I sauté them briefly, both out of habit and to speed the cooking along.

1½ tablespoons vegetable oil

1 medium-size onion, chopped

1 rib celery, chopped

1 medium-size carrot, peeled and diced

1 parsnip, peeled and diced

Handful green beans, ends trimmed and chopped

1 large all-purpose potato, peeled and diced

2 cups cored and thinly sliced green cabbage

2 cloves garlic, minced

8 cups beef stock

1 teaspoon fresh thyme leaves or
   ½ teaspoon dried

½ teaspoon salt, plus more to taste

Freshly ground black pepper to taste

1 cup diced cooked beef (optional)

¾ cup elbow macaroni or small shells

1. Heat the oil in a large soup pot over fairly high heat. Add all of the vegetables and the garlic and cook, stirring often, for 4 to 5 minutes.

2. Add the stock, thyme, salt, pepper, and beef, if using, to the pot. Bring the soup to a boil, then reduce the heat and simmer, partially covered, until the vegetables are just barely tender, 12 to 15 minutes. Taste, adding more salt and pepper if desired.

3. Add the macaroni or shells to the soup and continue to cook a few more minutes, until the pasta is tender. Serve piping hot.

MAKES 6 TO 7 SERVINGS

Wheaten Parker House Rolls

These are the rolls made famous by Boston's Parker House hotel. Beard called them one of America's most delicious rolls, and I agree heartily. (It probably didn't hurt matters, as he pointed out, that these "consume butter by the tons.") They're in the best tradition of an American dinner roll: soft, a tad sweet, with a delicious golden chewy crust. These are so good that it's entirely possible to eat three or four of them in a single sitting—and they freeze well—so don't be alarmed by the yield here; even a small family can go through thirty of these pretty quickly. Forming these into their traditional "lips" shape is half of the fun. Count on 3 to 4 hours from start to finish.

2 cups milk	**2 teaspoons salt**
$1/2$ cup (1 stick) unsalted butter	**$1/2$ cup whole wheat flour**
2 tablespoons sugar	**About 5 cups unbleached all-purpose**
$1/4$ cup water	**flour**
2 teaspoons (1 packet) active dry yeast	**Cornmeal or semolina, for dusting**

1. Heat the milk in a medium-size saucepan until the surface shimmers. Remove from the heat. Put 3 tablespoons of the butter and the sugar in a large bowl and pour the hot milk over it; stir, then let cool to body temperature.

2. While the milk cools, pour the water into a small bowl and sprinkle the yeast over the top. Stir to blend, then set aside for 5 minutes.

3. When the milk has cooled, stir in the dissolved yeast and salt. Stir in the whole wheat flour and 3 cups of the unbleached all-purpose flour, 1 cup at a time. Using a wooden spoon, beat vigorously for 100 strokes. Cover with plastic wrap and set aside this sponge for 15 minutes.

4. After 15 minutes, start adding the remaining unbleached flour about $1/3$ cup at a time, mixing well after each addition. When the dough is firm and kneadable, turn it out onto a floured work surface and knead for 10 minutes, using additional flour if necessary to keep the dough from sticking. Let the dough rest briefly every 3 or 4 minutes as you knead.

5. Place the dough in an oiled bowl, turning to coat the entire surface. Cover the bowl with plastic wrap and set it aside in a warm, draft-free spot until doubled in bulk, 60 to 90 minutes. Lightly butter a large baking sheet and dust with cornmeal or semolina.

6. When the dough has doubled, punch it down and turn it out onto a lightly floured work surface. Knead the dough for 1 minute, cover with plastic wrap, and let rest for 10 minutes. Melt the remaining 5 tablespoons butter.

7. Roll the dough out slightly more than $^1/_2$ inch thick on a floured work surface with a floured rolling pin. Using a $2^1/_4$- or $2^1/_2$-inch biscuit cutter (or water glass) cut the dough into circles, keeping the cuts as close together as possible. Leave the circles where they are, pick up all the scraps, and knead them into a ball. Cover with plastic wrap and set aside.

8. Brush the entire surface of each circle with a bit of melted butter. Working with one circle at a time, make a deep indentation across the diameter with a chopstick or the handle of a wooden spoon. Fold the circles in half, using the indentation as a hinge, so the buttered halves meet; you now have what looks like a big pair of lips. Place the lips on the prepared baking sheet flat side down. Repeat for the remaining circles, placing the lips so they barely touch. As you lay each one down—all pointing in the same direction—give the entire surface a light brushing with butter. When you start a second row, the edges should just barely touch.

9. Reroll and cut the scraps and place them on the sheet. Cover the rolls loosely with plastic wrap and set aside in a warm, draft-free spot until nearly doubled in bulk; it should take more than 30 minutes. Preheat the oven to 375 degrees F.

10. When rolls have doubled, put them in the oven and bake for 25 minutes. As soon as they come out, brush with more of the melted butter and serve at once, if possible, from a cloth-lined basket.

MAKES ABOUT 30 ROLLS

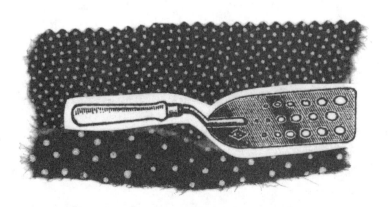

Marinated Cauliflower and Zucchini

One of my favorite old cookbooks is a compilation of James Beard's newspaper columns that he wrote years ago called *Beard on Food* (Knopf, 1974). I don't even know where that book is now; perhaps in that significant part of my cookbook collection that's in storage. I do, however, remember two things about the book: that it had the world's worst index—the referenced page numbers were famously inaccurate—and it had the first and best recipe I have ever used for marinated vegetables. This recipe is a descendent of that recipe. The vegetables turn out perfectly, crunchy and delicious. And since the vegetables stay that way, you can make this well ahead for later in the week, or just to pick at throughout the week. If you aren't using them all at once, just scoop out what you need from the marinade with a slotted spoon.

1 large head cauliflower	2 bay leaves
1 medium-size zucchini, ends trimmed and sliced into thin rounds	6 black peppercorns
	1¼ teaspoons salt
1 medium-size red onion, halved and thinly sliced into half moons	2 teaspoons fresh thyme leaves or 1 teaspoon dried
1½ cups dry white wine	1 tablespoon chopped fresh basil leaves or 1 teaspoon dried
¾ cup white wine vinegar or tarragon vinegar	1 cup cherry tomatoes, halved
⅓ cup olive oil	¼ cup chopped fresh parsley leaves

1. Cut the cauliflower into florets and put them in a large nonreactive pot with the zucchini and onion. Add the wine, vinegar, olive oil, and just enough water to cover. Add the bay leaves, peppercorns, salt, thyme, and basil.

2. Bring the liquid to a boil, then reduce the heat to moderately low and simmer gently, partially covered, until the cauliflower is just crisp-tender, about 15 minutes. Remove from the heat and transfer the vegetables and liquid to a pottery bowl to cool. When they're cooled, cover with plastic wrap and refrigerate overnight.

3. To serve, drain the vegetables (if you use it soon, the liquid can be used to cook another batch of vegetables) and transfer to a serving bowl. Toss in the tomatoes and parsley and serve cold or at room temperature.

VARIATION: I think it first appeared well after Beard's time, but today I sometimes make this with broccoflower instead of the cauliflower.

MAKES 6 SERVINGS

A CINCO DE MAYO FESTIVAL

Creamy Avocado "Gazpacho"
....
Pumpkin, Red Pepper, and Corn Quesadillas
....
Taco Chip Salad with Lime Vinaigrette
....

Cinco de Mayo commemorates the 1862 defeat of the invading French army over a poorly equipped army of 5,000 Mexican Indians. Over the years it has become a day when Mexican unity and national pride are given full expression with parades, song, dance, and feasting. This menu celebrates both Cinco de Mayo and the vivid colors of Mexican cooking, incorporating them into some new dishes you aren't likely find at your local Mexican restaurant. That's not to somehow suggest that everyday Mexican fare—tacos, burritos, enchiladas, and the like—is somehow beneath me. Far from it. I love those things and when they're well done I'm smitten. Even when they're not particularly well done, I'm still smitten. My kids won't hide from you the fact that one of our favorite places to eat on the run is Taco Bell.

Actually, I owe a debt of gratitude to Taco Bell. I borrowed the taco salad idea from them, in part because my kids are big fans of theirs. Taco salads are often made in those taco baskets, but my version just uses taco chips and a few bulky items like chicken, black beans, and lettuce, dressed with a zingy lime vinaigrette. It's almost a meal in itself.

The bread is a folded tortilla filled with vegetables and melted cheese, better known as a quesadilla, the Mexican version of the grilled cheese sandwich. You can imagine how good looking the filling is with chunks of pumpkin, red pepper, and corn bursting forth with every bite. They're pretty snazzy and I like to think they raise the bar for the creative quesadilla makers of the world. As for the cold avocado "gazpacho," try that last. It's just what your taste buds need to cool off after the spicy warmth of the quesadillas.

Creamy Avocado "Gazpacho"

This isn't your usual gazpacho by any means, but the fact that the soup is cold and full of diced vegetables reminded me of gazpacho, thus the name. It's one of those cool, colorful soups you will relish on a hot summer day when your mind could not be further from hot soup. If you're in a rush to eat this, you can skip the preliminary step of salting the chopped vegetables, but do salt first if you can. When the salt penetrates into the vegetables, their individual flavors stand out better in the soup. Thinning the soup with water, as opposed to milk, keeps the flavors crisp and sharp. Like most cold soups, you'll want to serve this in smaller, chilled bowls or custard cups.

1 cucumber, peeled, seeded, and finely
   diced
1 small zucchini, ends trimmed and
   finely diced
1 small green bell pepper, seeded and
   finely diced
1 rib celery, finely diced
4 scallions, white and light green parts
   only, thinly sliced
1/4 teaspoon salt
2 ripe avocados, halved and pitted

2 cups plain yogurt
Juice of 1 lemon
Juice of 1 lime
1 clove garlic, chopped
Small handful fresh cilantro leaves
Small handful fresh parsley leaves
1 teaspoon sugar
Freshly ground black pepper to taste
Thinly sliced cherry tomatoes or diced
   avocado, for garnish

1. Put all of the diced vegetables and scallions in a medium-size bowl. Toss with the salt. Set aside for 20 to 30 minutes.

2. Meanwhile, spoon the avocado flesh into a food processor. Add the yogurt, lemon and lime juices, garlic, herbs, and sugar. Process to a smooth puree, adding as much cold water as needed to make a thickish soupy texture. It will likely take no more than 1/2 cup at this point, though you may have to add more later. Season with pepper.

3. Add the avocado mixture and any liquid in the bowl to the vegetables. Stir well, adding more water if necessary. The soup should be thicker and more full-bodied than other cold and creamy soups you may have made, almost like the texture of a yogurt smoothie. Cover with plastic wrap and refrigerate up to 24 hours.

4. Ladle the soup into chilled bowls, adding the garnish of your choice.

MAKES 6 SERVINGS

Pumpkin, Red Pepper, and Corn Quesadillas

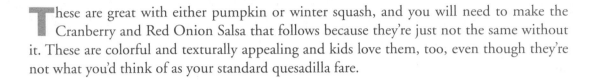

These are great with either pumpkin or winter squash, and you will need to make the Cranberry and Red Onion Salsa that follows because they're just not the same without it. These are colorful and texturally appealing and kids love them, too, even though they're not what you'd think of as your standard quesadilla fare.

1½ tablespoons vegetable oil

2 cups peeled and seeded pumpkin or winter squash cut into ¾-inch cubes

1 medium-size onion, halved and thinly sliced into half moons

1 small red bell pepper, seeded and sliced into ¼-inch-wide strips

1 large ripe tomato, cored, seeded, and coarsely chopped

¾ cup cooked corn kernels

½ teaspoon ground cumin

½ teaspoon ground coriander

½ teaspoon chili powder

Salt to taste

Four 8- or 9-inch flour tortillas

1½ cups grated Monterey Jack or smoked cheddar cheese

Cranberry and Red Onion Salsa (recipe follows)

1. Preheat the oven to 450 degrees F. Heat a large, heavy ovenproof skillet over high heat. Add the oil. Stir in the pumpkin and cook, stirring often, for 2 minutes. Add the onion and pepper and cook, stirring, for 2 minutes more. Stir in the tomato, corn, and spices and season with salt. Cook, stirring often, for 2 to 3 minutes. Transfer the skillet to the oven and roast until the pumpkin cubes are tender, about 8 minutes. Cover with a lid and set aside. Adjust the oven temperature to very low.

2. Place a large skillet over medium-high heat. Add 1 tortilla, sprinkling its surface with one quarter of the cheese. Strew one quarter of the pumpkin mixture over half the tortilla, then fold over to enclose. Heat about 30 seconds, then flip and heat the other side. Repeat for the remaining tortillas, cheese, and pumpkin mixture, keeping them warm in the oven as you go.

3. Cut the quesadillas into halves or thirds and transfer to a serving plate, serving the cranberry salsa on the side.

MAKES 4 TO 6 SERVINGS

Cranberry and Red Onion Salsa

¼ cup finely chopped red onion

¾ cup grated carrots

2 tablespoons chopped fresh parsley
leaves

¼ cup fresh lemon juice

1 tablespoon sugar

½ cup canned whole-berry cranberry
sauce

Salt to taste

1. In a small bowl, combine the onion, carrots, parsley, lemon juice, and sugar. Set aside to allow the sugar to dissolve, for 5 minutes.

2. Stir in the cranberry sauce and season with salt. Cover with plastic wrap and refrigerate for at least 1 hour before serving.

MAKES ABOUT 1 CUP

Taco Chip Salad with Lime Vinaigrette

This is not a true taco salad, which is to say a deep-fried taco basket full of salad stuff. No home cook I know would deep-fry a tortilla to do that; you'd have to take a sick day to find the time and then clean up the mess. But I know a lot of cooks who would do something like this and line a pretty Mexican-style salad with taco chips. Note that this calls for green leaf lettuce, but if I have some around I like to mix in a little shredded iceberg lettuce as well, for extra crunch. In the interest of saving time, I specify a fully cooked rotisserie chicken, one you can just pick up in the market. Any cooked chicken will do, however, just nothing with Asian or other competing spices that wouldn't work here.

LIME VINAIGRETTE

3 tablespoons olive or vegetable oil

1 tablespoon cider vinegar

Finely grated zest of 1 lime

1 tablespoon fresh lime juice

¼ cup seeded and diced ripe tomato

1 clove garlic, peeled

¼ teaspoon chili powder

¼ teaspoon ground cumin

Small handful fresh cilantro or parsley
leaves

Salt and freshly ground black pepper
to taste

SALAD AND ASSEMBLY
One 15-ounce can black beans, drained
  and rinsed well
2 medium-size ripe tomatoes, cored and
  cut into wedges
1 medium-size head green leaf lettuce,
  pulled apart into leaves and washed
1 small fully cooked rotisserie chicken,
  preferably barbecued, meat removed
  and chopped or cut into strips

1 small green or red bell pepper, seeded
  and finely diced
1 small red onion, finely diced
1 cup diced sharp cheddar or pepper
  jack cheese
Small bag baked tortilla chips

1. To make the vinaigrette, combine all of the dressing ingredients in a blender and process until smooth. Taste, adding more a bit more salt and pepper as needed. Transfer to a small serving bowl and set aside.

2. To assemble the salad, make a mound of the black beans in the center of a large serving platter. Make a ring of tomato wedges around the beans, laying them on a flat side.

3. Stack the lettuce leaves on top of one another and cut into thin strips; arrange in a circle around the tomatoes. Place the chunks of chicken meat here and there on top of the lettuce. Dampen the beans with a little of the dressing, then garnish the entire top of the salad with the bell pepper, onion, and cheese. Arrange a ring of tortilla chips around the lettuce. Serve with the dressing on the side.

MAKES 6 SERVINGS

SUMMER IN OUR SIGHTS

Cream of Watercress and Potato Soup

....

Dilly Cottage Cheese Biscuits

....

Strawberry, Cucumber, and Kiwi Salad

....

'm here to tell you that I never really had an appreciation for spring until I moved to New Hampshire. Now that I've been here twenty-two years, that appreciation is what you might call razor sharp.

Which is to say that when the first signs of spring start to appear up here, I'm nearly beside myself with gratitude and relief. It doesn't matter that the foods in the market are a good month or two ahead of our local schedule. At least I can start pretending winter is just about over and start cooking with a fresh new attitude.

This menu, then, is dedicated to a couple of those proverbial harbingers of spring many of us look forward to, strawberries and watercress. I've taken into account—let's be honest—that spring strawberries from California are but a shadow of what they'll be a couple of months hence. Still, they'll do for the time being and, with the blessing of balsamic vinegar, sugar, and the other good company they keep in this salad, the results are pretty darn good. Our soup features the wonderfully peppery flavor of watercress, which you can now buy in those handy bags in the salad department, if, that is, you don't have a secret supply in one of your local streams. Served with these little dill biscuits, this is a fine spring menu indeed.

Cream of Watercress and Potato Soup

Until recently here in rural New England it hasn't been easy to find a steady supply of watercress, but that's changed. Now you can find it almost without fail in the produce section along with those bags of prewashed salad greens (which, incidentally, is a huge market; in spite of their high cost versus whole heads of lettuce, Americans now spend more than a billion dollars a year on these bagged greens). Since watercress cooks down considerably, the major limiting factor as to how much you can include in this soup is cost. I buy a 4½-ounce bag and by the time I throw out the thick stems, there are probably only 2 cups lightly packed leaves. You can easily add twice that much if you like. This is a smooth, creamy soup with a subtle flavor and, once you've made it, my guess is that you'll want to make it again.

2 tablespoons unsalted butter

2 leeks, white part only, halved lengthwise, rinsed well, and chopped

1 tablespoon unbleached all-purpose flour

3 cups chicken or vegetable stock

1 large all-purpose potato

¼ to ½ teaspoon salt, to your taste

Freshly ground black pepper to taste

4 to 8 ounces watercress, to your taste or your pocketbook, thick stems discarded

¾ cup half-and-half or light cream

Several watercress leaves (optional), for garnish

1. Melt the butter in a medium-size saucepan over moderately low heat. Stir in the leeks, cover, and sweat, for 12 minutes.

2. Add the flour and cook, stirring, for 1 minute. Stir in the stock, potato, and ¼ teaspoon salt and season with pepper. Partially cover the pot and simmer for 10 minutes. Stir in the watercress and simmer, covered, until the potatoes are very tender, 5 minutes more.

3. Remove the soup from the heat and spoon the solids and a little of the broth into a food processor. Process until smooth, then stir the puree back into the broth. Heat several minutes, stirring, then serve. Garnish with watercress leaves, if desired.

MAKES 4 TO 5 SERVINGS

Dilly Cottage Cheese Biscuits

I've always liked recipes for what's commonly known as dilly bread. Sometimes it's a beaten (rather than kneaded) yeast bread, other times a quick bread, the common denominator seeming to be cottage cheese, dill, and sometimes other herbs. I thought the idea would translate well to a biscuit, and it did. This follows pretty straightforward biscuit procedure— you cut the butter into the dry mixture—but then, when you'd otherwise add the milk or buttermilk, you add cottage cheese that's been pureed with a little milk. This combination has a softening effect on the dough, so the biscuits are good and tender. And the cottage cheese helps them keep. These reheat nicely hours or even a day after, and many biscuits don't. Eat them plain with butter, perhaps with a dab of fruit preserves.

2 cups unbleached all-purpose flour	**$^1/_4$ teaspoon freshly ground black pepper**
$2^1/_2$ tablespoons sugar	**$^1/_4$ cup ($^1/_2$ stick) cold unsalted butter,**
$2^1/_2$ teaspoons baking powder	**cut into several pieces**
$^3/_4$ teaspoon salt	**$^1/_2$ cup grated cheddar cheese**
$1^1/_2$ teaspoons dill weed (or slightly	**$1^1/_4$ cups cottage cheese**
more, if fresh)	**$^1/_3$ cup milk**

1. Preheat the oven to 400 degrees F and very lightly butter a large baking sheet.

2. Sift the flour, sugar, baking powder, and salt together into a large bowl. Mix in the dill and pepper. Add the butter and cut or rub into the dry mixture with a pastry blender or your fingers until it resembles coarse meal. Mix in the grated cheese; set aside.

3. Puree the cottage cheese and milk together in a food processor. Make a well in the center of the dry mixture and add the cottage cheese mixture. Mix with a wooden spoon until the dough pulls together and there are no dry spots; it will be a little stiffer than other biscuit doughs you might have made. Let the dough rest for 3 minutes.

4. Turn the dough out onto a floured work surface and knead gently 3 or 4 times with floured hands. Pat the dough about $^3/_4$ to 1 inch thick. Cut into 2- to $2^1/_4$-inch rounds and place on the prepared baking sheet, leaving room between them.

5. Bake the biscuits on the center rack until golden, 15 to 17 minutes. Transfer to a cloth-lined basket and serve at once.

MAKES 12 TO 15 BISCUITS

Strawberry, Cucumber, and Kiwi Salad

This is an inspiration from my friend Jeff Paige, who was for years chef at the Canterbury Shaker Village in New Hampshire. If it sounds a little pretentious, fear not: this is plain good eating. When you mix these elements together and simply let them sit, a remarkable thing happens: they make their own dressing, and an excellent dressing at that. But don't wait too long—no more than 30 minutes—because you don't want the ingredients to get wilted and tired. Spoon the salad and its dressing over leaves of Bibb lettuce, and that's all there is to it.

2 large cucumbers, peeled, halved lengthwise, and seeded

Salt to taste

1 pint ripe strawberries, hulled and sliced

2 kiwi fruit, peeled, halved, and sliced into half moons

1 tablespoon sugar

1½ tablespoons balsamic vinegar

2 teaspoons olive oil

1 head Bibb lettuce, leaves rinsed well and dried

1. Halve the cucumber halves lengthwise, then place them side by side and cut them into dice. Transfer to a medium-size bowl and salt lightly. Add the strawberries, kiwi, sugar, vinegar, and olive oil; toss well. Cover with plastic wrap and refrigerate for 30 minutes, stirring once or twice.

2. To assemble the salad, arrange 2 or 3 lettuce leaves on individual salad plates. Spoon some of the salad mixture and its dressing over each salad, then serve right away.

MAKES 4 TO 6 SERVINGS

A FEW OF MY FAVORITE THINGS

Cream of Pea Soup with Mint Gremolata

. . . .

Apple Date Muffins

. . . .

Ranch Chicken Salad in Fanned Tomatoes

. . . .

As I say in the beginning of this book, the menus here are merely suggestions, various ways you *could* mix and match dishes. Sometimes, however—perhaps all of the time—we'd rather pick and choose and build a menu à la carte, adding stuff that just plain sounds good, whether or not they amount to a unified theme.

So it is with this menu: these are just things I like and I haven't lost sleep over whether or not they'll win any prizes for originality, goes-togetherness, or anything else. It's the sort of meal I might want fixed for me on Father's Day, one of the few days when a fellow can ask for his favorite things with selfish optimism.

Besides the flavor, it's the speediness of this soup I like. You more or less just boil up some peas in chicken stock, puree them, and you're there. We're talking maybe twenty minutes from start to finish and if you don't want to bother with the herb garnish, then don't.

These apple date muffins I've been making for years. My kids are crazy about them. Like I say, if the crumb topping makes the muffins seem too much like dessert, don't bother. My kids won't let me make these without the topping though. That's the best part, they say. I can't tell you how many times I've gone into the kitchen and found half a dozen or so decapitated apple muffins because someone has ripped off the tops.

Finally, I can never get enough chicken salad—plain, on sandwiches, or plunked on top of tomato, like I do it here. I dress mine with a creamy ranch dressing, add a little celery, and that's about it. If you haven't tried the ranch dressing yet, do. I'll bet you end up making it often and using it on salads of all sorts.

Cream of Pea Soup with Mint Gremolata

One of the easier soups I know, this tastes wonderful made with either fresh or frozen peas. Indeed, the season for fresh peas is so short, I almost always use frozen. The gremolata is simply a mixture of onion, parsley, mint, and lemon zest, all finely chopped and used as a garnish. When you puree the peas, leave a few whole ones in the broth for texture and interest.

CREAM OF PEA SOUP
2 tablespoons unsalted butter
1 medium-size onion, finely chopped
3¹/₂ cups chicken stock
3¹/₂ cups fresh or frozen peas
1 medium-size all-purpose potato, peeled and diced
¹/₄ to ¹/₂ teaspoon salt, or more to taste

Freshly ground black pepper to taste
³/₄ cup heavy cream

MINT GREMOLATA
Handful fresh parsley leaves
Handful fresh mint leaves
1 tablespoon chopped onion
1 lemon

1. Melt the butter in a large saucepan or medium-size soup pot over fairly low heat. Stir in the onion, cover the pan partially, and sweat the onion for 5 minutes.

2. Add the stock, peas, potato, salt, and pepper and bring to a lively simmer. Reduce the heat slightly, cover the pan, and simmer until the potato is soft, 10 to 12 minutes.

3. Using a large slotted spoon or skimmer, transfer most of the solids to a food processor, adding a ladleful of broth; the processor should be no more than one-quarter full. Process the peas until smooth, then add them back to the soup along with the heavy cream. Put the soup back on the burner and reheat it without boiling.

4. While the soup heats, make the gremolata by putting the herbs and onion in a pile on your chopping board. Finely grate about half of the lemon's zest on top of the pile, then mince everything well. Serve the soup with a sprinkling of the gremolata on top.

MAKES 5 SERVINGS

Apple Date Muffins

A great, grainy any-time-of-year muffin, these are so good at dinner that you'll be jump-ing out of bed in the morning to eat the leftovers, *if* you're lucky enough to have any. It sometimes strikes me as over-the-top to put a crumb topping on dinner breads—not always, mind you—but if you can be persuaded, this is a good candidate. (If you can be only half per-suaded, put it on the half of them you'll eat for breakfast the next morning.)

1 recipe Pecan Streusel (page 109) or granulated sugar, for sprinkling on top	1 large egg
	1/2 cup firmly packed light brown sugar
2 cups unbleached all-purpose flour	1 cup milk
1/2 cup whole wheat flour	1/3 cup plain yogurt
2 teaspoons baking powder	1/4 cup vegetable oil
1/2 teaspoon baking soda	1 medium-size crisp apple, peeled,
1/2 teaspoon salt	cored, and finely chopped
1/2 teaspoon ground cinnamon	1/2 cup finely chopped dates

1. Preheat the oven to 400 degrees F. Grease 12 muffin cups. Make the streusel if you're planning to use it.

2. Sift the flours, baking powder, baking soda, salt, and cinnamon together in a large bowl. In a medium-size bowl, whisk the egg until frothy, then whisk in the brown sugar, milk, yogurt, and oil.

3. Make a well in the center of the dry ingredients, add the liquid, and stir, using a wooden spoon, with a few swift strokes, just until blended. Fold in the apple and dates.

4. Divide the batter evenly between the prepared muffin cups. Cover with streusel or sprinkle with sugar and bake until the tops are golden brown and feel springy when gently prodded with a finger, about 20 minutes.

5. Let the muffins cool in the pan, on a wire rack, for several minutes, then transfer the muffins to a cloth-lined basket and serve at once. Or transfer back to the rack to cool.

MAKES 10 TO 12 MUFFINS

Ranch Chicken Salad in Fanned Tomatoes

This makes for an attractive presentation, the tomatoes sliced almost all the way through, separated, and a mound of chicken salad placed in the center. The beauty of this recipe is that the ranch dressing has got so much flavor that the chicken needs little else, other than some chopped celery and a little Parmesan cheese. Greens are optional here, but some shredded leaves do look pretty at the base of the tomato.

3 cups bite-size cooked chicken pieces

2 ribs celery, finely chopped

1/2 cup freshly grated Parmesan cheese

1 recipe Parmesan Peppercorn Ranch
   Dressing (page 239)

4 to 6 medium-size ripe tomatoes, to
   your taste, cored

Shredded lettuce greens (optional)

1. Combine the chicken, celery, Parmesan, and about 1 cup of the dressing in a large bowl. Toss well to coat evenly. Cover with plastic wrap and refrigerate if not using right away.

2. To serve, slice down through the top of the tomatoes with a sharp serrated knife, *but don't cut all the way through.* You'll want to make 3 evenly spaced cuts, leaving 6 wedge sections joined at the base by a little bit of tomato and skin. Place the tomatoes on individual salad plates and gently "fan" the sections by spreading them apart. Put a neat mound of chicken salad right in the center. If you're using the greens, make a circle of them around each tomato or put some underneath. Serve the salad with the extra dressing on the side.

VARIATION: If you'd like to use large tomatoes, slice off the top third of the tomato and hollow out some of the flesh. Mound the salad inside the tomato and put the top back on if you like. Don't put the tomato scoopings to waste; use them in soup or salad dressing or tomato sauce.

MAKES 4 TO 6 SERVINGS

SOUP HOT, SOUP COLD

The Bounty
of Summer in a
Bowl

thyme

basil

HERBS TAKE CENTER STAGE

Summery Cream of Spinach Soup with Lemon Basil

• • • • • • • • • • • • • •

Rosemary Semolina Scones

• • • • • • • • • • • • • •

Potato and Fresh Pea Salad with Dill

• • • • • • • • • • • • • •

Where would any of us be without fresh summer herbs? Fresh herbs put the spring back in our culinary step. They add little grace notes of flavor to our salads and soups, omelets, and fresh vegetables. And the nice thing is that anyone can grow them; you don't have to be a gardening whiz kid to grow a big pot of mixed herbs on your front porch or patio.

I count these three recipes high on my "can't miss" list of herbed favorites: a spinach soup with lemon basil, tender scones with a rosemary benediction, and a potato salad tossed with dill and a lovely pea-green vinaigrette. It's an ambitious menu for this time of year, but not overly so. The dry ingredients for the scones can be mixed ahead (you can even cut in the butter, too, if you refrigerate). And the potato and pea salad is uncomplicated and likes a few hours in the fridge anyway. Rather than try to bite this menu off in one piece, just whittle away at it over the day. It will come together nicely by dinner.

I mention this in the headnote, but it's worth repeating here: if the thought of a rosemary scone does nothing for you, keep an open mind. The first time I had one was at one of L.A.'s better eateries, for brunch. An editor friend of mine had been raving about this scone and it was one of the very reasons we had come. I remained skeptical up until the moment I took a bite, after which I couldn't get home fast enough to see if I could duplicate that blissful experience. (I suppose I could have simply asked for the recipe, but in my haste to ask for second and third helpings, it slipped my mind.) If you have an herb gardener friend, borrow a few sprigs of rosemary and return with a warm basketful of these scones. That should cement the friendship nicely.

Summery Cream of Spinach Soup with Lemon Basil

Perhaps you find yourself doing this too, but —to me—half the fun of shopping at farmstands in the summer is cooking in your head as you go. Of course, everything depends on what's there, what's priced right, and the quality of it all. Maybe you went with your heart set on green beans, only to see that they're a little tired, but that corn over there looks mighty fine. And don't you know that corn would taste wonderful steamed and served with potato salad made with those new potatoes over yonder. That big bargain bag of fresh spinach with your name on it? What a soup that would make, seasoned with the lemon basil up near the cash register whose aroma is driving you mad. That was precisely the scenario the first time I made this soup. I saw the spinach, then the basil, and the next thing you knew I had them in the pot. I kept it all very quick and simple, this being summer and all. I wanted to eat soup, not putter around a hot stove all afternoon. If this all sounds about right to you, try the soup, and don't worry if you don't have any lemon basil on hand. You can fake it with regular basil and a few gratings of lemon zest for garnish.

3 tablespoons unsalted butter

2 large onions

2 cloves garlic, bruised

5 cups hot chicken stock

1¼ to 1½ pounds fresh spinach, rinsed
   well and stems removed

½ cup heavy cream

3 tablespoons unbleached all-purpose
   flour

Salt and freshly ground black pepper
   to taste

½ lemon

Handful fresh lemon basil leaves

1. Melt the butter in a good-sized covered enameled casserole over moderate heat. Add the onions and garlic and cook, stirring, for 12 to 15 minutes; you want them to turn light golden but not brown and crispy.

2. Add about half of the chicken stock and all of the spinach to the pot. Bring to a boil, cover tightly, and steam over high heat until the spinach is cooked down and wilted, about 5 minutes. Remove from the heat.

3. Using a large slotted spoon, transfer the spinach and most of the other solids to a food processor; if a few onion or spinach floaters remain, that's fine. Process the spinach to a smooth puree and stir it back into the pot. Add the remaining stock and bring the soup to a simmer.

4. While the soup heats, whisk the cream and flour together in a small bowl. Scrape this mixture into the soup; whisk to blend. Bring the soup to an active simmer, then reduce the heat slightly and heat, stirring often, for 10 minutes. Taste the soup as it heats; season with salt and pepper.

5. Just before serving, squeeze the juice of the half lemon into the soup, but not all at once; do half, taste, then add the rest if you like. Stack the basil leaves, cut into threads, and sprinkle some over each serving.

MAKES 6 TO 8 SERVINGS

Rosemary Semolina Scones

I once had a scone like this at one of L.A.'s finest restaurants. Frankly, I was a little skeptical at first—a *rosemary* scone?—but the flavor turned out to be exquisite. Back home, I discovered how wonderful these are with butter and honey, not to mention how well they go with soups hot and cold. For a nice touch, mince extra rosemary with sugar. Glaze as directed, then sprinkle the herb-sugar on top and press it in lightly before baking.

1²/₃ cups unbleached all-purpose flour

¹/₃ cup semolina flour (available in health food stores)

3 tablespoons sugar, plus extra for sprinkling

1 teaspoon baking powder

¹/₂ teaspoon baking soda

¹/₂ teaspoon salt

Finely grated zest of 1 lemon

1 tablespoon minced fresh rosemary leaves or 1¹/₂ teaspoons minced dried

6 tablespoons (³/₄ stick) cold unsalted butter, cut into ¹/₄-inch pieces

¹/₂ cup sour cream

¹/₂ cup milk

1. Preheat the oven to 400 degrees F. Lightly grease a large baking sheet.

2. Sift the flours, sugar, baking powder, baking soda, and salt together into a large bowl. Add the lemon zest and rosemary. Scatter the butter over the dry ingredients and rub it in with your fingers, until the butter is the size of split peas.

3. Whisk the sour cream and milk together in a small bowl. Set aside 1¹/₂ tablespoons of this liquid. Make a well in the dry ingredients, add the rest of the sour cream mixture, and stir just until the dough pulls together in a shaggy mass. Let the dough rest for 3 minutes.

4. Gather the dough into a ball and knead gently several times, with floured hands, on a lightly floured work surface. Pat the dough out into a 7¹/₂-inch circle and cut into 8 wedges. Brush the pieces with the reserved sour cream mixture, then lightly sprinkle with sugar. Reassemble the pieces on the baking sheet, leaving ¹/₄ inch between them.

5. Bake until lightly browned and crusty, 17 to 18 minutes. Let cool briefly on a wire rack, but do eat them while still warm.

MAKES 8 SCONES

Potato and Fresh Pea Salad with Dill

Peas are just the right seasonal teammate for a summer potato salad. In this version, I take some of the peas and mash them with a fork, then include these mashed peas in the vinaigrette dressing. Adds a nice, light green hue and flavor. As with any potato salad, you may need to splash on a little extra vinegar, especially if the salad has been refrigerated for several hours ahead. I prefer summery red-skinned potatoes here, but you can use all-purpose potatoes if that's what you have on hand. You can't miss with a garnish of chopped hard-cooked eggs on this or most any other potato salad.

3 to 4 cups scrubbed potatoes, peeled
    and cut into ³/₄-inch dice
Salt
1 cup fresh peas (frozen will work fine,
    too)
3 tablespoons olive oil
2¹/₂ tablespoons red wine vinegar

2 teaspoons Dijon mustard
2 teaspoons chopped fresh dill or 1
    teaspoon dill weed
Freshly ground black pepper to taste
Chopped hard-cooked eggs or chopped
    fresh herbs (optional), for garnish

1. Bring the potatoes to a boil in a medium-size saucepan of salted water. Boil the potatoes until just tender, 5 to 8 minutes Quickly drain, then immediately spread them on a large baking sheet to cool.

2. Put the saucepan back on the heat with several inches of salted water. Bring to a boil, then boil the peas until tender, 4 to 8 minutes. Drain. Put about one third of the peas in a large bowl and mash them well with a fork. Whisk in the olive oil, vinegar, mustard, dill, and about ¹/₄ teaspoon salt. Add the potatoes and reserved peas; toss thoroughly but gently, adding more salt and pepper if needed.

3. Cover with plastic wrap and refrigerate until ready to serve. Taste again before serving, adding more salt, pepper, or vinegar as needed.

MAKES 6 SERVINGS

SEAFOOD CHOWDER AND CRACKERS

Cape Ann Seafood Chowder

• • • • • • • • • • • • • •

Grainy Parmesan Crackers

• • • • • • • • • • • • • •

Cold Broccoli Salad with
Creamy Mustard Dressing

• • • • • • • • • • • • • •

One of my favorite places in this country is a quiet little cape that sits in the shadow of its better-known cousin, Cape Cod, to the south. I'm referring to Cape Ann, a cluster of four small coastal communities on the north shore of Massachusetts. One of them, Rockport, used to be a famous granite exporter and you see lovely displays of the stone everywhere you go in town. Gloucester—the oldest commercial fishing town in the country—is also quite fetching, if a little rougher around the edges. Historically, the citizens of Gloucester honor St. Peter, the patron saint of fishermen, with a parade and other festivities on the last weekend in June, a fitting time to prepare this meal.

The centerpiece of this menu, then, is a chowder inspired by a place I love, and I think that's a nice way to cook. I like visiting an area, sampling the local cuisine, then spinning my own variations of dishes I've eaten there. After all, that's how cuisines move and evolve, when good cooks merge new ideas into old ones.

New Englanders have a penchant for plain crackers with their chowders. I think plain crackers are okay, but, not being a native, I'm also not bound to the silent code that says I will give them my unequivocal support. Frankly, I'm fonder of crackers with a little more crunch and flavor, like these Parmesan crackers. At the risk of sounding like a perfect dweeb, I like making my own crackers and I encourage you to try these because you might like cracker making too. A briny seafood stew and crunchy crackers beg for the company of something cold and creamy; I thought this cold broccoli salad, made with chickpeas and a sassy dressing, was just the ticket.

Cape Ann Seafood Chowder

This favorite chowder of mine represents an amalgam of variations and inspirations, based on a number of seafood chowders I've eaten on Cape Ann. I love the way this looks served in wide soup bowls, with the mussel shells peeking up out of it. Note that you shouldn't finish salting the soup until the very end because the final few minutes of cooking, with the seafood in the pot, will deepen the flavor and give it a briny taste.

2½ tablespoons olive oil

1 large onion, halved and thinly sliced
   into half moons

1 medium-size green bell pepper, seeded
   and cut into thin strips

8 ounces mushrooms, sliced

2 cloves garlic, chopped

1½ cups canned crushed tomatoes in
   puree

¾ cup vegetable stock

1 cup bottled clam juice

½ cup dry white wine

¾ teaspoon salt, plus more to taste

Freshly ground black pepper to taste

½ teaspoon dried basil

½ teaspoon dried oregano

½ teaspoon sugar

1 pound cod or haddock fillets,
   cut into 1½-inch chunks

1 pound fresh mussels, scrubbed and
   debearded (page 64), and those with
   broken shells discarded

Chopped fresh parsley leaves, for
   garnish

1. Heat the olive oil in a large, heavy enameled soup pot over moderate heat. Add the onion and bell pepper, and cook, stirring, until the onion is translucent, about 10 minutes. Stir in the mushrooms and garlic. Cover, reduce the heat slightly, and cook for several minutes, until the mushrooms give off some of their liquid.

2. Add the tomatoes, stock, clam juice, wine, salt, pepper, herbs, and sugar. Bring to a simmer, then simmer gently, partially covered, for 10 minutes.

3. Add the fish chunks to the soup, submerging them with a spoon. Scatter the mussels over the top and push them down into the broth also. Return to a simmer, then cover and gently simmer the soup about 7 minutes, very gently stirring it once or twice during the last couple of minutes.

4. Taste the soup, adding more salt or pepper if necessary. Serve piping hot, garnished with parsley, discarding any unopened mussels.

MAKES 6 SERVINGS

Of Mussels and Beards

That hairy little thing hanging from your mussels? It's called a byssus or, more commonly, the beard. The beard is the mussel's way of anchoring itself to solid objects and its steel wool–like fibers are incredibly strong. Greek fisherman are said to have made knit fishing gloves from it and passed them down for generations. The U.S. Navy is looking for ways to use the stuff for ship repairs.

Most every recipe you see for mussels will instruct you to remove the beards prior to cooking but don't be alarmed if your mussels are beardless. Sometimes the beards are removed prior to sale. And if the mussels are held in tanks before going to market, they may discard their own beards when they sense they no longer need them. When beards are present, they can be snipped off with scissors, but you will do a more thorough job by pulling the beards off because some of the beard is inevitably tucked inside the shell. Simply grasp the beard firmly and pull it from the broad end to the narrow end of the mussel, where the shell is hinged. Don't be surprised if the mussel puts up a bit of a fight. Just give the beard a good yank. Discard the beards, rinse the mussels well, and you're ready to use them.

Grainy Parmesan Crackers

These are very simple to make, very much like preparing a food-processor pie dough. This dough, however, is rolled even thinner than pie pastry and—unlike pie dough—is not prone to cracking apart and other sorts of ill behavior. These crackers can be rolled and immediately baked. Or you can refrigerate them, directly on the sheet, and then bake, which relaxes the dough somewhat and helps curtail the slight curling they do as they bake—not that there's anything wrong with that. In fact, the curl is quite charming. These are excellent with all sorts of soups.

$^1/_2$ cup whole wheat flour

$^1/_2$ cup unbleached all-purpose flour

$^1/_3$ cup fine-ground yellow cornmeal

$^1/_2$ teaspoon salt

$^1/_2$ teaspoon baking powder

$^1/_4$ cup freshly grated Parmesan cheese, plus extra to sprinkle on crackers

1 tablespoon olive oil

$^1/_3$ cup milk

1. Preheat the oven to 325 degrees F and get out a couple of large baking sheets.

2. Combine the flours, cornmeal, salt, baking powder, and cheese in a food processor; pulse briefly, to mix. With the machine running, add the olive oil in a gradual stream. Then add the milk in a gradual stream. When all the milk has been added, start pulsing the machine until the dough forms large clumps and looks like it wants to ball up around the blade.

3. Turn the dough out onto a floured work surface and divide into 4 equal parts. Squeeze each one several times—to sort of knead them—then wrap all but one of the pieces in plastic and set aside.

4. On a sheet of wax paper, roll the first ball of dough out with a lightly floured rolling pin into a very thin circle slightly less than $^1/_8$ inch thick. Sprinkle a little extra cheese over the dough and gently roll it into the top. Using a sharp knife or pizza cutter, cut the dough into 6 or 8 pie-like wedges. Transfer the wedges to the baking sheet, leaving just a little space between them. They won't spread. Poke each one several times with a fork, to prevent them from puffing up. Repeat with the remaining balls of dough.

5. Bake the crackers until they turn noticeably golden at the edges, about 20 minutes; don't underbake, because you want them to be good and crisp. Transfer to a wire rack and let them cool and crisp up before serving. Repeat for any remaining dough. These are best eaten the day they're made.

MAKES 24 TO 32 CRACKERS

Cold Broccoli Salad with Creamy Mustard Dressing

I love broccoli, hot or cold. So do my kids; it seems to be one of the more kid-friendly vegetables out there. Here's a salad that most people adore: cold broccoli, celery, and chickpeas tossed with a very mustardy dressing. If there's time to make them, or I have a package on hand, I'll sometimes mix in a handful of croutons just before serving (see page 26 for my homemade method). The pleasant crunch of the croutons is a wonderful texture contrast in this fairly rich-tasting, dense, and creamy salad.

1 large head broccoli	1 tablespoon tarragon vinegar or white wine vinegar
1/2 cup plain yogurt	1 rib celery, finely chopped
1/2 cup mayonnaise	1 cup canned chickpeas, drained and rinsed
2 tablespoons chopped fresh parsley leaves	1/2 cup finely chopped red onion
1 tablespoon chopped fresh basil leaves or 1 teaspoon dried	1/2 cup freshly grated Parmesan cheese
1 1/2 tablespoons Dijon mustard	Freshly ground black pepper to taste
1 teaspoon dry mustard	1 cup croutons (optional)

1. Bring a medium-size pot of salted water to a boil. Meanwhile, cut the broccoli into bite-size florets; peel and dice the stalks, if you like (see page 67). When the water boils, drop in the broccoli and boil just until crisp-tender, 3 to 4 minutes. Drain, then immediately spread on a baking sheet or platter to cool. Transfer to a bowl, cover with plastic wrap, and refrigerate.

2. In a large bowl, whisk the yogurt, mayonnaise, parsley, basil, mustards, and vinegar together. Add the celery, chickpeas, onion, cheese, and broccoli and toss together well, seasoning with pepper. Cover with plastic wrap and refrigerate at least 30 minutes before serving.

3. Just before serving, toss again with the croutons, if you're using them.

MAKES 5 TO 6 SERVINGS

Let's Talk About Stalks

In our rushed world, we often overlook some of the little blessings that come our way, like broccoli stalks. I don't want to sound too sentimental or sappy about it, but broccoli stalks should not be neglected as an important flavor ingredient in making soups and vegetable stock. It only takes a minute to peel your broccoli stalks and cut them into nice, neat little $1/2$-inch dice. Cut the very end off, as it tends to be woody and tough. Then peel the stalk with a vegetable peeler. These wonderful scraps can go in most chicken and vegetable soups and other pureed green soups. For instance, they would be a perfect little addition to Almost Instant Chicken and Rice Soup (page 133); just sweat them with the celery and onion.

A PASSION FOR PEACHES

Chilled Creamy Peach Yogurt Soup

• • • • • • • • • • • • •

Blueberry Lemon Scones

• • • • • • • • • • • • •

*Tomato, Feta, and Peach Composed Salad
with Peach Vinaigrette*

• • • • • • • • • • • • •

have a fondness for peaches that borders on an obsession. It reached its first apex when, as a young man, I would commute between New Jersey and Virginia Beach, where my girlfriend lived. There were peach farmstands scattered everywhere along this route. I'd stop at several of them on each trip and load up the back of my Toyota Corolla with bushel baskets full of dead-ripe peaches the size of softballs. And they were dirt cheap, too. What didn't end up in my stomach would go into preserves and stacks and stacks of peach pies I would make.

When I moved to New Hampshire, a good peach became harder to find. Until I found out that several farms in the southern part of the state grew wonderful peaches, I would have my sister ship them up from North Carolina by second-day mail. This arrangement worked pretty well but it was never quite enough to satisfy my hunger for them. And then there were a couple of occasions when my sister had sent really ripe fruit and the packages were delayed in what must have been some pretty hot trucks, because the boxes would arrive smelling rather foul and oozing liquid.

All this by way of letting you know that it's not so strange that I would offer you a menu with not one but two peach courses—a cold peach and yogurt soup and a composed salad with peach vinaigrette. If I could have figured a way to bake the peaches in the scones, I would have put them in there, too. As it is, blueberries hold up better in the baking and they make a nice seasonal counterpart to all this peachiness. And the colors—the light peach orange of the soup and the lemon-yellow scones studded with the blueberries—are just gorgeous together. An altogether wonderful menu to celebrate these sweet days of August.

Chilled Creamy Peach Yogurt Soup

I first learned about yogurt soups from my friend Jeff Paige, the former chef at the Canterbury (New Hampshire) Shaker Village. Jeff is a gifted cook, and those gifts haven't gone unnoticed: he has cooked for President George Bush (the elder), for members of the European Parliament, and Julia Child once featured him on one of her cooking shows. He was also lucky enough to train directly under the last two living Shaker eldresses before their passing in the early '90s. Did the Shakers really make yogurt soups? Jeff doesn't think so. But he doesn't think they'd be opposed to the idea either, since they were experimental cooks who embraced good ideas. In any case, Jeff makes a wonderful strawberry yogurt soup that he served to visitors to the Shaker Village; this recipe is adapted from that model. Main rule: Be sure your peaches are absolutely fresh, ripe, and juicy—only the best will do here. This soup needs to chill for at least 4 hours before serving.

2½ pounds ripe peaches (6 or 7
    medium-size ones), peeled
¾ cup sugar
Juice of 1 lemon
⅛ teaspoon pure vanilla extract

1½ cups plain yogurt
1 to 2 cups lemonade, to your taste
Chopped fresh lemon thyme or mint
    leaves (optional), for garnish

1. Cut the peaches into large chunks over the bowl of a food processor, discarding the pits. Add the sugar and lemon juice and process into a smooth puree. Pour the puree into a medium-size bowl. Whisk in the vanilla and yogurt. Stir in 1 cup of the lemonade. Cover with plastic wrap and refrigerate for at least 4 hours. Chill the bowls you plan to serve this in.

2. Just before serving, check the consistency. If it seems to need some thinning—it shouldn't be very thick—stir in enough of the remaining 1 cup of lemonade to achieve the correct texture. Serve in the chilled bowls, garnishing with lemon thyme or mint, if desired.

MAKES 6 TO 8 SERVINGS

Blueberry Lemon Scones

These are gorgeous: a crusty, golden exterior and pale lemon interior, shot throughout with fresh blueberries. Serve these in a small wicker basket lined with a decorative cloth, with a crock of softened butter—and honey or blueberry preserves on the side. You could use raspberries in place of the blues, but they'll likely get somewhat crushed when you handle the dough. They'll still taste wonderful, however.

2¼ cups unbleached all-purpose flour

¼ cup sugar

1 teaspoon baking powder

1 teaspoon baking soda

½ teaspoon salt

Large pinch of ground nutmeg

Finely grated zest of 1 lemon

6 tablespoons (¾ stick) cold unsalted
    butter, cut into ¼-inch pieces

1 cup fresh blueberries (the smaller
    ones are best here), picked over
    for stems

½ cup sour cream

½ cup milk

1 large egg yolk

1 teaspoon pure lemon extract

A little extra milk and sugar,
    for glaze

1. Preheat the oven to 400 degrees F. Lightly oil a large baking sheet and set aside.

2. Sift the flour, sugar, baking powder, baking soda, salt, and nutmeg together into a large bowl; add the lemon zest. Add the butter and cut into the dry ingredients with a pastry blender or use your fingertips until the mixture resembles coarse crumbs. Gently mix in the blueberries.

3. In a small bowl, whisk together the sour cream, milk, egg yolk, and lemon extract. Make a well in the dry mixture and add the liquid all at once. Stir with a wooden spoon just until dough pulls together in a shaggy mass. Let rest for 3 minutes.

4. Scrape the dough onto a floured work surface. Using floured hands, gently knead the dough 4 or 5 times into a ball. Pat the dough out into an 8-inch circle. Slice the dough into 8 wedges, as you would a pie. Brush each one with milk and sprinkle with sugar. Reassemble the wedges on the prepared baking sheet, leaving about ½ inch between the pieces.

5. Bake the scones on the center rack of the oven until golden brown and crusty, about 15 minutes. Transfer the scones to a wire rack. These are best served warm, or at least within an hour of baking.

MAKES 8 SCONES

Tomato, Feta, and Peach Composed Salad with Peach Vinaigrette

This was inspired by a recipe I saw for feta cheese, honey, and coarsely ground pepper. It got me playing around with the concept of using salty feta cheese with ripe fruit. The contrast played quite well and particularly well with peaches. If you like, add a few diced cooked beets. There's flexibility here in your choice of greens: I like a mix of milder and more peppery greens.

SALAD

4 to 5 medium-size ripe tomatoes, cored and thinly sliced

One 6- to 8-ounce block feta cheese, cut into thinly sliced squares

1 head Boston lettuce

Handful watercress, large stems removed

3 medium-size ripe peaches

PEACH VINAIGRETTE

2 medium-size very ripe peaches, peeled

2 tablespoons fresh lemon juice

1 teaspoon finely grated lemon zest

1 tablespoon honey

Pinch of salt

3 tablespoons olive oil

1 tablespoon chopped fresh basil or lemon basil leaves

3 tablespoons fresh orange juice, or more to taste

Sugar to taste

Freshly ground black pepper to taste

1. Select a large presentation plate. Around the outside of the platter, arrange the tomato and feta cheese slices in an overlapping row. Rinse and dry the greens, tearing the Boston lettuce into large pieces. Toss with the watercress and spread in the center of the plate. Peel the peaches if they have thick skins; otherwise, don't bother. Pit, then slice the peaches and place them here and there over and around the lettuce.

2. To make the vinaigrette, pit, then cut the peaches into chunks, dropping the flesh into a medium-size bowl. With your hands, break the peaches into small pieces. Whisk in the lemon juice, zest, honey, olive oil, and basil. Whisk in the orange juice, 1 tablespoon at a time, until the dressing tastes right and seems to have the proper texture. Add sugar as needed, by the 1/2 teaspoon. It should be sweet, mildly tart, and with just enough body to coat the greens.

3. Spoon the dressing lightly over the tomatoes and feta, drizzle some over the greens and peaches, then toss the greens lightly. Any extra dressing can be served on the side. Garnish the salad with pepper as needed, then serve.

MAKES 6 SERVINGS

THREE AMERICAN CLASSICS

Cream of Broccoli and Fontina Soup

* * * * * * * * * * * * * *

Cinnamon Raisin Bran Muffins

* * * * * * * * * * * * * *

The Great American Iceberg Salad

* * * * * * * * * * * * * *

Treasured recipes are like treasured cars, movies, or songs: their appeal endures and even sometimes gets stronger as the years go by. So it is with the menu I've selected here. These are recipes that have been around for years, never drifting far from our thoughts and plates, even as the likes of fancy foods, gourmet foods, and fashionable foods have come and gone. American classics that they are, these three have a patriotic flavor that's suitable for the Fourth of July, Flag Day, or even Election Day.

The only problem with some of the classics, I've noticed, is that we occasionally start to take them for granted. Thus, it is not uncommon to see sloppily made examples that can give these standards a bad name. Cream of broccoli soup is one good example. I can't tell you how many times I've ordered it in restaurants, hoping for the best, but all too often being served a pasty thick mess that should bring shame to our collective culinary soul. My purpose here, then, is to show that the standards, if made with care, can be every bit as good as the food we think of as "gourmet." A gourmet is someone who takes care with his food, treats it with respect and takes pleasure in it, whether it's a pricey cut of meat, a peanut butter and jelly sandwich, or a bowl of soup.

Cream of Broccoli and Fontina Soup

Smooth and creamy, with just the right amount of body, this is the way I like a cream of broccoli soup. Some of the vegetable pieces are left whole—you pluck them out of the simmering broth and set them aside—and the rest are pureed and poured back into the soup. Fontina is a relatively mild cheese. If you want to make this a bit zippier, and taste closer to the standard recipes of this sort, substitute extra-sharp cheddar cheese and add a teaspoon or so of Dijon mustard.

4 cups chicken stock	2½ tablespoons unbleached
1 head broccoli	all-purpose flour
1 medium-size all-purpose potato, peeled	1½ cups milk or light cream
and diced	Pinch of ground nutmeg
Salt to taste	2 cups grated fontina cheese
3 tablespoons unsalted butter	½ teaspoon dried basil
1 large onion, finely chopped	Freshly ground black pepper to taste

1. Bring the chicken stock to a gentle simmer in a medium-size saucepan. As it heats, cut the broccoli into small florets; peel and dice the stalks, then add the florets, stalks, and potato to the stock. Add about ¼ teaspoon salt, cover partially, and bring the liquid to an active simmer.

2. When the vegetables are barely tender, scoop about 1 cup of them out of the stock with a slotted spoon and set aside. Continue to simmer, covered, until the vegetables are soft, about 5 minutes longer. Remove from the heat.

3. Meanwhile, melt the butter in a large saucepan or medium-size soup pot over moderate heat. Stir in the onion and cook, stirring, until translucent, 8 to 9 minutes. Stir in the flour and cook for 1 minute, stirring. Add the milk or cream and nutmeg and cook, stirring, until thickened. Stir in the cheese about half at a time.

4. Once the cheese has been added, ladle most of the broth into the cheese mixture. Transfer the remaining broth and solids to a food processor—filling it no more than about one-quarter full—and process until smooth. Add the puree and reserved vegetable pieces back to the soup. Stir in the basil and season with pepper and more salt if necessary, then gently heat for several minutes before serving.

MAKES 6 SERVINGS

Cinnamon Raisin Bran Muffins

Bran used to be considered horse feed until the early '90s, when it became a sort of heart-healthy horse feed before dropping off the gourmet radar screen to be replaced by something else, maybe sun-dried tomatoes or olive oil, about the time everyone got sick of seeing recipes for Bran-Dusted Chicken Breasts and Bran Ratatouille. Once the dust settled, bran muffins managed to emerge with their reputation intact, probably because it's the most legitimate use there is for the stuff. The best bran muffins are made at home. Almost all the bakery ones I've tried are dry and taste rather like horse feed muffins, the exception being a bran muffin my friend Bev makes from a boxed mix, believe it or not, which is the one I've tried to copy here: dense, moist, and fruity. The applesauce helps, in that regard, as do the moistened raisins. As might be expected, these are very healthy for you, but not nearly so much for me because I tend to slather them with lots of butter. Note that this makes 9 muffins because you fill the muffin cups right up.

1 cup raisins	³/₄ cup oat bran or wheat bran
1 cup unbleached all-purpose flour	1 large egg
¹/₂ cup whole wheat flour	1 cup sweetened applesauce
2¹/₂ teaspoons baking powder	¹/₂ cup firmly packed light brown sugar
¹/₂ teaspoon salt	¹/₃ cup flavorless vegetable oil
¹/₂ teaspoon ground cinnamon	2 tablespoons molasses

1. Preheat the oven to 375 degrees F and grease 9 muffin cups. Put the raisins in a small bowl and cover with hot water. Set aside to plump.

2. Sift the flours, baking powder, salt, and cinnamon together into a large bowl; stir in the bran and set aside.

3. Beat the egg lightly in a medium-size bowl. Whisk in the applesauce, brown sugar, oil, and molasses. Make a well in the center of the dry ingredients, add the liquid, and stir with a wooden spoon until evenly blended. Drain the raisins and stir into the batter.

4. Divide the batter evenly between the 9 muffin cups, filling them nearly to the top. Bake for 22 minutes; when done, the tops will be springy to the touch. Let the muffins cool in the pan, on a wire rack for 5 minutes, then transfer the muffins to the rack.

MAKES 9 MUFFINS

The Great American Iceberg Salad

Fashions come and go in the food world. For many years it was fashionable to put down iceberg lettuce, passing it off as trivial and tasteless compared to some of the hip greens that were coming to market. And even though there was an element of truth to some of the criticism—the charms of iceberg are more tied to its texture than any actual flavor—I was glad when the name calling started to die down so we could all start eating it again. That said, here's my take on one of the best things you can do with iceberg: serve it with sliced tomato, hard-boiled egg, and maybe a few strips of ham, with the requisite Thousand Island dressing. My mom was crazy about this when I was a kid and she served it all the time, though I don't remember much caring for it back then. Nowadays I love it, however, and every time I eat it I think of the kitchen I grew up in, all Formica, stainless steel, siblings galore, and, of course, my mom. Note: If you have the time, do make the dressing ahead and refrigerate it for a couple of hours to firm up the texture. And no fair using any low-fat ingredients; we never would have done that back in the 1960s.

THOUSAND ISLAND DRESSING
3/4 cup mayonnaise
1/4 cup sour cream
1/3 cup chili sauce, preferably Heinz
2 tablespoons finely chopped pitted
    green olives
2 tablespoons seeded and finely chopped
    green bell pepper
2 tablespoons minced red onion
1 to 2 tablespoons minced fresh parsley
    leaves, to your taste

Salt and freshly ground black pepper
    to taste

SALAD AND ASSEMBLY
1 head iceberg lettuce
4 to 6 hard-cooked eggs, to your taste
2 to 3 medium-size ripe tomatoes or
    1 pint cherry tomatoes
1 cucumber, sliced
Thin strips thick-cut deli ham or
    turkey (optional)

1. To prepare the dressing, combine all of the dressing ingredients in a medium-size bowl and mix together well. Cover with plastic wrap and refrigerate.

2. To assemble the salad, core the lettuce and cut into reasonably sized wedges. Arrange the wedges on individual (preferably chilled) salad plates. Add some of each of the remaining ingredients: the eggs should be peeled and halved or quartered, the tomatoes cut into wedges. Don't make a fancy presentation; remember, this salad is from a time when salads were not works of art.

3. Spoon some dressing over the iceberg wedge and on the side of the plate and serve.

MAKES 4 TO 6 SERVINGS

Muffin Musings

If you've been to your local kitchenwares shop lately, you've probably noticed that muffin pans come in an amazing and sometimes bewildering range of shapes and sizes. You'll still find the standard 1/2-cup capacity size. But you'll see mini and maxi versions that hold nearly a cup of batter, with many sizes in between. There are muffin cups that bake into more or less just the wide tops of the muffin. And glazed muffin cups that look like little flower pots.

If, like me, you sometimes find all of this a little confusing, don't worry too much, any pan will work so long as you adjust the baking time accordingly. Obviously, the smaller the pan, the less baking time is required. Those mini muffins will do the job in about 15 minutes. The larger cups may need as much as 30 minutes. It's not difficult to check: just lift out a muffin with the help of a fork, then score it with the fork and gently open. You'll be able to tell if it is done.

While we're on the subject, remember that you can adjust the yield of your muffin recipes simply by using more or less batter per cup, again adjust the baking time as necessary. Traditionally, muffin cups are filled two thirds to three quarters full. A tea-party muffin, however, might be more appropriately petite if you only filled the cup half way. And a muffin you'd take on a hike could be boldly fist-size; fill the cups nearly the entire way. If you end up with unused muffin cups in the pan, put a little water in each of them. The steam will help make a good crust and it will protect the cup from the intense heat of the oven.

A LITTLE HELP FROM MY FRIENDS

Deborah's Bulgur Buttermilk Herb Soup

• • • • • • • • • • • • • •

Jeff's Whipped Cream Biscuits

• • • • • • • • • • • • • •

Brother Victor's French-Style Potato Salad

• • • • • • • • • • • • • •

One of the best things about being in the food business is other people in the food business. Food people—be they writers, editors, restaurateurs, or chefs—are, on the whole, the most generous, helpful, loyal lot you'd ever care to meet. Naturally, there are those with whom we develop a special connection, either by their writings or by meeting them. This menu was inspired by three friendships of my own.

I'm not the only one who thinks highly of Deborah Madison's cooking. She is perhaps the most highly regarded vegetarian cookbook author today, having written first *The Greens Cookbook* (Bantam Books, 1987) and more recently the wildly successful *Vegetarian Cooking for Everyone* (Broadway Books, 1997). What I love most about Deborah is the way she is able, through her writings and recipes, to capture the essence of good flavor and good cooking. Deborah and I have never met, but we've spoken with one another several times over the years about various projects and interests. It was Deborah who inspired this Bulgur Buttermilk Herb Soup.

I've known Chef Jeffrey Paige for many years now. Formerly the chef at the Canterbury Shaker Village, he is one of the smartest, hard-working, and most capable chefs in the country today. I can't tell you the number of times I've called him for cooking advice of one sort or another and he's never failed to help me out, even at his busiest. Among many things culinary, Jeff knows more about Shaker cooking than anyone in the country. Nowadays he's the co-owner and chef at his own restaurant, Cotton, in Manchester, New Hampshire. Jeff tipped me off to these ethereal biscuits on the menu.

Finally, Brother Victor-Antoine d'Avila-Latourrette is another special friend, a gifted cook and holy man who lives under the order of St. Benedict at his monastery in upstate New York. If his name is familiar, that's because this simple monk has a string of successful cookbooks, including his classic *From a Monastery Kitchen* (Triumph Books, 1997) and his wonderful *Twelve Months of Monastery Soups* (Broadway Books, 1998). I've met and written about Brother Victor, so I know firsthand what a fine person and cook he is. He is best known for simple dishes with direct flavors, like this potato salad recipe I adapted from one of his own.

Thanks to the three of you fine cooks, and all my other good cooking friends. This menu is dedicated to all of you.

The Old-Fashioned Bread Basket

Throughout this book you will see the phrase "transfer the bread to a cloth-lined basket" any number of times. This is a suggestion with both practical and symbolic meaning. It's practical because a cloth-lined basket is probably the best short-term method for trapping the heat of the muffins, biscuits, scones, or rolls in question. And a basket makes the bread easy to pass at the table. Symbolically, a cloth-lined basket is an invitation to sit a while, relax, and enjoy your meal. It's a welcoming gesture on the cook's part, a detail that may appear small on the surface but speaks volumes about the hospitality that's been extended, and not just to special guests—a bread basket should be a family tradition as well. So next time you break bread, break out the basket and cloth first.

Deborah's Bulgur Buttermilk Herb Soup

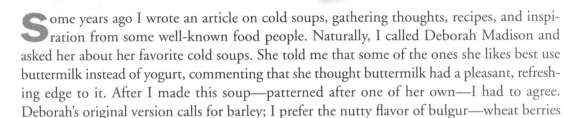

Some years ago I wrote an article on cold soups, gathering thoughts, recipes, and inspiration from some well-known food people. Naturally, I called Deborah Madison and asked her about her favorite cold soups. She told me that some of the ones she likes best use buttermilk instead of yogurt, commenting that she thought buttermilk had a pleasant, refreshing edge to it. After I made this soup—patterned after one of her own—I had to agree. Deborah's original version calls for barley; I prefer the nutty flavor of bulgur—wheat berries that have been steamed, dried, and then chopped to a fine or somewhat rougher grind. Use the latter here. One of Deborah's trademarks is lots of good fresh herbs, so do use them here; the soup just isn't the same with dried herbs. For best results, let this refrigerate overnight so the flavors can merge and mingle.

½ cup medium-coarse bulgur

¼ cup finely diced red onion

3 cups buttermilk

½ teaspoon turmeric

¼ cup finely chopped fresh parsley
  leaves

2 tablespoons finely chopped fresh dill
  or ½ teaspoon dill weed

1 tablespoon finely chopped fresh
  cilantro leaves

1 tablespoon snipped fresh chives

Salt and freshly ground black pepper
  to taste

Dash of sweet paprika or herb
  blossoms (optional), for garnish

1. Rinse the bulgur in a sieve, then transfer it to a bowl. Add enough lightly salted water to cover by a couple of inches. Let it sit at room temperature for a couple of hours, until the bulgur is swollen.

2. Using your hands, scoop up the bulgur and squeeze it well to express as much water as possible, transferring it to a large bowl as you do this. Stir in the remaining ingredients except for the optional garnish. Taste, adding salt and pepper as needed. Cover with plastic wrap and refrigerate overnight if possible, or at least for 4 to 5 hours. Serve in chilled bowls, garnished with the paprika or herb blossoms. Chive blossoms, cilantro flowers, or mustard petals are all good.

MAKES 6 SERVINGS

Jeff's Whipped Cream Biscuits

Maybe you've had cream biscuits or cream scones before, but not this good. This recipe, adapted from one in Jeff Paige's *The Shaker Kitchen*, is the lightest, richest, most melt-in-your mouth biscuit going. As Jeff points out, using cream in biscuits is not a Shaker exclusive, but he thinks that whipping it beforehand probably is. The result? Biscuits so light that they nearly levitate. Note that these use cake flour, which is made from a soft wheat that yields an ultra-light and tender biscuit. You may, however, substitute 2 cups unbleached all-purpose flour, replacing 2 tablespoons of the flour with 2 tablespoons cornstarch to help mimic the softening properties of the cake flour. My favorite thing on these biscuits is a dab of peach preserves. With all that cream, they really don't need any butter.

2 cups cake flour	**¾ teaspoon salt**
1½ tablespoons sugar	**1¼ cups heavy cream**
1 tablespoon baking powder	

1. Preheat the oven to 425 degrees F and get out a large baking sheet. There's no need to grease it.

2. Sift the flour, sugar, baking powder, and salt into a large bowl. Using an electric mixer, in a medium-size bowl whip the heavy cream just until it holds soft peaks. Make a well in the center of the dry mixture and add the whipped cream. Stir briskly with a wooden spoon, just until the dough pulls together in a uniform, shaggy mass.

3. Turn the dough out onto a floured work surface. With floured hands, knead the dough 4 or 5 times, then pat the dough out to a thickness of ¾ inch. Using a smallish biscuit cutter, cut the dough into rounds and transfer them to the baking sheet, leaving a little room between them. Reroll and cut any scraps and put them on the sheet, too.

4. Bake the biscuits until light golden, 15 to 16 minutes. Transfer the biscuits to a wire rack or cloth-lined basket and serve as soon as possible.

MAKES 12 TO 14 BISCUITS

Brother Victor's French-Style Potato Salad

You can see the influence here, with the olives and capers, of Brother Victor's upbringing in France. This presents best if it is dressed and tossed at the last moment.

1½ pounds small red-skinned potatoes

6 small ripe tomatoes, cored and quartered

6 hard-cooked eggs, peeled and quartered

1 small red onion, sliced and separated into rings

½ cup pitted black olives, halved

2 to 3 tablespoons capers, to your taste, drained

⅓ cup olive oil

3 tablespoons tarragon vinegar

1 tablespoon Dijon mustard

Salt and freshly ground black pepper to taste

1. Put the potatoes in a large pot of salted water and bring to a boil over high heat. Cook the potatoes at a boil until they are tender at the center when you poke them with a cake tester, 15 to 20 minutes. Drain, let cool slightly, then peel the potatoes, cut them into bite-size chunks, and place in a large salad bowl. Add the tomatoes, eggs, onion, olives, and capers.

2. In a small bowl, whisk together the olive oil, vinegar, and mustard. Pour the dressing over the salad and toss gently, to coat evenly. Season with salt and pepper. Taste, adding a bit more vinegar if necessary. Cover with plastic wrap and refrigerate if not serving right away.

MAKES 6 SERVINGS

TIME FOR TOMATOES!

Zingerman's Bulgarian Cucumber Soup

• • • • • • • • • • • • •

Tomato Upside-Down Bread

• • • • • • • • • • • • •

Trumped-Up Tabbouleh

• • • • • • • • • • • • •

Here we have a true celebration-of-summer menu. Generally speaking, I have a limited appreciation for cold soups—precisely the few I've included in this book—but this cold cucumber soup is one of my favorites and it anchors the menu perfectly in the season.

I've chosen a tomato bread to go with the soup. I've generally been underwhelmed by breads with tomatoes *in* them; I much prefer this bread with tomatoes *on* it. If you've ever made an upside-down cake, you can imagine how this is done, with the tomato slices placed in the pan before the batter is poured on. If all this sounds a bit iffy or contrived, it did to me at first, too. But once I made it, I was quickly hooked. Do give this a try.

Perhaps some will be put off by the thought of serving a tomato bread along with a tabbouleh, which also has tomatoes in it, but it doesn't bother me at all. This is the tomato season, after all—why try to hide the fact that we're all working overtime to use them up as quickly as we can? The "trumped-up" part? That would be the pesto and garbanzo beans, the former because it says "summer" like nothing else can; the latter because I like them and they provide enough bulk that I can expect a little left over for lunch the next day. In summer, for a salad like this, I wouldn't bother to cook up dry garbanzo beans; it's hardly worth the trouble. Give yourself a break and use canned beans, well rinsed.

Zingerman's Bulgarian Cucumber Soup

This recipe was generously given to me by Ari Weinzweig, one of the founding partners of the famous Zingerman's deli in Ann Arbor, Michigan. Ann Arbor is a pleasant, leafy college town, but not the sort of place where you'd expect to find one of the premier delis in the entire country. But that's precisely where you'll find Zingerman's, located in a former corner grocery just a short stroll from the center of the University of Michigan campus. Once his customers have tried this cold cucumber soup, says Ari, they keep coming back for more. Since Ari gave me this recipe, it's become one of my favorite summer soups. (To get a Zingerman's catalog, call 313-769-1235.)

3 medium-large cucumbers, peeled and
  seeded
2 cups plain yogurt
One 8-ounce container sour cream
1 cup milk
3 tablespoons olive oil

1 or 2 cloves garlic, to your taste,
  minced
2 tablespoons chopped fresh dill
1 cup walnuts, toasted (page 218),
  cooled, and coarsely chopped
Salt and freshly ground black pepper
  to taste

1. Coarsely chop 1 1/2 of the cucumbers and process until smooth in a food processor. Cut the remaining 1 1/2 cucumbers into 1/2-inch dice. Combine the cucumber puree and pieces in a large bowl. Stir in the remaining ingredients, adding salt and pepper to taste.

2. Cover and refrigerate for at least several hours, or preferably overnight, before serving. Taste again before serving, adding more salt and pepper if necessary.

MAKES 6 SERVINGS

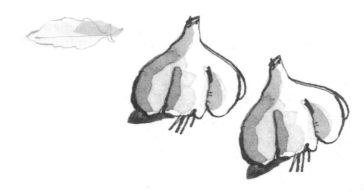

Tomato Upside-Down Bread

Every few years, when I have enough new material to offer on the subject, I end up writing an article about what I like to call harvest breads—inventive ways to work fresh produce into homemade breads; one of these days there'll be enough for a book. Apart from a few clunkers that never made it into print, I've been really pleased with the marriages I've arranged between the garden and loaf pan, or muffin tin, as the case may be. Here's one recent experiment I was particularly happy with, and one that will no doubt catch your eye if you grow a summer garden: there's a layer of tomatoes under the batter, which itself is flecked with fresh herbs and grated zucchini. It's a true celebration of the harvest, all in one loaf. The finished bread is inverted, cut into slices, and served warm.

3 to 4 large ripe tomatoes, cored and
 thinly sliced
1 tablespoon unsalted butter, softened
1³/₄ cups unbleached all-purpose flour
³/₄ cup fine-ground yellow cornmeal
2¹/₂ teaspoons baking powder
1 teaspoon salt
1 teaspoon fresh thyme leaves

1 teaspoon fresh chopped marjoram
 leaves
¹/₄ teaspoon freshly ground black
 pepper
2 large eggs
¹/₂ cup vegetable oil
³/₄ cup milk
1 tablespoon sugar
1 cup grated zucchini

1. Preheat the oven to 400 degrees F. Spread the soft butter on the bottom and sides of a 9 x 13-inch baking pan. Arrange the tomato slices in the bottom of the pan in rows, overlapping them slightly end to end and side to side. Bake for 30 minutes, then remove from the oven.

2. While the tomatoes bake, prepare the batter. Sift the flour, cornmeal, baking powder, and salt together into a large bowl. Add the herbs and pepper. In a medium-size bowl, whisk the eggs, oil, milk, and sugar together; stir in the zucchini. When the tomatoes are done, make a well in the dry ingredients, add the liquid, and stir just until blended. Transfer the batter to the pan, mounding it here and there over the tomatoes and spreading evenly with a spoon.

3. Bake until golden brown, about 25 minutes. Immediately invert the bread onto a baking sheet. Let cool briefly, then slice into squares and serve.

MAKES ABOUT 12 SERVINGS

Trumped-Up Tabbouleh

You've had tabbouleh; here it is with bells and whistles—feta cheese, chickpeas, and pesto. If you have extra, a dollop of pesto on each serving is a nice touch. Serve on salad greens, or without.

1¼ cups medium-coarse bulgur

2 cups warm water

½ cup prepared pesto, store-bought or homemade (page 94)

3 to 4 tablespoons fresh lemon juice, to your taste

1 pint cherry tomatoes, halved

One 19-ounce can chickpeas, drained and rinsed

4 or 5 scallions, white and light green parts, to your taste, thinly sliced

2 to 3 tablespoons finely chopped fresh parsley leaves, to your taste

Salt and freshly ground black pepper to taste

1 cup crumbled feta cheese

1. Pour the bulgur into a medium-size bowl; cover with the warm water. Set aside for 45 minutes. When grains are tender-chewy, drain through a sieve. Squeeze the bulgur between your hands to express as much water as possible. Transfer the bulgur to a large salad bowl.

2. Whisk the pesto and 3 tablespoons of the lemon juice together in a small bowl. Pour over the bulgur and toss well. Add the tomatoes, chickpeas, scallions, and parsley and season with salt and pepper. Toss again. Taste, adding more lemon juice, if necessary. Spoon the salad onto individual serving plates and garnish with the feta cheese.

MAKES 6 SERVINGS

POTLUCK POSSIBILITIES

One Good Gazpacho
....
Cheddar, Onion, and Sour Cream Drop Biscuits
....
*Two-Bean Summer Salad with
Cumin-Dill Dressing*
....

Summer is full of pressing questions, like what trashy new paperback we should bring to the beach, what summer blockbuster is worth our time and money, and what we should bring to next week's potluck. After all, as good local cooks we have reputations to uphold. We can't bring the same dishes year after year, lest someone accuse us of being a one-string fiddle.

Here is a menu rife with potluck possibility. Everyone likes a good gazpacho, so I call this One Good Gazpacho. Gazpacho is tricky. You don't want to make it too early in the season or everyone will know you're cheating and using tomatoes from away. This will not enhance your standing among cooks. Make it too late in the season, however, and people are starting to suffer from gazpacho ennui. My point? Your timing has to be right with this one if you're potluck bound.

This drop biscuit is something that's easy to mix up, bake, and carry along. Because they're savory biscuits, with cheddar and onions, you have the option of reheating them off to one side of the grill that fires perpetually at every potluck I've ever been to. You will look quite cool doing this and others will marvel at your resourcefulness.

Finally, you will find here my entry in the great bean salad division. I'm not making fun of bean salads. I like them and, when they're well made, I can eat my way through an entire potluck and not touch anything but.

One Good Gazpacho

Gazpacho has become a summer right of passage, and for good reason: you'd be hard pressed to find a single dish that captures more good summer flavor. There's some disagreement as to whether gazpacho is actually a salad or a soup, and one's point of view is usually pretty apparent in the finished dish, thinner and soupy, or thick and chunky. I like the middle ground myself, neither too thin nor too thick. Since there's such variation between the size and relative flavor of the ingredients, this is a soup that needs to be tweaked and adjusted more than most to get the flavor just right. So don't be surprised if it needs more lemon juice, vinegar, salt, or pepper. Also, don't wait until just before serving to add them, or the seasonings will not be well integrated. Rather, taste and add any additional seasoning incrementally as the soup chills. Some purists blanch at the notion of thinning the texture with tomato juice, but I actually like a little V-8 in here. For a seafood variation, you can add a small can of clams and their juice.

6 large ripe tomatoes

1 large cucumber, peeled, seeded, and chopped

1 large green bell pepper, seeded and diced

1 medium-size red onion, minced

3 tablespoons red wine vinegar

2 tablespoons olive oil

Juice of ½ lemon

2 to 3 tablespoons chopped fresh parsley leaves, to your taste

2 tablespoons chopped fresh basil leaves or 2 teaspoons dried

Salt and freshly ground black pepper to taste

V-8 juice or tomato juice, as needed

Chopped fresh basil or parsley leaves or both, for garnish

1. Peel the tomatoes by submerging them in boiling water for 15 to 30 seconds. Remove to a colander and rinse under cold running water. The skins should slip right off.

2. Core the tomatoes and gently squeeze out the seeds. Chop half of the tomatoes coarsely and puree the other half in a food processor. Combine the puree and chopped tomatoes in a large bowl.

3. Blend the remaining ingredients together with the tomatoes. If you like, thin with a little V-8 or tomato juice. Cover with plastic wrap and refrigerate for several hours before serving. Serve in bowls or glass goblets, garnished with fresh herbs.

MAKES 6 TO 8 SERVINGS

Cheddar, Onion, and Sour Cream Drop Biscuits

If you've ever eaten at a Red Lobster restaurant, you've probably tried one of those big cheese biscuits they bring you at the beginning of the meal. I'm quite fond of them myself and I thought it would be fun to come up with something similar; this is as close as I've gotten so far. This is a drop biscuit, meaning that you don't roll and shape the dough; it's too wet for that. Rather, you just spoon it onto a baking sheet and bake, a time-saving grace worth noting. Since the dough is wetter than it is for a regular biscuit, they spread more than they rise and that's nice, since you end up with more crusty surface area. Inside, you have sautéed onions, cheddar cheese, and garlic, for savory measure and good soup compatibility.

5^1/$_2$ tablespoons cold unsalted butter	^{1}/$_2$ teaspoon salt
1 large onion, finely chopped	2 teaspoons chopped fresh basil
1 clove garlic, minced	leaves or ^{1}/$_2$ teaspoon dried
2 cups unbleached all-purpose flour	1 cup grated sharp cheddar cheese
1 tablespoon sugar	^{3}/$_4$ cup sour cream
1 teaspoon baking powder	^{2}/$_3$ cup milk
^{3}/$_4$ teaspoon baking soda	

1. Melt 1^1/$_2$ tablespoons of the butter in a skillet over moderate heat. Add the onion and cook, stirring, until translucent, about 8 minutes. Add the garlic and cook, stirring, for 30 seconds, then remove from the heat. Preheat the oven to 425 degrees F and lightly grease 1 or 2 large baking sheets.

2. Sift the flour, sugar, baking powder, baking soda, and salt together into a large bowl; add the basil. Cut the remaining 4 tablespoons of butter into pieces and add to the dry mixture. Using your fingers or a pastry blender, break the butter into fine bits with the flour until the mixture resembles a fine meal. Mix in the cheese.

3. Blend the sour cream and milk together in a small bowl. Make a well in the center of the dry mixture, add the liquid, and stir with a wooden spoon until evenly blended and no dry streaks remain. Set the dough aside for 5 minutes.

4. Using a large spoon, scoop blobs of dough onto the baking sheet, leaving a couple of inches between them; you can either use 2 baking sheets or bake a second batch after the first is done. Bake until golden and crusty, about 15 minutes. Eat right away or transfer biscuits to a wire rack to cool.

MAKES ABOUT 16 BISCUITS

A Drop Biscuit Strategy

....

As I've noted here, drop biscuits are a couple of steps faster to the oven than traditional biscuits: no shaping and cutting. That's a plus, especially in the summer when we're all looking for ways to get out of the kitchen a little quicker.

No matter the time of year, however, you can turn almost any regular biscuit into a drop biscuit simply by adding a bit more liquid, increasing it by roughly 25 percent. Thus, if a biscuit calls for 1 cup buttermilk, add $1\frac{1}{4}$ cups. In every case, you can expect the final product—as with the Cheddar, Onion, and Sour Cream Drop Biscuits—to spread more, with a surface of crusty peaks and valleys. The somewhat flattened size isn't quite so handy for splitting and buttering, but better for dunking. You win some, you lose some.

Two-Bean Summer Salad with Cumin-Dill Dressing

One of the best things about summer potlucks are all the bean salads you get to sample. Bean salads reveal a lot about a cook and an astute observer can sometimes match up the bean salad with its cook of origin. If a certain gardener-cook is crazy about the thin French-style green beans he grows, his bean salad will be easy to spot. The lady friend who has been dating that cheese maker in Vermont? You know hers will have the chunks of fresh goat cheese. The mom with six kids? That's probably hers over there, with all canned beans and the bottled dressing. Frankly, I'm not sure what this one says about me; perhaps little other than the fact that I have an inclusive mentality when it comes to them. And that I like cumin. Here I roast it briefly, to remove the raw edge and intensify the flavor. If you happen to have cumin seeds around, you can use them instead; increase the quantity slightly.

SALAD

¾ **pound fresh green beans, ends trimmed and snapped into bite-size pieces**

Salt

One 19-ounce can chickpeas, drained and rinsed

½ **red bell pepper, seeded and finely diced**

1 cucumber, peeled, seeded, and diced

8 to 10 cherry tomatoes, halved

3 to 4 tablespoons finely chopped red onion, to your taste

CUMIN-DILL DRESSING

⅔ **cup plain yogurt**

2 tablespoons sour cream

1 teaspoon ground cumin

¼ **teaspoon sweet paprika**

2 to 3 tablespoons chopped fresh dill, to your taste

Salt and freshly ground black pepper to taste

Fresh lemon juice to taste

1. Bring a large saucepan of salted water to a boil. Add the green beans, return to a boil, and cook until just tender, 7 to 10 minutes. Drain, then run cold water over the beans to stop the cooking. Spread on paper towels and pat dry. Transfer to a large bowl. Add the chickpeas, bell pepper, cucumber, tomatoes, and onion. Mix well.

2. To make the dressing, blend the yogurt and sour cream together in a small bowl. Put the cumin and paprika in a small skillet. Over moderate heat, toast the spices, stirring often, until fragrant, about 2 minutes. Blend into the yogurt mixture along with the dill.

3. Scrape the dressing over the salad; adjust the flavor with salt, pepper, and lemon juice as needed. If there's time, cover with plastic wrap and refrigerate at least 30 minutes before serving. Taste again and correct seasonings just before serving.

MAKES 6 SERVINGS

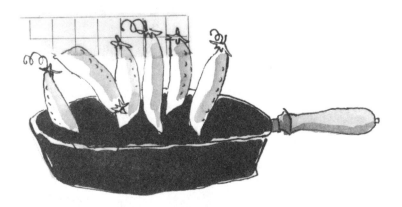

A BEST OF SUMMER TRIO

Summer Squash Lemon Soup with Pesto Foam

....

Fresh Corn and Cheddar Spoonbread

....

Marinated Goat Cheese and Tomato Salad

....

If I had to, and you threw in some good crusty bread and fresh peaches for my sweet tooth, I could survive summer quite nicely with three items: pesto, fresh corn, and fresh tomatoes. I love these things in all permutations: pesto slathered on my corn, scraped corn kernels with pesto dressing, tomato and pesto sandwiches. You get the idea. And now you understand why I call this a best of summer menu.

I had also thought of calling it a spoonbread menu, simply to call your attention to this wonderful half-bread, half-pudding dish. I first tried it when I was in the Navy living in Mississippi back in the early 1970s. As you know, corn- and corn-type breads are big down there. I had a lot of southern buddies who would carry on and on about their mama's corn-bread—or "cone-brad," whose meaning took this New Jersey kid months to translate. It was one of these buddy's mama who first turned me on to the stuff. I've been an inveterate fan ever since.

Not to overlook a lemony squash soup and a fresh tomato salad, the former with the unusual twist of pesto whipped cream stirred in at the very end for a burst of richness and herbal flavor.

Summer Squash Lemon Soup with Pesto Foam

I follow the mainstream food press just well enough to know that foams are in these days. I understand a chef in Spain started this whole craze and now chefs everywhere are foaming up soups, sauces, and lots more with CO_2 cartridges, apparently leaving their customers— from what I hear—foaming at the mouth for more. I like a good foam as much as the next cook, but one of the few I know is whipped cream, like I use here. It is blended with pesto, then spooned into this gorgeous and simple summer squash soup, which is plenty good enough on its own, so if you decide to skip the pesto foam, you won't have any regrets. To serve the soup, bring it just to the boiling point, then add a dollop of the cream to each portion at the table, because watching it melt into the hot soup, starburst fashion, is one of the great things about it.

2 tablespoons unsalted butter

1 large onion, finely chopped

4 cups tender, small yellow summer
   squash cut into small dice

1 clove garlic, minced

Salt and freshly ground black pepper to
   taste

4 cups chicken stock

1 tablespoon fresh lemon juice

Finely grated lemon zest to taste

1/2 cup well-chilled heavy cream

1 teaspoon sugar

1/2 cup prepared pesto, store-bought
   or homemade (page 94)

1. Melt the butter in a medium-size soup pot or large saucepan over moderately low heat. Add the onion, squash, and garlic, salt lightly, and add pepper. Cover and sweat the vegetables, stirring occasionally, for 10 minutes.

2. Add the chicken stock, lemon juice, and lemon zest. Bring to a simmer, then cover and simmer for 10 minutes.

3. While the soup simmers, whip the cream in a medium-size bowl with an electric mixer until it holds its shape well, adding the sugar as you beat. Gently fold in the pesto. Cover with plastic wrap and refrigerate if not using soon.

4. When you're ready to serve the soup, bring it to a near boil. Ladle into bowls, then pass the pesto foam at the table and let each person spoon a large dollop into their own bowl.

MAKES 5 TO 6 SERVINGS

A Penchant for Pesto

If there's a use for basil that's half as delicious as pesto, I'd like to know about it. Pesto is the standard bearer for herbal sauces. For the truly addicted like myself, a spoonful can turn a plate of hot pasta into a near-religious experience. I spread it on bagels and toast, and mix it with cottage cheese and chopped veggies to make a sandwich spread.

In the soup and bread arena, pesto has many uses. Perhaps the best-known soup of Nice is *soupe au pistou*, a type of minestrone in which a quantity of pesto is stirred into the pot near the end, or blended into individual bowls by the spoonful. Try it the next time you make vegetable soup, passing a bowlful of pesto at the table.

Pesto is also lovely on flatbreads, such as the Push-Button Rosemary Flatbread (page 151). Use a little less olive oil, then brush on several generous spoonfuls of pesto before the dough's last rising. When I make pizza—often with that same flatbread dough—I like to add a healthy slug of pesto to the marinara sauce. Sometimes I'll make sandwiches with focaccia, slathering the bread with pesto, and layering on grilled vegetables.

All of this comes with a price, either at the supermarket—where you can generally find several varieties of pesto—or at home, where you'll need to make it yourself with some decidedly uncheap ingredients. Supermarket brands are pretty good, but making your own yields a wonderfully fresh flavor that you won't find in the store-bought versions. If you'd like to try, the Basic Pesto (page 95) is a simple recipe I've been using for years.

Basic Pesto

**3 cups packed fresh basil
leaves**

**2 to 3 cloves garlic, to your
taste, peeled**

²/₃ cup olive oil

**¹/₄ cup walnut pieces or pine
nuts (optional)**

¹/₈ teaspoon salt

**³/₄ cup freshly grated
Parmesan cheese**

1. In a blender or food processor, process the basil, garlic, olive oil, nuts (if using), and salt until smooth, stopping occasionally to scrape down the sides.

2. Scrape the mixture into a small bowl and stir in the Parmesan. Cover and refrigerate, tightly covered, until using. If you're not using within several days, freeze the pesto. It will keep for 2 to 3 months.

MAKES ABOUT 1 CUP

Fresh Corn and
Cheddar Spoonbread

Doubtless you've eaten your share of cornbreads and the occasional corn pudding too. But have you ever tried spoonbread, that tasty in-between cousin? Spoonbread may sound like nothing so much as a dish with a textural identity crisis, but it's actually one of the world's most underrated fork-breads, a wholesome and ethereal cloud of well-being. I first learned about spoonbreads when I lived in the southern United States, where they take their cornmeal seriously. A cook there once told me to think of spoonbread as a sort of cornmeal soufflé. Unlike your usual soufflé, however—where the egg whites are folded into a flour-thickened base—spoonbread is built on a seasoned cornmeal porridge known as a rick. Baked in a shallow casserole, spoonbread emerges from the oven dramatically puffed, though this stage is only a fleeting feast for the eyes: within moments it gently sighs and settles, ready to be spooned forth. It isn't quite the same if you wait more than 5 or 10 minutes to serve it, after which this cloud starts to lose its lovely cush.

2 tablespoons unsalted butter

1 small onion, minced

1½ cups fresh-cut corn kernels

3 cups milk

¾ cup fine-ground yellow cornmeal

1 teaspoon salt

Large dash of cayenne pepper

2 teaspoons Dijon mustard

2 cups grated extra-sharp cheddar cheese

2 teaspoons chopped fresh dill or other fresh herb

5 large eggs, separated

1. Preheat the oven to 375 degrees F and butter the bottom only of a 3-quart baking dish or gratin. Put a second casserole or a jelly-roll pan, large enough to hold the baking dish, on the center rack of the oven and pour in enough hot water to come not quite halfway up the sides.

2. Melt the butter in a medium-size skillet over moderately low heat. Stir in the onion and corn and cook gently, stirring often, for 3 to 4 minutes. Set aside.

3. Whisk the milk and cornmeal together in a medium-size saucepan over moderate heat. Switch to a wooden spoon and stir almost nonstop until the mixture thickens to a porridge-like consistency. Remove from the heat and stir in the salt, cayenne, mustard, cheese—half at a time—and herbs until smooth. Stir in the egg yolks and sautéed mixture.

4. Beat the egg whites in a large bowl with an electric mixer until they hold firm peaks. Fold one third of the whites into the cornmeal mixture, then fold in the remaining whites until no white streaks remain. Scrape the mixture into the prepared baking dish and place the dish in the water bath. Bake until golden and puffy, about 35 minutes. Serve at once.

MAKES 6 TO 8 SERVINGS

Marinated Goat Cheese and Tomato Salad

Goat cheese is great and I really love it, aside from the fact that it can sometimes be dry and, well, a little goaty-tasting. Marinating it helps in both departments by lubricating the cheese and infusing it with other flavors, in this case, basil and fennel seed, which add sparkle and manage to tame the flavor, too. After the olive oil is used in the marinade, it is recycled and blended with honey and lemon juice to make the dressing for the salad. If you like, add a few bitter greens to balance the slight sweetness of the dressing. If you plan to feed more than four people with this, you will need a second log of goat cheese.

1/2 cup olive oil

1/2 teaspoon crushed fennel seeds (see note)

Small handful fresh basil leaves chopped or 1/2 teaspoon dried

Freshly ground black pepper, preferably coarsely ground, to taste

One 4-ounce log goat cheese

1 head Boston lettuce, leaves rinsed and dried

2 to 3 medium-size ripe tomatoes, cored and cut into wedges

2 1/2 to 3 tablespoons fresh lemon juice, to your taste

1 tablespoon honey

Salt to taste

Vinegar of your choice (optional) to taste

1/4 cup chopped pecans or walnuts (optional), toasted (page 218), for garnish

1. Blend the olive oil, fennel seeds, basil, and pepper in a small bowl. Pour half of it into a small pie plate. Slice the goat cheese into 8 rounds and lay them in the oil. Drizzle the rest of the oil over the slices. Cover with plastic wrap and let marinate at room temperature for 2 hours.

2. When you are ready to serve the salad, arrange the salad greens on individual serving plates in a fan fashion. Place several tomato wedges and 2 rounds of goat cheese on each plate. Set aside the oil marinade, pouring it into a small bowl.

3. Warm the lemon juice and honey together in a small skillet just long enough to liquefy the honey. Whisk this into the marinade, adding a pinch or two of salt. Taste the dressing, adding more lemon juice or a touch of vinegar if necessary. Spoon the dressing over the greens and tomatoes just before serving. Garnish with the pecans or walnuts if you are using them.

NOTE: To crush fennel seeds, put them on a chopping board or counter, cover with a sheet of wax paper, then roll up and pound them gently with a rolling pin.

MAKES 4 SERVINGS

AN EAR-IE SOUP GOES UP IN SMOKE

Smoky Fresh Corn Chowder
· · · · · · · · · · · · ·
Raspberry Muffins
· · · · · · · · · · · · ·
Pesto Potato Salad
· · · · · · · · · · · · ·

For a lot of people, summer officially begins when the first local corn on the cob goes on sale. For them, corn is the first letter in the first line of the chapter on summer cooking, perhaps because—unlike nearly every other vegetable—it defies you to let it venture very far from its source. Corn's sweetness is notoriously ephemeral, quickly slipping into a starchy slide the moment it is picked. Some cooks go to extreme measures to seize corn's flavor at its fleeting peak. Armed with cell phones, they make frantic calls. "Okay, honey, I'm at the farmstand. The kids are putting the corn in the bag. Okay, I'm giving him the money. Put the water on to boil right...NOW!"

I do love fresh corn on the cob, but the season is barely off the ground when I'm getting bored and digging out my recipes for corn chowder. Like tomatoes in a sauce, chowder is second nature for corn, a natural expression of its juicy sweetness. And I do mean juicy, as you're well aware if you've ever sliced kernels off the cob.

And if you haven't, well, this is a fine time to start with the smoky fresh corn chowder on the menu. I'm not sure what it is about corn and smoke, but it's a match made in heaven. Our soup gets the smoke from bacon and smoked cheddar. And I mention in the headnote that you could add some grilled corn kernels too, if that appeals.

If corn is in season, then pesto fans everywhere are indulging in their annual ritual, pounding and processing great piles of fresh basil into their favorite sauce. It makes a fabulous potato salad dressing, with the addition of cherry tomatoes and feta cheese. Why not bring the whole feast, including a basket of the warm raspberry muffins, out to the back deck and just bask in these glorious corn days of summer?

Smoky Fresh Corn Chowder

Some corn chowders are soft and delicate in flavor; not this one. It has an unabashed smoky personality, thanks to the bacon and smoked cheddar cheese. If I want to get fancy, I'll sometimes grill up some green peppers ahead of time, peel and seed them, and make a puree to use as a garnish. I just put it on the table and let people serve themselves. Here's another possibility: grill up some ears of corn, peeling back the husks for the last minute or so to give the kernels a bit of char. When cool enough to handle, cut off the kernels and use them as a garnish.

2 slices bacon, cut crosswise into 1-inch
   pieces
1 large onion, chopped
1 clove garlic, minced
4 large ears corn, kernels cut off the
   cobs
Salt to taste
5 cups chicken stock
½ cup heavy cream

3 tablespoons unbleached all-purpose
   flour
4 to 5 ounces smoked cheddar
   cheese, to your taste, grated
1 teaspoon Dijon mustard
Freshly ground black pepper to taste
Chopped fresh parsley leaves or dill,
   for garnish

1. Heat a large, heavy enameled soup pot over moderate heat. Add the bacon and fry until crisp. Add the onion and cook, stirring, until translucent, about 8 minutes. Add the garlic and corn, salt lightly, and cook, stirring, for 2 minutes. Add the chicken stock and bring to a near boil. Simmer the soup until the corn has lost its raw taste, 8 to 10 minutes.

2. Whisk the cream and flour together in a small bowl. Add to the soup and heat for 10 minutes, under salting the soup slightly, to taste. Stir the cheese into the soup, in a couple of batches, until it melts. Stir in the mustard and season with pepper. Serve hot, garnished with the fresh herbs.

MAKES 6 SERVINGS

Raspberry Muffins

Sweet and dessert-like, these muffins have shiny golden domes and big raspberry-red freckles. If you grow mint or lemon thyme, finely chop a little and add it to the batter.

- 2 cups unbleached all-purpose flour
- 2/3 cup sugar, plus extra for sprinkling on top
- 2 1/2 teaspoons baking powder
- 3/4 teaspoon salt
- 1/8 teaspoon ground nutmeg
- 1 large egg
- 1 1/4 cups milk
- 1/4 cup sour cream
- 1/4 cup (1/2 stick) unsalted butter, melted and cooled
- 1/2 teaspoon pure vanilla extract
- Finely grated zest of 1 lemon
- 1 cup fresh raspberries

1. Preheat the oven to 400 degrees F. Grease a 12-cup muffin pan and set it aside.

2. Sift the flour, sugar, baking powder, salt, and nutmeg together into a large bowl. In a medium-size bowl, whisk the egg until frothy, then whisk in the milk, sour cream, butter, vanilla, and lemon zest.

3. Make a well in the center of the dry mixture and add the liquid all at once. Stir with a wooden spoon until the batter is uniformly mixed; gently fold in the berries. Divide the batter evenly between the cups, filling them each about two thirds full. Generously sprinkle the tops with sugar.

4. Bake the muffins on the center rack of the oven until golden brown, about 22 minutes. The tops should feel springy to the touch. Let cool in the pan, on a wire rack, for 5 minutes, then remove the muffins to a cloth-lined basket and serve warm or let them cool further on the rack.

MAKE 10 TO 12 MUFFINS

Pesto Potato Salad

When I want to make an impressive "cheater's" summer potato salad, this is generally the one I make. The cheating part is the fact that, if you don't mind forking over the three or four bucks for a package of prepared pesto, you don't even have to make a dressing: just boil the potatoes, squeeze some lemon juice over them, and toss with the pesto. Add a pint of cherry tomatoes and a crumbled block of feta for garnish, and you're in business.

2½ pounds red-skinned potatoes
   (7 medium-size ones), scrubbed
Salt
1 lemon, halved
¾ cup prepared pesto, store-bought
   or homemade (page 94), at room
   temperature

Freshly ground black pepper to taste
1 pint cherry tomatoes
4 ounces feta cheese, coarsely
   crumbled

1. Put the potatoes in a large saucepan and add enough lightly salted water to cover. Bring to a boil, reduce the heat to moderately low, and simmer, covered, until potatoes are just tender (check with the tip of a paring knife), 20 to 25 minutes. Drain. When cool enough to handle, cut into bite-size pieces (peeling the potatoes, if desired) and spread the pieces on a baking sheet. Squeeze lemon juice over the pieces. Let cool.

2. When the potatoes have cooled, transfer to a medium-size bowl. Add about two thirds of the pesto and toss well to coat evenly. Season with salt and pepper. Transfer to a shallow serving dish. Cover with plastic wrap and refrigerate for at least 1 hour or as long as overnight.

3. When ready to serve, halve the tomatoes and scatter them over the top. Top with the cheese, then dot the top with the remaining pesto. Toss gently, then serve.

MAKES 6 SERVINGS

A HOME GARDENER'S SHOWCASE

Simple Cream of Summer Tomato Soup
....

Zucchini Muffins with Walnuts and Thyme
....

Very Celery and Pickle Salad
....

I am not a gardener, though I did take one good stab at it early in my career as a New Englander when I moved here more than twenty years ago. I began, as many do, in a sort of springtime trance. Birds were singing, a warm hypnotic New Hampshire breeze was lapping at my face. I drove down to the local nursery and walked out with a shovel, a rake, and some packets of seeds. Then I came home and proceeded to thrash my way through a 10-foot-square patch of earth in the side yard that had more in common with asphalt than actual dirt. Before long I discovered that the spot I had picked got very little sun, thanks to a towering pine tree I had somehow overlooked. I'll spare you the rest of the sordid details, other than to mention that when my more experienced neighbors were harvesting produce by the armload, I was making trips to the market. That's when I decided that this cook would be better off cultivating friendships with good gardeners rather than the garden itself.

And it has pretty much worked out that way. Some of my best friends are gardeners, so I'm never too far from a few good homegrown tomatoes, zucchini, or raspberries. What doesn't come my way through friends, I can find at one of the local farmstands. The one thing I do grow, however, is herbs—a few big baskets of them on my steps right off the kitchen.

This is a menu I thought home gardeners and herb growers like myself would gravitate toward. It incorporates at least two vegetables that are usually plentiful in the home garden, zucchini and tomatoes, and seasons them with some of my favorite herbs—thyme, dill, and mint. The mint goes in a crunchy celery salad; the zucchini and thyme in the muffins; the dill and tomatoes in the soup. Nothing takes too long to prepare and, if you have a patio or deck, I'd take the whole thing out there with a frosty pitcher of lemonade.

Simple Cream of Summer Tomato Soup

When you're using fresh, ripe, local tomatoes, you don't need a lot of other fanfare to make a good cream of tomato soup—just butter, fresh herbs, and heavy cream. This one is pretty quick. You could pick some garden-ripe tomatoes just before lunch and have this on the table in about 20 minutes. If you like, you can use yellow or orange tomatoes for a change of pace.

2½ tablespoons unsalted butter

1 medium-size onion, finely chopped

1 rib celery, finely chopped

1 clove garlic, minced

1 tablespoon unbleached all-purpose flour

4 large, ripe tomatoes, cored, peeled, seeded, and chopped

1 teaspoon sugar, plus more to taste

½ teaspoon salt, plus more to taste

3 cups chicken stock

¾ cup heavy cream

1 tablespoon chopped fresh dill, parsley, or basil leaves

Freshly ground black pepper to taste

1. Melt the butter in a large saucepan or medium-size soup pot over moderate heat. Stir in the onion and celery, cover, and sweat the vegetables for 5 minutes. Stir in the garlic and flour and cook, stirring, another minute.

2. Stir the tomatoes, sugar, and salt into the sweated vegetables. Increase the heat and bring the tomatoes to a boil. Cover, reduce the heat slightly, and cook the tomatoes at a lively simmer until they're quite saucy, 8 to 10 minutes. Remove from the heat.

3. Working in two batches, transfer the contents of the pan to a food processor. Process the soup to a smooth puree, returning it to the saucepan.

4. Stir the chicken stock into the soup. Heat the soup through, then add the cream and herbs and season with pepper. Heat the soup thoroughly, without letting it boil, adding more salt and pepper if needed. Serve, garnished with extra chopped herbs, if you have some on hand.

MAKES 5 TO 6 SERVINGS

Tomatoes, with a Peel

Whenever you use fresh tomatoes in soup, you should weigh the benefit of first peeling them versus the amount of time needed to do it. I have no set rules about this and, more often than not, if I'm only using one or two of them in a recipe, I don't bother. If you get up to 3 or more tomatoes—as in the Simple Cream of Summer Tomato Soup on page 103—the landscape changes. The problem is, when you leave the skins on, they tend to form papery little flecks in the broth; the more tomatoes there are, the more flecks there are. It helps if you chop the tomatoes finely before adding them, but the skins can be a turnoff in any amount. Bottom line: it's your choice whether or not to peel your tomatoes, but if you do, here's an easy way how. Bring a medium-size saucepan of water to a rolling boil. Gently drop the tomatoes, one or two at a time, into the water. Count to fifteen, remove the tomatoes with tongs or a slotted spoon, and place in a bowl. The skins will quickly shrivel and you can slip them right off.

Zucchini Muffins with Walnuts and Thyme

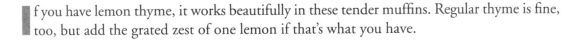

If you have lemon thyme, it works beautifully in these tender muffins. Regular thyme is fine, too, but add the grated zest of one lemon if that's what you have.

2⅓ cups unbleached all-purpose flour

2½ teaspoons baking powder

1 teaspoon salt

Pinch of ground nutmeg

2 large eggs, lightly beaten

½ cup milk

⅓ cup vegetable or sunflower seed oil

½ cup sugar

1 teaspoon pure vanilla extract

1 cup grated zucchini

½ cup chopped walnuts

1 teaspoon fresh thyme or lemon
thyme leaves

1. Preheat the oven to 375 degrees F and grease a 12-cup muffin pan.

2. Sift the flour, baking powder, salt, and nutmeg into a large bowl; set aside. In a medium-size bowl, whisk the eggs together with the milk, oil, sugar, and vanilla. Make a well in the center of the dry ingredients, add the liquid, and stir several times with a wooden spoon. Add the zucchini, walnuts, and thyme and blend with a few more strokes, mixing just until blended.

3. Divide the batter evenly between the muffin cups—if they're on the large side, you may only need 9 of them—filling them three quarters full, and bake until crusty and done, the tops will be springy to the touch, 22 to 25 minutes.

4. Let cool briefly in the muffin pan, then transfer the muffins to a wire rack. These are best eaten warm.

MAKES 9 TO 12 MUFFINS

Very Celery and Pickle Salad

I like chopped celery salads better than celery sticks because they're easier to eat and you can mix in a good dressing and accompaniments, in this case, pickles and scallions. The mint lends this a sweet, summery lift and the mustard and pickles give it a sassy little edge. When I want a fast 5-minute salad, I'll often make this one.

4 cups ¼-inch-thick slices celery

1 cup diced bread-and-butter pickles

5 scallions, white part only, thinly sliced

2 tablespoons chopped fresh mint leaves

2 tablespoons chopped fresh parsley leaves

3 tablespoons olive oil

2 tablespoons cider vinegar

2 teaspoons Dijon mustard

1 teaspoon sugar

Dash of cayenne pepper

1. Mix the celery, pickles, scallions, and herbs in a large bowl.

2. In a small bowl, whisk together the olive oil, vinegar, mustard, sugar, and cayenne pepper. Pour the dressing over the salad and toss well to coat evenly. Cover with plastic wrap and refrigerate if not serving right away.

VARIATION: One-half cup or so of diced crisp apple is a good addition and it sweetens the salad just a bit.

MAKES ABOUT 5 SERVINGS

A SYMPHONY OF SUMMER FRUIT

Cold Cantaloupe and Peach Soup

··············

Chunky Banana Bread with Pecan Streusel

··············

Bibb Lettuce Salad with Raspberries and Figs

··············

What is summer if not a celebration—at long last—of the year's best fruit? For months we wait, only to be teased and taunted by second-rate fruit, like rock-hard plums, imitation peaches, and raspberries from the other side of the globe that are suffering from the worst sort of jet lag.

Then along comes summer, just in time, and we can start eating real fruit again. This menu celebrates those real fruits of summer, as well as one winter stalwart most of us appreciate: the banana. Is this too much fruit for one menu? Maybe. But that's okay. There's no rule that says every menu has to be perfectly balanced between sweet and savory elements. Sometimes we can just have fun and include what we like.

So what we have here is a peach soup, and I'll say it again—don't even try this without perfect fruit; you'll only be disappointed and write me nasty letters. The banana bread is unusual in that it uses chunks of banana, not just mushed banana; I like the way you take a bite and get a mouthful of banana pieces. And the salad, which you might want to serve first, on its own, is a little fancier than some I do, but I like the way figs and raspberries go together. Note that I use dried figs, not fresh. I love fresh figs, but, because they're so fragile, they're just too hard to come by where I live.

Cold Cantaloupe and Peach Soup

The success of any cold fruit soup rests squarely on the quality of the fruit—there's simply no way around it. It's not like a less-than-perfect tomato where you're sneaking a slice onto a BLT. The fruit *is* the soup, thus it has to be juicy, at the height of ripeness, and free of bruises or blemishes (those can always be cut out, of course). Most melons make wonderful cold soups because they are very juicy. A melon passes the juiciness test—you probably know this—when you pick one up in the market and you're pleasantly impressed by its heft, like a little grandchild or niece you haven't held in some time. The best melons are coming to market around the same time as the first good peaches, so this is a cold soup opportunity not to be missed. Instead of adding sugar as you go, just wait until all of the ingredients are pureed, then stir in the sugar. It may need very, very little if the fruit is perfect. The garnish of plain yogurt and chopped mint is just the right touch.

1 ripe cantaloupe, halved and seeded

2 or 3 good-size ripe peaches, peeled and pitted

Juice of 2 oranges

Juice of 1 to 2 lemons, to your taste

Sugar to taste

1/2 cup plain yogurt, or more to taste

8 to 10 fresh mint leaves, to your taste

1. Cut the cantaloupe flesh into large chunks and place in a food processor; process to make a smooth puree. Transfer to a medium-size bowl you'll refrigerate the soup in.

2. Cut the peaches into chunks and puree with the orange juice and juice of 1 lemon. Stir into the melon puree. Taste, then add enough sugar—by the teaspoon—to give the soup a pleasant sweetness. Add more lemon juice, as needed.

3. Cover the soup with plastic wrap and refrigerate several hours or overnight. When ready to serve, taste once more and make slight corrections, if needed, with the sugar and lemon juice. Serve in small chilled bowls or ramekins. Put a dollop of yogurt in the center of each serving. Mince the mint leaves with 1/4 teaspoon sugar, then sprinkle a little over each portion.

MAKES 6 SERVINGS

Of Cold Fruit Soups and Garnishes: A Chilling Revelation

What do you get if you cross a cold fruit soup with your freezer? You get sorbet, or something akin to it, and that can be a delightful little bonus when you're making cold fruit soup. Icy sorbet shavings taste delicious strewn over a bowl of fruit soup at the last moment. They add a contrasting texture and another layer of refreshment.

How to accomplish this little trick? It couldn't be simpler; just spoon a ladle's worth of soup into a small bowl. Place it in the freezer and stir with a fork every 20 minutes or so, more frequently the longer it has been in there. You want to keep it stirred so you end up with shavings and not a solid block. Then spoon some of the shavings over each portion at serving time.

Freezing dulls the flavors of the puree somewhat, so consider stirring an extra bit of sugar and lemon juice into the portion you plan to freeze.

Chunky Banana Bread with Pecan Streusel

Ultra-moist and tender, this has mashed banana and banana pieces in the bread, with an inviting sweet-crunch of pecans on top. Like the cold soup, it should really be made at least several hours or a day ahead. This keeps very well in the refrigerator; I've kept it around for up to 4 days and it was barely showing its age.

BANANA BREAD

2 cups unbleached all-purpose flour

1 teaspoon baking powder

1/2 teaspoon baking soda

1/2 teaspoon salt

1/2 cup (1 stick) unsalted butter,
  softened

1 cup sugar

2 large eggs, at room temperature

1 teaspoon pure vanilla extract

Finely grated zest of 1 lemon

1 cup (about 3 medium-size) mashed
  ripe bananas, plus 1 whole medium-
  size banana

1/2 cup sour cream, at room temperature

PECAN STREUSEL

3 tablespoons sugar

2 tablespoons unbleached all-purpose
  flour

2 tablespoons cold unsalted butter,
  cut into several pieces

1/2 cup pecan halves or pieces

1. Preheat the oven to 325 degrees F. Grease a 5 x 9-inch loaf pan and set aside.

2. Sift the flour, baking powder, baking soda, and salt together into a medium-size bowl. Using an electric mixer, cream the butter in a large bowl, gradually adding the sugar. Add the eggs, one at a time, beating well after each addition. Blend in the vanilla and lemon zest.

3. Blend the mashed banana with the sour cream in a small bowl. Blend one third of the dry mixture into the creamed butter mixture. Blend in half the banana mixture, another third of the dry, the rest of the banana, then the remaining dry mixture, blending well after each addition. Peel and quarter the whole banana lengthwise and cut into 1/2-inch chunks. Fold the chunks into the batter.

4. Scrape the batter into the prepared pan and smooth the top. For the streusel, put the sugar, flour, and butter in a food processor and pulse until crumbly. Add the pecans and pulse until finely chopped. Spread the streusel evenly over the batter, pressing it in lightly. Bake on the center rack of the oven until a tester inserted in the center of the loaf comes out clean, about 1 hour and 10 minutes. Let cool in the pan on a wire rack for 10 minutes. Turn the bread out of the pan and cool completely on the rack before slicing.

MAKES 10 TO 12 SERVINGS

Bibb Lettuce Salad with Raspberries and Figs

If you like, add some bitter greens to this as well, like radicchio or escarole; they go well with the sweetness of the dressing and fruit. I prefer dried Mission figs here but any kind will do. Since the dried figs need to cook and then soak, start this a couple of hours before you plan to eat.

6 to 8 dried figs, stemmed and
    quartered
About 1½ cups ruby port
2½ tablespoons balsamic vinegar
1 cup fresh raspberries
1 tablespoon sugar
1½ tablespoons olive oil

Handful cherry tomatoes, halved
Fresh lemon juice to taste
Salt and freshly ground black pepper
    to taste
Fresh orange juice (optional) to taste
1 large or 2 smaller heads Bibb lettuce,
    leaves rinsed well and dried

1. Put the figs in a small nonreactive saucepan and add enough port to cover. Bring the port to a simmer, reduce the heat to low, and cover. Simmer very gently for 10 minutes, then remove from the heat. Let the figs cool to room temperature, covered.

2. Using a slotted spoon, transfer the figs to a small bowl. Add the vinegar to the port still left in the saucepan. Bring to a boil and boil until reduced by about half. Remove from the heat.

3. Put about half of the raspberries in a medium-size bowl. Add the sugar, then mash the raspberries with a fork. Stir in the reduced port liquid from the saucepan. Stir in the olive oil. Add the figs and cherry tomatoes; taste, adding lemon juice a teaspoon at a time, as needed. Add a pinch of salt and dash of pepper. (If the dressing needs to be thinned or mellowed, add orange juice.)

4. Arrange several lettuce leaves on individual salad plates. Spoon some of the fruit mixture and its dressing over the leaves, then garnish each salad with some of the remaining raspberries.

MAKES 4 TO 5 SERVINGS

LATE SUMMER LOAFING

Parsley and Noodle Soup
····················
Blueberry-Lemon Poppy Seed Bread
····················
Whole Wheat Bread and Tomato Salad
····················

Here is another end-of-summer grouping, one that fits into that distinct two- or three-week time frame when the last of the blueberries and vine-ripe tomatoes are available, but the weather is getting cool enough that you're in the mood for hot soups again.

This menu is unique in that the salad course is a bread salad. How do you choose a bread course when the salad itself is already heavy on bread? Simple. You turn the bread course into dessert by serving a sweet, cake-like bread, which is what I've done here. So, instead of serving the blueberry bread with the meal, serve it after, with hot coffee and tea.

One of the best things about this soup is that it solves the common problem of what to do with potato water, typically left over from making mashed potatoes. I know a lot of people just throw it down the drain, and I have, too, because there are times when I don't want to refrigerate it for days until I'm inspired to make a big pot of soup. I like to think that this soup provides that incentive.

Now that the availability of good bread in this country has improved, you see a lot more recipes around for bread salad. If you haven't made bread salad before, summer is the right time since the more fresh, juicy vegetables you can include, the better. Once you're familiar with the method, you'll see how easily it can be adjusted by adding or substituting other vegetables.

As I mentioned earlier, the blueberry bread is sweet and dessert-like, though that's never stopped me from serving it with a little something extra; a bowl of mixed berries, chunks of watermelon, or sliced fresh peaches. All are good accompaniments. If you'd like, you can put fresh blackberries in the bread instead of blueberries, or fresh raspberries earlier in the summer.

Parsley and Noodle Soup

One of the simpler soups I make, this is little more than potato broth with thin spaghetti and a lot of parsley thrown in. I grew up on Campbell's Chicken Noodle Soup, for which I still have a soft spot, and this soup has an uncanny—you might say—resemblance to it, if you include a little chicken broth or add a chicken bouillon cube. Don't be tempted to use thick spaghetti or some other thick pasta; it takes forever to cook in the starchy potato water, for some reason. And don't use more noodles, either, or else they absorb too much of the broth. If I feel a sore throat coming on, this is the soup I make. It has amazing restorative qualities.

About 5 cups potato water (see page 167)

¹/₃ to ¹/₂ bunch fresh parsley

About ¹/₈ pound thin spaghetti

Salt and freshly ground black pepper to taste

1 tablespoon unsalted butter

1. Heat the potato broth in a large saucepan. If you haven't already made the broth, cut off the stems of the parsley—they hold lots of flavor—and add them to the potatoes. Alternatively, you can make a little bundle of them, tied together with kitchen string, and add to the simmering broth. Just remove them before serving the soup.

2. Finely chop the parsley leaves and add them to the simmering broth. Break the spaghetti into short pieces—an inch or so long—and drop them into the broth. Bring to a low boil, then keep the temperature there while the noodles cook with the pot mostly covered; you don't want to lose too much liquid at this point. Taste the soup as it cooks, seasoning with salt and pepper.

3. Remove the soup from the heat and add the butter. Serve hot, as soon as the butter melts.

MAKES 4 TO 5 SERVINGS

Blueberry-Lemon Poppy Seed Bread

Large or small, fresh or frozen—use any blueberry you like here. This bread will keep 4 to 5 days in the refrigerator, but chances are slim you'll have any left over the day after, let alone several days. Try this with soft, honey-sweetened cream cheese.

2 cups unbleached all-purpose flour

1 teaspoon baking soda

1/2 teaspoon ground nutmeg

1/4 teaspoon salt

1/4 cup poppy seeds

1/2 cup (1 stick) unsalted butter, softened

1 cup sugar, plus more for sprinkling, if desired

2 large eggs, at room temperature

1 teaspoon pure vanilla extract

Finely grated zest of 1 lemon

2/3 cup buttermilk

1 1/2 cups fresh blueberries, picked over for stems

1. Preheat the oven to 325 degrees F. Grease and lightly flour a 5 x 9-inch loaf pan and set aside.

2. Sift the flour, baking soda, nutmeg, and salt into a medium-size bowl. Mix in the poppy seeds. Set aside.

3. Using an electric mixer, in a large bowl cream the butter, gradually adding the sugar. Add the eggs, one at a time, beating well after each addition. Blend in the vanilla and lemon zest.

4. Mix half of the dry ingredients into the creamed mixture. Blend in the buttermilk, then the rest of the dry ingredients, mixing just until uniform. Gently fold in the blueberries.

5. Scrape the batter into the prepared pan and smooth the top; tap the pan on the counter, to settle the batter. Sprinkle the top with sugar, if desired, for a crustier top. Bake until a tester inserted into the center of the bread comes out clean, 50 to 60 minutes. Let cool in the pan, on a wire rack, for 10 minutes, then turn the bread out and place on the rack. Let cool before slicing.

MAKES 10 TO 12 SERVINGS

Whole Wheat Bread and Tomato Salad

Doubtless you've seen versions of this in your cookbook cruising. It often goes by the name of panzanella or *insalata de pane*. Frugal cook that I am, I love the premise: give slightly old bread new life by mixing it with juicy vegetables, olive oil, vinegar, and herbs. Bread soaks up seductive liquid, takes on wonderful flavor, and everyone lives happily ever after, or at least thoroughly enjoys the meal at hand. The key here is to not moisten the bread too much. I've made versions that called for far too much water to be added to the bread right off the bat, and that can make for one wet salad. I prefer a kinder, gentler approach; you let the vegetable juices and dressing soak into the bread first. Then, and only then, do you add water to moisten the bread. Your choice of bread is important. Use only a good, firm country sourdough. Use a soft, cheap, faux wheat bread and it will quickly turn into little wet cotton balls.

½ **pound slightly dry whole wheat bread**
3 good-size cucumbers
1 large red bell pepper, seeded and
  finely diced
1 small zucchini, finely diced
1 small red onion, halved and thinly
  sliced into half moons
2 to 3 pounds small, ripe tomatoes, to
  your taste
1 cup good-quality olives, halved and
  pitted

¼ **teaspoon salt, plus more to taste**
⅓ **cup olive oil**
2 tablespoons red wine vinegar
1 clove garlic, minced
2 to 3 tablespoons chopped fresh
  parsley leaves, to your taste
2 to 3 tablespoons chopped fresh
  basil leaves, to your taste
Freshly ground black pepper to taste

1. Trim the crusts from the bread and cut into large cubes; you should have about 4 cups. Spread on a baking sheet and set aside. If the bread isn't fairly dry, this can be done early and left to sit for part of the day.

2. Peel, halve, and seed the cucumbers. Cut in ½-inch-thick slices and transfer to a large salad bowl. Add the bell pepper, zucchini, and onion. Core and slice the tomatoes into eighths and add them along with the olives. Stir in the salt. Set aside for 15 minutes.

3. Add the bread to the salad and toss well. Cover with plastic wrap and set aside for 10 minutes so the bread can absorb the juice.

4. Whisk the olive oil, vinegar, and garlic together in a small bowl. Drizzle over the salad and mix well. Toss in the herbs and season with pepper and more salt, if necessary. Set aside for several minutes, then check the bread; it should be nicely dampened. If it seems somewhat dry, sprinkle the salad with water—1 tablespoon at a time—until you've achieved the right texture.

MAKES 6 SERVINGS

VARIATIONS: Add 1 cup canned chickpeas (drained and rinsed) to the salad, or pieces of leftover chicken.

And Speaking of Good Bread...

...we're fortunate to be living in a time of a widespread bread renaissance in this country. Gone are the days when France and the rest of Europe could make the claim to the best breads in the world. A new generation of bakers in this country has learned to make breads as good as any you'll find. They've often traveled and worked abroad to learn these methods, to research ovens, and they've brought their expertise home, to our advantage.

Which is to say that on those occasions when you don't have the time or inclination to make bread to go with one of these meals, support your local bread artisans and buy one of their loaves. Nearly every large city and now many rural areas are home to a variety of small bread bakers. Their breads tend to be of the slow-rising sourdough persuasion, precisely the sort of bread that works best in the Whole Wheat Bread and Tomato Salad (page 114). You should also be aware that several recipes in this book work well, too, including Cuban Bread (page 24) and Ciabatta (page 166).

FROM SWISS CHARD TO PUMPKIN

The Simmering Shades of Autumn

CORN CAKES AND APPLE SOUP

Squash, Cider, and Apple Soup

. . . .

New England Fresh Corn Cakes

. . . .

*End of Summer Salad with
Blueberry Balsamic Vinaigrette*

. . . .

It is, hands down, the most bittersweet time of year, when August melts into September, leaving you with a trail of fond summer memories and a revived spirit for the months ahead. I love these weeks: the bugs are gone. The air is once again as crisp as a just-picked McIntosh apple. The skies are bluer than ever beside the yellows and reds of changing leaves. It's prime time to be outside and I relish the afternoons when I can take an hour or two off to go watch one of my kids play field hockey or soccer.

Producewise, the last of the local corn and blueberries is overlapping with the first of the new apples and squash and there's a small window of opportunity when we can bring all these elements together at the dinner table. This menu opens that window and looks at some delicious possibilities.

You'll notice pancakes on this menu. That's right, pancakes for dinner is an old New England tradition, so it isn't too unusual to think about eating them with soup, and especially one that's slightly sweet and laced with boiled cider. The two work beautifully together at the same meal. However, if it seems more appropriate, wait until after your salad and soup and have the pancakes for dessert.

Blueberries usually go in the pancakes, but in this case I've put them in the vinaigrette, and why not? They're attractive and sweet, and this sweetness makes for a pleasing balance to the acidity of the vinegar and the saltiness of the blue cheese. You might be tempted, but no sneaking the blueberry vinaigrette onto the pancakes. You'll want to serve those with maple syrup.

Squash, Cider, and Apple Soup

I like to mix storage vegetables, like carrots and squash, with fruit in soups. The result is often a sweet-and-savory soup that I find very satisfying, and that many people find quite surprising. This has to be one of my favorites in the genre: butternut squash mixed with apples and reduced cider. (You can, of course, use another winter squash; delicata squash is wonderful here, too.) The real flavor kicker comes from the reduced cider mixture—just pour it into a skillet or wide saucepan and let it boil down while the vegetables cook. The finished soup is laced with cinnamon and clove and, at that point, the aroma becomes too much to resist.

2 tablespoons unsalted butter

1 large onion, finely chopped

3 cups peeled and diced butternut squash

2 large apples (any kind), peeled, cored, and chopped

3 cups chicken or vegetable stock

1/4 teaspoon salt

1 bay leaf

1 1/2 cups fresh cider

2 tablespoons firmly packed light brown sugar

1/4 teaspoon ground cinnamon

Large pinch of ground cloves

1. Melt the butter in a medium-size soup pot or large saucepan over moderate heat. Stir in the onion, cover, and sweat for 10 minutes.

2. Add the squash, apples, stock, salt, and bay leaf to the pot. Bring to a boil, reduce the heat to moderately low, cover, and simmer the soup until the squash and apples are very soft, about 20 minutes. Remove from the heat.

3. As the soup simmers, pour the cider into a medium-size skillet, bring to a boil, and reduce to 4 or 5 tablespoons; you don't have to be too precise about it. Remove from the heat.

4. Remove the bay leaf from the soup, then spoon the solids into a food processor. Process the mixture until smooth, then stir it back into the broth. Add the reduced cider. Reheat the soup, stirring in the brown sugar and spices. Serve piping hot.

MAKES 5 TO 6 SERVINGS

New England Fresh Corn Cakes

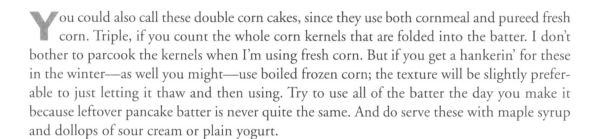

You could also call these double corn cakes, since they use both cornmeal and pureed fresh corn. Triple, if you count the whole corn kernels that are folded into the batter. I don't bother to parcook the kernels when I'm using fresh corn. But if you get a hankerin' for these in the winter—as well you might—use boiled frozen corn; the texture will be slightly preferable to just letting it thaw and then using. Try to use all of the batter the day you make it because leftover pancake batter is never quite the same. And do serve these with maple syrup and dollops of sour cream or plain yogurt.

1¼ cups unbleached all-purpose flour
¼ cup fine-ground yellow cornmeal
1 teaspoon baking powder
½ teaspoon baking soda
½ teaspoon salt
2 cups fresh-cut corn kernels (from 3 to 4 large ears)

2½ tablespoons sugar
2 large eggs
½ cup milk
½ cup sour cream
¼ cup vegetable oil, plus extra for frying

1. Sift the flour, cornmeal, baking powder, baking soda, and salt together into a large bowl; set aside.

2. Put 1⅓ cups of the corn kernels and the sugar in a food processor and process to make a rough puree; set aside.

3. Whisk the eggs together in a medium-size bowl until frothy. Add the pureed corn, milk, sour cream, and oil; whisk thoroughly. Make a well in the center of the dry mixture. Add the liquid and remaining ⅔ cup corn kernels and mix until evenly blended.

4. Preheat one or two large skillets over moderate heat. Add a little oil to the pan and spread it around (a brush is handy). Ladle the batter into the hot pan, using about ¼ cup per cake. Cook until holes appear on the surface and the edge is somewhat dry looking, about 1½ minutes on the first side. Flip and cook on the second side until pancakes are done, about 1 minute. Serve at once on warm plates.

MAKES ABOUT 12 PANCAKES

End of Summer Salad with Blueberry Balsamic Vinaigrette

This blueberry vinaigrette was inspired by something I saw in my friend Jeff Paige's book on Shaker cooking, *The Shaker Kitchen* (Clarkson Potter, 1994). Apparently, this is the sort of thing—if more in spirit than actually to the letter—the Shakers would have dreamed up. It's wonderful, almost good enough to eat without the salad part. Note that small wild Maine blueberries are much preferable here to the larger cultivated ones.

BLUEBERRY BALSAMIC VINAIGRETTE

⅔ cup small blueberries, picked over for stems

⅓ cup dry white wine

1½ tablespoons sugar

3 tablespoons olive oil

1½ tablespoons balsamic vinegar

1½ to 2 tablespoons orange juice, preferably fresh, to your taste

A few gratings of orange zest

SALAD AND ASSEMBLY

1 head Bibb lettuce, leaves washed and dried

1 carrot, peeled and grated

1 ripe pear, peeled, cored, quartered, and sliced crosswise

½ cup crumbled blue cheese

½ cup chopped walnuts, preferably toasted (page 218)

Handful fresh blueberries, for garnish

1. To make the vinaigrette, put the blueberries, wine, and sugar in a small nonreactive saucepan. Bring to a boil, then boil for several minutes, until the wine is reduced by about half. Remove from the heat and transfer to a small bowl. Whisk in the remaining dressing ingredients. Cover with plastic wrap and refrigerate until needed.

2. To assemble the salad, make sure the lettuce leaves are good and dry, then arrange a couple of leaves on each salad plate. Scatter some of the carrot, pear, blue cheese, and walnuts over the leaves, then spoon some of the blueberry vinaigrette over each salad. Garnish each salad with fresh blueberries and serve.

MAKES 4 TO 5 SERVINGS

THE ABCs OF ALPHABET SOUP

Alphabet Ham and Bean Soup
....
Stuffed Pita Pizza Breads
....
A Kid's Antipasto Plate
....

I like to see kids in the kitchen. It feels very natural to someone like myself who grew up there, not actually cooking so much as hanging out with my mom and dad and six siblings. It was a large kitchen in a big old Victorian with twenty rooms. I miss it, and I know that my fond associations with it had an influence on my choice of a career as a food writer.

Like me, my own kids have always gravitated toward the kitchen and cooked with me, much more so when they were younger. Today they're all teenagers and there are many more important things to do in life than cook with Pop. That's okay with me, though. I know someday, when they're adults, they'll come back to the kitchen and make lots of good meals there.

I think it's important to give kids the opportunity to help with mealtime. I don't think kids should ever be forced to cook because there's no surer way to turn them off to cooking. But we should encourage them if they show an interest, and be clever enough to find age-appropriate tasks and recipes they can follow. Gradually, as one small success leads to another, they'll enjoy the time they spend cooking and view their efforts with pride. And that's good material for growing into a confident, self-sufficient adult.

Here is a menu that the kids can have a hand in putting together. It's a fun back-to-school menu because it can tie in with spelling lessons. Among the kid-friendly projects here is an easy way to make a stuffed pizza, using pita bread. Kids will have fun with this one. Heck, *I* have fun with this one. The soup is one we all learned to spell with: alphabet soup. I wish I had a nickel for every time I peered down into my soup spoon as a little boy and shouted *There it is! K-E-N-N-Y!* As for our salad, I don't know too many adults who think washing lettuce is a gas; kids don't think so either. This kid's antipasto plate is a lot more fun. Kids can include what they want and in the end they've created something of their own design, which, of course, makes it taste even better. Be alert for all the kid-cooking opportunities in this menu, like grating vegetables and stuffing the breads. They'll need supervision with the soup, of course; never leave children unattended near the stove. But most importantly, enjoy yourself and your child's company, and don't make a big deal of any messes that happen. (I know one cooking mom who throws a big canvas tarp on the floor when her kids cook, says a couple of Hail Marys, and then just enjoys herself. I like that attitude.)

Alphabet Ham and Bean Soup

The alphabet pasta, of course, is what makes this so much fun to eat; you get to spell your name as you slurp. Note that I use several grated vegetables here in case you have willing younger children who aren't quite old enough to entrust with knives. Older kids can chop the vegetables—the onion and celery—that need chopping, and dice the ham.

1½ tablespoons unsalted butter or vegetable oil

1 medium-size onion, finely chopped

1 rib celery, finely chopped

1 medium-size carrot, peeled and grated

1 medium-size parsnip, peeled and grated

1 medium-size all-purpose potato, grated

5½ cups beef or chicken stock

1 cup diced ham

1 teaspoon fresh thyme leaves or ½ teaspoon dried

¼ to ½ teaspoon salt, plus more to taste

Freshly ground black pepper to taste

½ cup uncooked alphabet pasta

1 cup cooked cannellini (white kidney) beans, drained and rinsed

½ cup canned tomato puree or tomato juice

1. Melt the butter or heat the oil in a medium-size soup pot or large saucepan over moderate heat. Stir in the vegetables, cover, and sweat the vegetables, stirring a few times, for 3 minutes.

2. Add the stock, ham, thyme, salt, and pepper, bring to a simmer, then cover and gently simmer the soup for 5 minutes. Stir in the alphabet pasta. Increase the heat to moderately high and continue to simmer the soup, partially covered, until the pasta is tender, 8 to 10 minutes.

3. When the pasta is tender, stir in the beans and tomato puree and simmer 5 more minutes before serving.

MAKES 5 TO 6 SERVINGS

Stuffed Pita Pizza Breads

This is supposed to be a kid's bread, so I'm almost embarrassed to admit how much I like to eat these little stuffed pizzas. If you've never made anything like this, you'll be impressed. Personally, I've always found pita bread sort of dry and underwhelming; this treatment renders it soft and appealing. First, you stuff the insides with tomato sauce, grated cheese, and pepperoni. Then you brush the outside with olive oil and pan-cook the bread for a couple of minutes on each side. What you end up with is something like a pita calzone. There's room here for personal flights of fancy: throw in a few olives, sautéed mushrooms, finely chopped bell pepper, or whatever the kids want or will eat. Note that the quantities you'll need for each ingredient depend on the size of your pita bread. Use small or large breads.

3 pita breads, cut in half
1½ to 2 cups prepared tomato sauce (the thicker the better), as needed
2 to 3 cups grated mozzarella, Monterey Jack, or cheddar cheese, as needed

Small package sliced pepperoni
¼ to ½ cup olive oil, as needed

1. Start heating a large, heavy skillet; cast iron is best here. Take one of the pita halves and spoon about ¼ cup of the sauce into the middle, spreading it out with the spoon. Add a small handful of the cheese and some pepperoni, spreading them around as well.

2. Brush one side of the bread with olive oil. Put the bread in the skillet, oiled side down. Brush oil on the second side. At this point, cook the bread as you would a grilled cheese sandwich, a minute or so on each side, flipping it once. When done, the cheese should be melted and the outside perhaps darker, though by no means burned.

3. Transfer the breads to a serving plate and serve at once, repeating for the remaining breads. If you'd rather, hold the cooked breads in a low oven while you finish cooking the last batches.

MAKES 6 SERVINGS

A Kid's Antipasto Plate

This is less a recipe than it is a discussion of the ways kids might go about designing their own antipasto plates. You, as the adult, should allow as much kid discretion as possible, only drawing the line when they start wanting to smear peanut butter and jelly on the prosciutto. I used to do this sort of thing with my own kids all the time. We called it a goodie plate and it would have grapes, raisins, celery sticks, chunks of cheese—whatever was on hand and struck our fancy. You can be as formal or casual as you like. Your child's personality will emerge in the process: some will want to arrange things in neat little rows, others just jumble them on the plate in groups, still others will only want to throw the grapes across the room at a sibling. In the end, you would hope to create an attractive platter of things to nibble on, with a more or less unified flavor scheme. Or, if not so much unified, then not outrageously un-unified. The stuffed dates mentioned below are made by blending a little bit of honey into cream cheese; you can use this mixture on the celery sticks, too. Here, then, are some suggestions.

- Cream cheese–stuffed dates (Medjools are best)
- Thinly sliced fennel bulb
- Cubes of cheddar or Monterey Jack cheese impaled on toothpicks
- Seedless red or green grapes
- Apple and pear slices
- Cubes of ham on toothpicks or slices of pepperoni
- Celery sticks, plain or filled with sweetened cream cheese
- Carrot sticks
- Pecans, walnuts, almonds, or pine nuts
- Cucumber slices
- Moist dried fruits such as halved figs or strips of apricot or pear
- Pickles

Don't feel as though you have to include lots of the above. Three or four items on the plate will do nicely, more if you like. This can be assembled several hours ahead of serving, covered with plastic wrap, and refrigerated. Bring to room temperature about 30 minutes before serving.

Kids in the Kitchen: A Primer

Whether you're making soup and bread from this book, or a Sunday breakfast, it takes a clear head and a clean kitchen to cook with kids. I've spent years cooking with my own kids, so I have a few opinions about what works and what doesn't. I've boiled them down to five rules.

1. *Get out the goods.* Kids—especially young ones—have limited attention spans. They want to cook, not wait around while you search for the baking powder. Plan accordingly. Gather your ingredients, dig out the biscuit cutter, and find the baking sheet before you say, "Let's make biscuits!" When they're cooking, kids like to stay focused on the destination. Side trips only distract.

2. *Do a dry run.* If your destination is something good to eat, the recipe is your map. Study it before you set out. Are the directions clear to you? Try to visualize the steps a recipe involves. Tune into age-appropriate tasks you can assign. Your job is to orchestrate. To do that, you need to know the score.

3. *Show and tell.* Even if a child can read, you're still the mouthpiece who makes the recipe come to life for a young cook. Your words are his or her barometer of how things are going. So keep up the chatter. Explain or demonstrate steps as you work, highlighting what may be obvious to you, though not to your child. Be positive and specific—"You did a good job measuring that flour!"—and bite your tongue when mistakes happen. They will, but that's how all cooks learn.

4. *Put safety first.* Kitchens are safe places with some potentially unsafe tools and situations parents must stay alert to. Let common sense prevail. Young children should never stand in front of an open oven. Older kids, on the other hand, are usually sure-footed enough to slide a tray of biscuits into a hot oven—so long as they wear oven mitts and you're there to supervise. Again, be verbal. Tell your child that the biscuit cutter is sharp. Don't assume he or she knows.

5. *Have fun.* Remember, whatever else they might gain in the process, kids will keep coming back to cook only if they're having fun. And they'll only have fun if you do. Bottom line: don't sweat the small stuff. Value the process more than the outcome. So what if your biscuits are a little misshapen? They'll probably look better next time. And besides, misshapen biscuits taste great.

CURRYING FLAVORS

Curried Carrot and Pineapple Soup

· · · · · · · · · · · · ·

Curried Potato-Stuffed Breads

· · · · · · · · · · · · ·

Carrot and Cucumber Raita

· · · · · · · · · · · · ·

I don't think I know anyone who isn't fond of Indian food. How could you not be? The colors of the various curries and curry spices are so vibrant. The aromas make you weak in the knees. And it has what a lot of what many other cuisines lack: drama. It was this drama that first drew me in. When I was a kid, I used to frequent a small Indian restaurant near where I lived in New Jersey. You would walk into the place and it was like being transported to another world. Sitar music would be playing, sizzling food would come flying out the kitchen door—held aloft by turbaned waiters—and great hot, puffy breads would be delivered to your table within moments. On top of that, it was reasonably priced.

I'm certainly no authority on Indian food, but I do have a repertoire of Indian dishes I like to make. Some are more authentic than others, which are more self-styled. A couple of the recipes here fall into the latter category. Like the soup. I've never actually seen a recipe for a curried carrot and pineapple soup in an Indian cookbook, but there's no quibbling with the flavor. I think you'll enjoy it. The bread, too, is my cheater's version of something you will find in Indian restaurants—vegetable-stuffed breads. The cheating part is the way I use store-bought tortillas to make them, but you can—if you're so inclined—use the traditional chapati breads (page 242) to make a more authentic version of these. Incidentally, the plain chapatis would be a good menu substitution for the stuffed breads.

Curried Carrot and Pineapple Soup

This soup has lots of carrots, so it must be good for your vision. It's a great winter soup, for those times when nothing in the produce section looks all that fresh and appealing except for the root vegetables. Or when you're scrounging around the refrigerator looking for something to make soup with and all you can find is a bag of carrots. Indeed, I was in the midst of just such a predicament when I came up with the soup; about the only other thing I had on hand was a can of crushed pineapple, and what a fine match it was. (Good thing it wasn't a can of blueberries.) The curry was just the right seasoning to tie the carrots and pineapple together.

2 tablespoons unsalted butter

1 large or 2 medium-size onions, chopped

1 tablespoon curry powder

1 teaspoon ground ginger

5 large carrots, peeled and sliced

1 large all-purpose potato, peeled and diced

1 bay leaf

4$\frac{1}{2}$ cups chicken stock

$\frac{1}{2}$ teaspoon salt

One 8-ounce can crushed pineapple

Freshly ground black pepper to taste

1. Melt the butter in a large saucepan or medium-size soup pot over moderate heat. Add the onion and cook, stirring, until softened, 8 to 9 minutes. Add the curry powder and ginger and cook, stirring, for 30 seconds. Add the carrots, potato, bay leaf, stock, and salt and bring the soup to a boil. Reduce the heat to moderately low, cover tightly, and simmer until the carrots are very tender, about 20 minutes.

2. Using a large slotted spoon, transfer the soup solids to a food processor, adding a ladleful of the broth. Add the pineapple, then process the solids to a smooth puree. Stir the puree back into the soup. Reheat and taste the soup, adding more salt, if necessary, and pepper as needed. Serve piping hot.

MAKES 6 SERVINGS

Curried Potato-Stuffed Breads

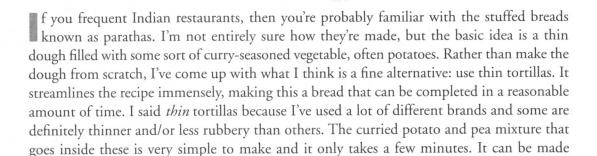

If you frequent Indian restaurants, then you're probably familiar with the stuffed breads known as parathas. I'm not entirely sure how they're made, but the basic idea is a thin dough filled with some sort of curry-seasoned vegetable, often potatoes. Rather than make the dough from scratch, I've come up with what I think is a fine alternative: use thin tortillas. It streamlines the recipe immensely, making this a bread that can be completed in a reasonable amount of time. I said *thin* tortillas because I've used a lot of different brands and some are definitely thinner and/or less rubbery than others. The curried potato and pea mixture that goes inside these is very simple to make and it only takes a few minutes. It can be made ahead, if you like, and rewarmed when the breads are assembled. Please note that if you brush the exterior of these with butter, you'll get a soft-textured bread; if you heat them without it, you'll get a crisper bread. Both are good.

3 large all-purpose potatoes, peeled and cut into chunks
1 cup frozen peas
2 tablespoons olive oil
1 cup finely chopped onions
2 teaspoons curry powder
1/4 cup water

1/2 teaspoon salt
2 tablespoons sour cream or plain yogurt
Three 9- or 10-inch thin flour tortillas
A little soft butter for brushing on the breads (optional)

1. Bring the potatoes and peas to a boil in a large saucepan of salted water. Boil until the potatoes are tender, about 10 minutes. Drain and transfer the vegetables to a medium-size bowl.

2. Heat the olive oil in a medium-size skillet over moderate heat. Add the onions and cook, stirring, until translucent, 7 to 8 minutes. Add the curry powder and cook, stirring, for 30 seconds. Stir in the water and cook several more seconds, letting some of the liquid evaporate. Scrape the onions into the potatoes. Add the salt and sour cream or yogurt and mash well with a potato masher.

3. Working with one tortilla at a time, spread the potato mixture thickly and evenly over half of the tortilla. Fold in half to enclose. Get a cast-iron skillet fairly hot, then lay the bread in the pan and heat until golden brown and crispy, about 1 1/2 minutes on each side. Cut in half and serve. (If you're using the butter, brush or spread a little of it on both sides before heating. Use slightly less heat.)

MAKES 6 SERVINGS

Carrot and Cucumber Raita

This is one of the best-known Indian salads, though it is not what we typically think of as a salad in this country. It's a creamy base of yogurt into which vegetables, seasonings, and spice are mixed. This is the fast version. There's another way of doing this that takes just a little longer, gives slightly better results, and I recommend particularly if you aren't serving this at once. Just follow the recipe, but instead of mixing everything in at the same time, put the cucumber in a bowl, salt lightly, and refrigerate for 30 minutes to get some of the water out of it. Drain, then proceed. Even though I add a little sugar to this, don't substitute sweetened yogurt because there's only enough sugar in here to take the edge off the yogurt, not to actually sweeten it. Some like to use toasted cumin seeds in raita, instead of ground, but I don't think it makes much difference.

2 large cucumbers, peeled, halved, and
   seeded
2 large carrots, peeled and grated
1/4 cup minced red onion
2 cups plain yogurt
2 tablespoons chopped fresh cilantro or
   parsley leaves

2 teaspoons sugar
1/2 teaspoon ground cumin
A little finely grated orange zest
Salt to taste

Combine all of the ingredients in a medium-size bowl; stir to blend. Serve at once or cover with plastic wrap and refrigerate until serving, up to several hours.

MAKES 5 TO 6 SERVINGS

A QUICK CHICK 'N' RICE TRIO

Almost Instant Chicken and Rice Soup

· · · · · · · · · · · ·

Best Parmesan Garlic Bread

· · · · · · · · · · · ·

Cherry Tomato Salad

· · · · · · · · · · · ·

Sometimes, oftentimes perhaps, we'd like to get a homemade meal on the table without having to run a gauntlet of fussy techniques, ingredient lists that never end, ingredients we probably don't have or never heard of. This is a menu for those times. It makes no apologies—nor should you—for any of the convenience items that make an easy menu possible: instant rice, store-bought bread, and the like. I've also pared slicing, dicing, mincing, and other such obstacles to mealtime down to a minimum. All you have to do is make a short shopping list and grab a few items at the supermarket after work, or when you're shuttling kids home from field hockey games or soccer practice.

By design, this menu doesn't break any new gastronomic ground. I mean, what's the use of a making a quick soup meal if you've got to spend 30 additional minutes convincing your kids to eat the blessed radicchio and strawberry salad with rosewater vinaigrette? Rather, it goes straight to what most of us like best: chicken soup, garlic bread, a simple tomato salad. And if the latter isn't one your kids will go for, well, there are plenty more salads in this book that they'll find to their liking. And hardly any of them use radicchio.

Almost Instant Chicken and Rice Soup

If you happen to have some chicken on hand that you can dice up and add to this, wonderful. But remember that the whole theme here is *easy does it*, so don't bother cooking any or running out for a rotisserie chicken if there's none on hand.

2 tablespoons unsalted butter, melted

2 ribs celery, finely chopped

1 medium-size onion, finely chopped

1 medium-size carrot, peeled and grated

1 bay leaf

1/4 teaspoon salt, plus more to taste

5 cups chicken stock

1 cup instant rice

2 to 3 tablespoons chopped fresh
   parsley leaves, to your taste

Freshly ground black pepper to taste

1. Melt the butter in a medium-size soup pot or large saucepan over moderately low heat. Stir in the vegetables and bay leaf; salt lightly. Cover, then sweat the vegetables until they're good and soft, 10 to 12 minutes.

2. Add the stock and bring to an active simmer; cover and simmer for 5 minutes. Stir in the rice and parsley and season with pepper. Cover, then remove from the heat and let sit undisturbed for about 7 minutes before serving.

MAKES 4 TO 5 SERVINGS

Best Parmesan Garlic Bread

Any good French or Italian-style bread will work here. If using the latter, just cut it into thick pieces. Make this in your oven or toaster oven.

1 long loaf soft French bread

3 tablespoons olive oil

2 tablespoons unsalted butter

3 cloves garlic, minced

Freshly ground black pepper to taste

1 cup finely grated Parmesan cheese

1. Preheat the oven or toaster oven to 400 degrees F. Cut the bread into several sections, then halve each of the sections lengthwise. Place the bread on a baking sheet, cut sides up, and toast the pieces until they're light golden.

2. While the bread is toasting, warm the olive oil, butter, and garlic together in a small saucepan until the butter melts. When the bread is golden, spoon some of the butter mixture over the inside of each section. Dust with pepper and sprinkle on the Parmesan cheese. Put the bread back in the oven for several minutes, until it turns a shade or two darker. Serve at once.

MAKES 4 TO 6 SERVINGS

Cherry Tomato Salad

There are just enough tomatoes here to serve four. If you want to pad it and add a leafy green element, increase the dressing ingredients just a tad, proportionally, and serve over thin wedges of iceberg lettuce. Or just toss a few torn lettuce leaves into the mix right before serving. This will hold for a little while in the fridge, perhaps 15 minutes, but don't let it sit much longer than that or the dressing will get watery.

1/3 cup mayonnaise

2 teaspoons red wine vinegar or tarragon vinegar

2 tablespoons chopped fresh parsley leaves

1 teaspoon dried basil

1 teaspoon Dijon mustard

1 pint cherry tomatoes, halved

1/4 cup finely chopped red onion (optional)

Salt and freshly ground black pepper to taste

1. In a small bowl, whisk together the mayonnaise, vinegar, herbs, and mustard.

2. Add the cherry tomatoes—and onion, if you're using it—and toss well. Season with salt and pepper. Cover with plastic wrap and refrigerate if not serving right away.

MAKES 4 SERVINGS

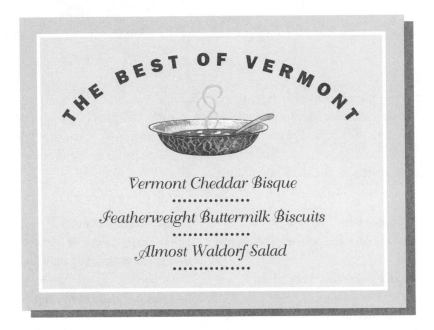

THE BEST OF VERMONT

Vermont Cheddar Bisque

....

Featherweight Buttermilk Biscuits

....

Almost Waldorf Salad

....

Even if you've never been to Vermont, you've been there. For many people, Vermont is the symbol of the way America used to be, where—like Garrison Keillor's Lake Wobegon—all the women are strong, all the men good looking, and all the children above average. Because I live next door in New Hampshire, I can tell you that many of these stereotypes are true. Vermont is a great place—fetching, energetic, politically active, and aware.

Among the many things Vermont is praised for are its native food products, nearly all of it well deserved. You would be hard-pressed to find a state, and citizenry, more supportive of their local food producers and artisans. Excluding maple syrup, Vermont is probably best known for its apples and cheese, primarily the well-aged, sharp cheddars you can find in every village store across the state. These aren't the anonymous, standard-issue cheddars you get in the grocery store; these cheeses have character. They're a little crumbly under the knife, and the flavor is what you'd call snappy, the very qualities that endear them to the local apples. Everyone in Vermont knows that apples and cheese have a natural affinity. Old-time Vermonters still take slabs of hot apple pie and lay slices of cheddar on the crust, only digging in when the cheese is nearly melted. Others use grated cheddar in apple muffins or top apple cobbler with cheddar biscuit dough.

What I do here is serve them separately—the cheddar in a thick, rich bisque; the apples in a crisp update of Waldorf salad. If Vermont makes the ultimate cheddar, I like to think of this as the ultimate farmhouse cheddar soup, something you might find on the menu of a country inn. Since it reminds me of Welsh rarebit, which is most at home on split biscuits, I made the biscuits so you can drop pieces into the soup for a sort of reverse rarebit experience.

Vermont Cheddar Bisque

No one has ever asked me, but I've thought about what I'd like to eat for my last meal and I'm pretty sure it would be Welsh rarebit on toast points. I think it's the ideal comfort food and I've loved it ever since I was a kid, when my mom would prepare it weekly. This soup is just a step or two removed from the Welsh rarebit I love. The flavor is virtually the same; it's just thinner, though still quite full-bodied, and not quite so rich—less cheese, no egg yolks. And there are potatoes in here, something you won't find in real rarebit. Still, this is rich enough that you won't need huge servings; small bowls will do.

1½ cups peeled potatoes cut into
  ½-inch dice

2 cups chicken stock

¼ cup (½ stick) unsalted butter

1 cup finely chopped onions

3 tablespoons unbleached all-purpose
  flour

1½ cups milk

2 teaspoons Dijon mustard

1½ cups grated extra-sharp cheddar
  cheese

Salt and freshly ground black pepper
  to taste

Pinch of cayenne pepper

1. Combine the potatoes and stock in a medium-size saucepan. Cover, bring to a simmer, and let simmer until the potatoes are tender, 8 to 10 minutes. Remove from the heat.

2. Meanwhile, melt the butter in a large saucepan over moderately low heat. Add the onions and cook, stirring, until translucent, 6 to 8 minutes. Add the flour and cook, stirring, for 1 minute. Add the potatoes and stock and continue to cook over moderate heat, stirring, until thickened.

3. Stir the milk into the soup. Heat, stirring, for 7 to 8 minutes, then take off the heat and stir in the mustard and cheese, about half at a time. Season to taste with the salt, black pepper, and cayenne pepper and serve piping hot.

MAKES 4 TO 5 SERVINGS

Featherweight Buttermilk Biscuits

Thes are my favorite plain biscuits, though "plain" hardly does them justice; perhaps "basic" is a better choice of word. I like a little cornstarch in these because it makes them even more tender and light, though those qualities are nearly as much a function of how they're handled as of what they're made of. Which is to say, you should handle and work the dough minimally—just enough to make it feel smooth and supple. You can put anything on these: preserves, slices of ham and cheese, honey, you name it.

2 cups unbleached all-purpose flour

1 tablespoon sugar

1 tablespoon cornstarch

2 teaspoons baking powder

1/2 teaspoon baking soda

1/2 teaspoon salt

1/4 cup (1/2 stick) cold unsalted butter, cut into 1/2-inch pieces

3/4 cup chilled buttermilk

1. Preheat the oven to 425 degrees F. Sift the flour, sugar, cornstarch, baking powder, baking soda, and salt into a large bowl. Add the butter and cut it into the dry mixture with a pastry blender, or rub it in with your fingers, until the mixture resembles a coarse meal; the butter will be in tiny bits and flakes.

2. Make a well in the center of the dry mixture and add the buttermilk all at once. Stir, using a few rapid strokes, until a dough forms. Let rest for 2 minutes. Very lightly oil a baking sheet.

3. Turn the dough out onto a floured work surface. Knead the dough gently, 5 or 6 times, with floured hands, then pat it down to a thickness of 1 inch. Using a 2-inch-diameter biscuit cutter, cut into rounds and place them on the baking sheet. Gather and re-roll the scraps and cut them as well.

4. Bake the biscuits on the center rack of the oven until golden, 13 to 14 minutes. Transfer to a cloth-lined basket and serve at once.

MAKES ABOUT 12 BISCUITS

TIP: If you don't have a biscuit cutter, remove both ends from a tomato paste can, wash well, and use it. Works like a charm.

Almost Waldorf Salad

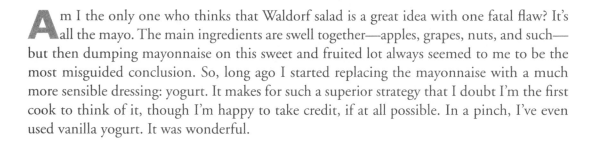

Am I the only one who thinks that Waldorf salad is a great idea with one fatal flaw? It's all the mayo. The main ingredients are swell together—apples, grapes, nuts, and such—but then dumping mayonnaise on this sweet and fruited lot always seemed to me to be the most misguided conclusion. So, long ago I started replacing the mayonnaise with a much more sensible dressing: yogurt. It makes for such a superior strategy that I doubt I'm the first cook to think of it, though I'm happy to take credit, if at all possible. In a pinch, I've even used vanilla yogurt. It was wonderful.

2 large crisp apples, quartered, cored, and cut into chunks

2 ribs celery, finely chopped

1 cup red or green seedless grapes, halved

½ cup raisins

½ cup coarsely chopped walnuts, toasted (page 218) if desired

1 cup plain yogurt

2 to 3 teaspoons sugar (optional), to your taste

Combine all of the ingredients in a medium-size bowl and mix well, coating everything evenly with the yogurt. Serve immediately, or cover with plastic wrap and refrigerate until serving.

MAKES 5 TO 6 SERVINGS

A NOD TO FARM AND GARDEN

Farm-Style Cream of Chicken Soup

· · · · · · · · · · · ·

Sage Dumplings

· · · · · · · · · · · ·

Chopped Salad with Port Dressing

· · · · · · · · · · · ·

Alas, we are no longer a nation of farmers. The statistic one often hears cited is that one hundred years ago, ninety-five percent of us lived on farms and nowadays it is just the reverse, with only five percent of us living on farms. Whatever the numbers, you get the point: most of our produce today comes from Big Farming.

My chicken soup with dumplings harkens back to a different age of farming, Small Farming, if you will. These were farms like the one Lassie and Timmy grew up on, where the chickens would scatter whenever someone drove in the driveway.

This is different from chicken and dumplings, in that you don't end up with a whole chicken in the pot, just little pieces of it. The dumplings are gently coaxed into the pot at the very end, then the broth is enriched with a little cream and served with the dumplings. It's delicious. Along with this hearty soup I like to serve chopped salad. As I note, chopped salads are experiencing a comeback nowadays and they're getting quite upscale in certain venues. But all those nicely cut fresh veggies remind me of a farm garden, so I think it's appropriate here. And if the port dressing sounds a little too precious for an old-fashioned farm meal like this, just serve it with another; Parmesan Peppercorn Ranch Dressing (page 239) would be great.

Farm-Style
Cream of Chicken Soup

This is one soup you can't—shouldn't—make without the benefit of homemade stock, with its depth and complexity of flavor. You'll need the chicken pieces anyway because the broth should have lots of meltingly tender chunks of chicken floating around in and among the dumplings. Think of this as a weekend soup project and not something you'll knock out after you get home from work. This is a *cream* of chicken soup: heavy cream is stirred in just after the dumplings come out. If that sounds too rich for your liking, simply skip that part and serve this great broth without it.

1 recipe Basic Chicken Stock (page 4), chicken pieces reserved	Salt and freshly ground black pepper to taste
2 tablespoons unsalted butter	1 recipe Sage Dumplings (recipe follows)
1 large onion, chopped	1/2 cup heavy cream
2 cups thinly sliced mushrooms	1 1/2 tablespoons unbleached all-purpose flour
1 clove garlic, minced	

1. Prepare, cool, refrigerate, and skim the stock as instructed; set aside. Pick the meat off the bones of the chicken, reserving 2 cups of it.

2. Melt the butter in a large soup pot over moderate heat. Stir in the onion and cook, stirring, for 7 minutes. Stir in the mushrooms and garlic and continue to cook, partially covered, for 3 to 4 minutes.

3. Add the stock to the soup pot and bring to a lively simmer. Taste the stock, seasoning with salt and pepper as needed. Stir in the reserved chicken.

4. While the soup heats, prepare the sage dumplings.

5. When the soup reaches a gentle boil, gently add the dumpling batter to the stock by the spoonful; you should get 8 dumplings. Reduce the heat slightly and cover tightly. Simmer the dumplings for 10 minutes without removing the lid; you want to keep all the steam trapped inside.

6. Turn the oven onto low and get out a pie plate. In a small bowl, whisk together the cream and flour; set aside.

7. After 10 minutes, lift the dumplings out of the soup with a large slotted spoon, transferring them to the pie plate. Place the dumplings in the oven. Quickly whisk the cream and flour into the broth and bring to a boil; boiling will help cook out any lumps. Gently boil the broth for 2 minutes, whisking occasionally.

8. To serve, put 1 or 2 dumplings in individual wide soup bowls and ladle the broth around them. Serve at once.

MAKES 5 TO 6 SERVINGS

Sage Dumplings

The sage makes these dumplings taste like they came right from a farm kitchen; the sour cream renders them soft and gives a slight tang. To get these into the soup properly, spoon the dough up, place the spoon right over the simmering broth, then gently push the dumpling into the soup. You don't want them to hit the broth with a splatter. Just imagine a large man rolling into a pool from the deck as opposed to belly-flopping from the high dive.

1 cup unbleached all-purpose flour
1½ teaspoons baking powder
Scant ½ teaspoon salt
½ teaspoon crumbled dried sage
¼ teaspoon dried thyme

⅛ teaspoon freshly ground black
    pepper
1 large egg
¼ cup milk
2 tablespoons sour cream

1. Sift the flour, baking powder, and salt into a medium-size bowl. Mix in the herbs and pepper.

2. In a small bowl, whisk the egg, milk, and sour cream together.

3. Make a well in the center of the dry ingredients, add the liquid, and stir briefly, just until the dough is uniformly mixed. Finish cooking as instructed in the soup recipe.

MAKES 8 DUMPLINGS

Chopped Salad with Port Dressing

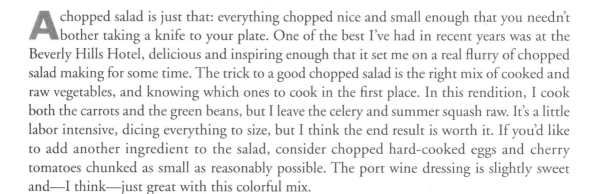

Achopped salad is just that: everything chopped nice and small enough that you needn't bother taking a knife to your plate. One of the best I've had in recent years was at the Beverly Hills Hotel, delicious and inspiring enough that it set me on a real flurry of chopped salad making for some time. The trick to a good chopped salad is the right mix of cooked and raw vegetables, and knowing which ones to cook in the first place. In this rendition, I cook both the carrots and the green beans, but I leave the celery and summer squash raw. It's a little labor intensive, dicing everything to size, but I think the end result is worth it. If you'd like to add another ingredient to the salad, consider chopped hard-cooked eggs and cherry tomatoes chunked as small as reasonably possible. The port wine dressing is slightly sweet and—I think—just great with this colorful mix.

SALAD
1½ cups ½-inch green bean pieces
2 medium-size carrots, peeled and cut
   into small dice
1 head romaine lettuce, heart only
2 ribs celery, cut into small dice
1 medium-size or 2 small yellow summer
   squash, cut into small dice
3 medium-size dill pickles, cut into small
   dice

PORT DRESSING
⅓ cup olive oil
5 tablespoons ruby port
2 tablespoons red wine vinegar
1 tablespoon Dijon mustard
2 teaspoons tomato paste
2 teaspoons sugar
½ teaspoon Worcestershire sauce
Salt and freshly ground black pepper
   to taste

1. Bring to a boil 2 small saucepans of lightly salted water. When the water boils, add the green beans to one and the carrots to the other. Boil both about 5 minutes, then drain them separately. Briefly rinse with cold running water. Drain thoroughly and let cool.

2. Stack the romaine lettuce leaves and slice in half lengthwise, then slice crosswise into ¼-inch-wide strips. Neatly mound the lettuce in the center of a serving platter. Arrange neat groupings of the vegetables and pickles around the greens. Cover with plastic wrap and refrigerate if not serving within 10 minutes.

3. To make the dressing, whisk all of the dressing ingredients together in a small bowl. Taste and adjust the seasonings as needed. Just before serving, toss the salad at the table and serve with the dressing on the side.

MAKES 4 TO 5 SERVINGS

OF BISQUE-QUICK AND FALL COLORS

Curried Pumpkin and Cheddar Bisque

••••••••••••••••

Molasses Soda Bread

••••••••••••••••

Green Bean and Carrot Salad with Apple Vinaigrette

••••••••••••••••

Have you ever thought about the importance of color in the way we perceive and relate to food? Good chefs give a lot of thought to the harmony of color on your plate. So do editors. I write for food magazines and when an editor asks me to do a story on fall desserts or soups or whatever, she will often say "Use a lot of different colors" or "Don't make everything brown," the point being that, even if it tastes good, dark or otherwise muted food doesn't always make the best first impression.

I was thinking of such things when I put this menu together because the colors here take you from one end of autumn to the other, from the early fall greens to the darkness of late November. The concept of four distinct seasons is a handy one, but it doesn't do enough to capture the diversity we experience within each one. I was hoping this menu might.

Early fall is more like late summer. The trees and lawns are still as green as this green bean salad, whose grated carrots suggest the first turning foliage. Mid-fall is more about pumpkins. Come October you see them everywhere on porches, flanking driveways, in windows with scary carved faces. You see them in soup, too, like this one, flavored with curry and cheddar cheese. By November, the leaves and lawns have all turned brown, like molasses soda bread. Don't get the wrong impression—this bread is anything but drab. It's handsome, grainy, and its earthy darkness only makes the rest of the meal look all the more vivid. If you haven't made a soda bread before, this would be a great time to start. You'll love how simple all these recipes are and how great they taste.

Curried Pumpkin and Cheddar Bisque

When I'm making a smooth pumpkin soup—as opposed to leaving in chunks—I'll often just open a can of pumpkin puree; as canned foods go, it is quite acceptable as a substitute for fresh and you'd scarcely know the difference, especially when you're using a dominant seasoning like curry. Like most soups, this one tastes best if you can make it ahead and let it sit for a few hours or overnight. The cheddar is a nice touch at the end, especially if you're serving crunchy croutons with this.

2 tablespoons olive oil

1 large onion, finely chopped

1 rib celery, finely chopped

1 small green bell pepper, seeded and finely chopped

1 bay leaf

1 tablespoon unsalted butter

1½ tablespoons mild curry powder

2 cloves garlic, minced

5 cups chicken stock

1 cup frozen corn kernels

½ teaspoon salt, plus more to taste

2 cups canned pumpkin puree

½ cup canned crushed tomatoes in puree

½ teaspoon crushed or powdered dried sage

6 ounces extra-sharp cheddar cheese, grated, for garnish

1. Heat the olive oil in a medium-size soup pot or large saucepan over moderate heat. Stir in the onion, celery, bell pepper, and bay leaf and cook, stirring, until the onion is translucent, about 8 minutes. Add the butter, curry powder, and garlic and cook gently, stirring, for 1 minute.

2. Add the stock, corn, and ½ teaspoon salt; bring to a boil. Stir in the pumpkin, crushed tomatoes, and sage. Simmer, stirring occasionally, for 15 minutes, adding more salt, if necessary. When ready to serve, stir well (the ingredients tend to settle) and serve in warm bowls with some of the grated cheddar sprinkled over the top.

MAKES 6 TO 8 SERVINGS

Molasses Soda Bread

Yet another soda bread I'm quite fond of, this one is dark, handsome, and crusty. The molasses makes it just a little sweet, which I think tastes great with the curry-sharpness of the pumpkin soup. In fact, I play up the sweetness by serving this with a crock of cold Spiced Ginger Apple Butter (recipe follows). As with other soda breads, you have to wait until this is almost cool before slicing. Otherwise, it may seem underdone.

Cornmeal or semolina, for dusting
1/2 cups rolled (old-fashioned, not instant or quick-cooking) oats
1 3/4 cups buttermilk
1/4 cup molasses
2 tablespoons vegetable oil
3 cups unbleached all-purpose flour

1/2 cup whole wheat flour
1 tablespoon sugar
1 1/2 teaspoons salt
1 teaspoon baking soda
1 teaspoon baking powder
1 cup raisins

1. Preheat the oven to 400 degrees F and lightly oil a large baking sheet. Sprinkle the sheet with cornmeal or semolina and set aside.

2. Put the oats in a medium-size bowl. Stir in the buttermilk, molasses, and oil; set aside. Mix the dry ingredients together in a large bowl. Make a well in the center of the dry mixture and add the liquid all at once; add the raisins. Stir briskly with a wooden spoon until the dough pulls together in a shaggy mass. Let rest for 3 minutes.

3. Flour your work surface and hands. Scoop half of the dough onto the floured surface and knead gently; if dough is a little sticky, a dough scraper might help. Knead about 1 minute, shaping into a ball. Place on the prepared baking sheet. Using a sharp, serrated knife, make 2 parallel slashes on the surface of the dough, about 3/4 inch deep. Repeat with the other half of the dough and place on the sheet; leave plenty of room between the loaves.

4. Bake for 20 minutes, then reduce the oven temperature to 375 degrees F and bake until dark and crusty, about 20 minutes more. When done, the bottom should sound hollow when tapped. Cool the loaves on a wire rack before slicing. (The loaves are best if they're eaten within 24 hours.)

MAKES 2 LOAVES

Spiced Ginger Apple Butter

I f you've ever made applesauce, you've come within one step of making apple butter, which is essentially sauce cooked down to a thicker consistency. It doesn't really require any more of your time, however, because you do this last part in the oven. If you have any left after teaming it with the Molasses Soda Bread, use it with muffins and biscuits.

3 to 4 pounds apples (use a mix of them), peeled, cored, and cut into large chunks
1½ cups cider

2 tablespoons minced candied ginger
⅓ cup sugar
1½ tablespoons fresh lemon juice

1. Preheat the oven to 375 degrees F. Combine the apples, cider, and ginger in a large nonreactive covered pot. Bring to a boil. Cover, reduce the heat, and cook at a low boil, stirring occasionally, until the apples turn to mush, 20 to 25 minutes. Remove from the heat and stir in the sugar and lemon juice. Transfer about half of the apple mixture to a food processor and process to a fine puree. Pour into a medium-large shallow casserole. Repeat for the remaining apple mixture, pouring it into the same casserole.

2. Put the casserole in the oven and bake for 30 minutes, stirring once or twice. Reduce the oven temperature to 350 degrees F and cook, stirring occasionally, until the apple butter has darkened, thickened, and reduced by nearly one-half, another 45 to 60 minutes. Remove from the oven and let cool. Transfer to jars and refrigerate. This will keep in the refrigerator for at least 1 week.

MAKES 2½ TO 3 CUPS

Green Bean and Carrot Salad
with Apple Vinaigrette

Dressing the green beans while they're hot allows the apple-sweet vinaigrette to permeate them. The carrots add a dash of color, the nuts a little bit of crunch. It's optional, but a scattering of blue cheese makes a tasty garnish.

APPLE VINAIGRETTE
2 tablespoons olive oil
1½ tablespoons apple jelly
1 tablespoon cider vinegar
2 teaspoons Dijon mustard

ASSEMBLY
1 to 1¼ pounds fresh green beans,
   ends trimmed

2 medium-size carrots, peeled and
   grated
Salt and freshly ground black pepper
   to taste
1 lemon
⅓ cup walnuts or pecans, preferably
   toasted (page 218) and chopped
A little crumbled blue cheese for
   garnish (optional)

1. Make the vinaigrette in a large bowl—the green beans will go in it too—by whisking together the dressing ingredients. Set aside.

2. Bring a medium-size pot of salted water to a boil. Add the beans and boil until tender, 5 to 10 minutes. Drain, add the beans to the vinaigrette, and toss well. Set aside to cool for 10 minutes.

3. Add the carrots, season with salt and pepper, and toss well. Grate a little lemon zest into the beans and add a teaspoon or two of lemon juice, as needed. Refrigerate for at least 30 minutes.

4. Just before serving, toss the nuts with the beans. Transfer to a serving platter and garnish with the blue cheese, if using.

MAKES 4 TO 6 SERVINGS

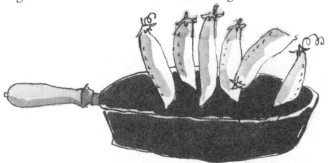

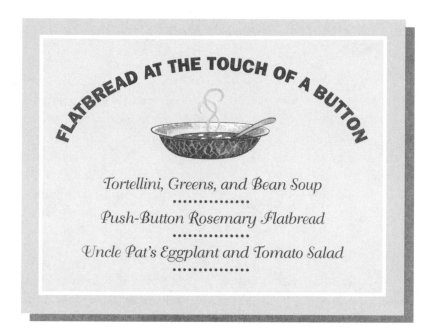

FLATBREAD AT THE TOUCH OF A BUTTON

Tortellini, Greens, and Bean Soup

•••••••••••••••

Push-Button Rosemary Flatbread

•••••••••••••••

Uncle Pat's Eggplant and Tomato Salad

•••••••••••••••

Most of the bakers I know personally are Old School Bakers, which in my case—to hear my kids tell it—isn't all that different from just plain old. Old School Bakers like to make all kinds of breads, but even if we don't make that much of it anymore, we consider ourselves yeast bread bakers first and foremost. We make it from scratch and we make it by hand. New School Bakers, on the other hand, have embraced their electric bread machines. Like other OSBs, I used to think bread machines were for sissies and cheaters, a classic case of technological art imitating real life. But I don't think that anymore because I realize that bread machines have introduced many home cooks to homemade bread, and spurred many of them to try making it by hand.

Besides, I've recently come to realize just how handy one of my other machines is for making flatbread and pizza dough: my food processor. To be sure, there are differences between a bread made by hand and one made in the food processor, but they tend to be negligible. And I find that the more I make flatbread dough in the processor—just as I found when I started making pizza dough by hand—the better I get at it.

Here, then, is a menu built around a bread that you can like because it tastes good, saves you time, and puts homemade bread even closer within reach for most of us. Play around with it, take notes, and finesse it as you see fit once you've worked a few times with the basic recipe. In the end I'll bet you like it and start using it for pizzas and other things, too.

Not to overlook the fine soup on this menu, always a hit with kids and anyone else who likes tortellini. Eat it in the good company of Uncle Pat's marinated eggplant salad and you have the makings of a great meal.

Tortellini, Greens, and Bean Soup

Tortellini is probably my favorite pasta for soup because the shape is so neat and you get a little bonus with the filling. This is a hearty soup, and because of the quantity of tortellini used, the result is almost more of a brothy pasta main dish than it is a soup with tortellini, though that's by no means a bad thing. I buy the fresh tortellini that comes in a 9-ounce package, which is plenty for 6 servings. But if you aren't feeding that many, you might want to use less since it will absorb a lot of liquid if you have tortellini sitting in the leftovers. Better to simmer some fresh tortellini in the soup when you reheat it (adding a bit more chicken stock if you don't have much broth left).

2 tablespoons olive oil or unsalted butter

1 large onion, chopped

1 rib celery, finely chopped

3 cloves garlic, minced

Salt

6 cups chicken stock

1 teaspoon dried basil

One 9-ounce package fresh tortellini (cheese or meat)

2 to 3 cups stemmed and chopped spinach or Swiss chard, to your taste

Freshly ground black pepper to taste

1 cup canned chickpeas, drained and rinsed

1 tablespoon tomato paste

Freshly grated Parmesan cheese, for garnish

1. Heat the olive oil or butter in a large saucepan or medium-size soup pot over moderately low heat. Add the onion, celery, and garlic; salt lightly. Cover tightly and sweat the vegetables for 10 minutes.

2. Add the stock and basil and about 1/4 teaspoon additional salt to the soup (depending on the saltiness of the stock). Bring to a boil. Add the tortellini and greens. Return the soup to a boil, boil for 1 minute, then reduce the heat to moderately low and simmer, partially covered, for 5 minutes. Taste the broth, adding pepper as needed and a bit more salt, if necessary.

3. After 5 minutes, stir the chickpeas and tomato paste into the soup. Simmer 5 more minutes. Serve piping hot, passing the Parmesan cheese at the table.

MAKES 6 SERVINGS

Push-Button Rosemary Flatbread

I've become quite enamored of this food-processor bread dough and spoiled by all the things you can do with it, including using it for pizza, calzone, focaccia, and other flatbreads. This rosemary flatbread is one of the easiest ways to prepare it. The finished bread is an inch or so thick with a gorgeous golden crust that softens somewhat as the bread cooks. If you like, press a handful of sliced pitted olives into the surface about 5 minutes before baking. You can also dust the surface with freshly grated Parmesan cheese as it comes out of the oven.

Do use *unbleached* all-purpose flour here, rather than bleached all-purpose; the former makes a better, more resilient food-processor dough. And don't be tempted to process the dough longer than specified, in hopes of eliminating the little bit of kneading. It won't be the same, and you may end up overheating, tearing, or otherwise damaging the dough.

. . . .

³/₄ cup warm water (105 to 115 degrees F)
1¹/₂ teaspoons active dry yeast
1 teaspoon salt
¹/₂ teaspoon sugar
2 teaspoons olive oil, plus extra for brushing on crust

1³/₄ cups plus 1 tablespoon unbleached all-purpose flour
Cornmeal or semolina, for dusting
1 teaspoon fresh chopped rosemary leaves or ¹/₂ teaspoon crushed dried

. . . .

1. Pour the water into a food processor. Sprinkle the yeast over it, then add the salt, sugar, and olive oil. Process briefly, to mix. Let rest for 1 minute.

2. Add the 1³/₄ cups flour and process for two 4-second bursts, waiting 15 seconds between each. Shake on the last tablespoon flour and process for one additional 4-second burst. Let the dough rest in the processor for 1 minute. While you're waiting, lightly oil a medium-size bowl.

3. Turn the dough out onto a lightly floured work surface; it will be a tad sticky. Knead gently with floured hands for 30 to 45 seconds. Place the dough in the oiled bowl, rotating the dough to coat the entire surface with oil. Cover the top of the bowl with plastic wrap. Set the bowl aside in a warm, draft-free spot and let rise until doubled in bulk, 1 to 1¹/₂ hours. Lightly oil a large baking sheet and dust with cornmeal or semolina.

4. When the dough has doubled, punch it down gently and knead into a ball. Place the dough in the middle of the prepared baking sheet, cover loosely with plastic wrap, and let rest for 15 minutes.

5. Smear your fingers with olive oil and press the dough into a circle about 10 inches in diameter, making little dimples all over it. Sprinkle the rosemary over the dough and drizzle with another tablespoon or so olive oil. Cover loosely with plastic wrap and let rest in a warm spot for 20 minutes. Meanwhile preheat the oven to 400 degrees F.

6. After 20 minutes, place the baking sheet in the oven and bake for 25 minutes. The bread is done when it is golden brown and has a hard, crusty crust (it will soften after you take it out of the oven). Serve right away, breaking it into large pieces rather than cutting it.

MAKES 6 SERVINGS

Uncle Pat's Eggplant and Tomato Salad

I didn't know my friend Barb's Uncle Pat, but based on the way he could make a salad, I think I would have liked him. This is one of the few recipes I've ever seen that uses raw eggplant. It gets cut into little rectangles, then is quick-pickled overnight in equal parts vinegar and water. The pieces are squeezed to express out most of the liquid, and finally are mixed with onion, fresh herbs, olive oil, and tomatoes. It's a summer standard around here and most people I've offered this to just love it. But you probably do have to be an eggplant lover to appreciate it. You'll need to start this a day ahead.

2 medium-size eggplants, peeled

2¹/₂ cups water

2¹/₂ cups red wine vinegar

1 teaspoon salt

2 ribs celery, chopped

1 small red onion, finely chopped

1 medium-size green or red bell pepper, seeded and diced

¹/₄ cup chopped pitted green or black olives

2 tablespoons chopped fresh parsley leaves

2 tablespoons chopped fresh basil leaves

¹/₄ cup olive oil

Salt and freshly ground black pepper to taste

1 to 2 cups cherry tomatoes, to your taste, halved

Fresh lemon juice to taste

Crumbled feta cheese to taste

1. Cut the eggplants into lengthwise slabs about ¹/₂ inch thick. Cut each slab lengthwise into ¹/₂-inch-wide strips, then cut the strips about 1¹/₂ inches long. Put the eggplant pieces in a large glass or pottery bowl and add the water, vinegar, and salt. Mix everything together with your hands. Cover the eggplant with a plate and weigh it down with a can or two, to submerge the pieces. Refrigerate overnight.

2. The next morning, drain the eggplant. Using your hands, squeeze out most of the liquid. Place the eggplant in a large bowl and mix with the remaining ingredients up to the salt and pepper. Cover with plastic wrap and refrigerate for 1 hour or longer.

3. Just before serving, add the tomatoes and lemon juice to the eggplant and toss well. Stir in the feta cheese or pass it separately at the table.

MAKES 6 SERVINGS

TAKING TIME FOR YEAST BREAD

Tomato-Vegetable Lentil Soup

. . . .

Oatmeal Hearth Loaves

. . . .

Pears and Apples Salad with
Toasted Walnut Dressing

. . . .

By design, there are only a handful of yeast breads in this book. Yeast breads are wonderful, but even a dedicated home baker like myself often has trouble finding a three- or four-hour block of time to schedule a yeast bread into. If this were a bread cookbook, that would be one thing. But it isn't. It's a book in which bread is a more or less equal player with the two other players on the team, soup and salad. And if my aim is to help you get dinner on the table in a reasonable amount of time, there's only so much yeast bread baking a cook can entertain.

This menu, with these old-fashioned oatmeal loaves, is one of several notable exceptions. Our aim here is not getting dinner on the table quickly; it is simply to enjoy getting it there. For yeast bread bakers, this means some beloved rituals—the dissolving of the yeast. The mixing and the kneading and even the choosing of the pottery bowl we like to let our dough rise in. Even if we haven't made yeast bread in a year or two, it all comes back again immediately. Like riding a bike, once you've done it you never forget how.

The oatmeal bread featured here makes handsome, fragrant loaves like those you'd find at a good local bakery. It's a soft loaf, so leftovers will make great sandwich bread. And need I mention that it goes splendidly with the vegetable-lentil soup? Probably not. I should point out, however, that the oats are a natural ally to the walnuts in our pear and apple salad, the toastiness of the walnuts playing off the earthy goodness of the grain.

Tomato-Vegetable Lentil Soup

Short of relying on canned beans, using dried lentils is the easiest way to make a from-scratch bean soup since they cook so much faster than other beans and don't need a preliminary soaking. When I want to make an especially good-tasting soup but I don't want to work too hard at it, I'll often turn to this one. My kids love the meatless version (with vegetable stock).

2 tablespoons olive oil

1 large onion, chopped

1 rib celery, thinly sliced

1/2 green bell pepper, seeded and diced

Salt to taste

5 cups vegetable or chicken stock

3/4 cup dried lentils, rinsed and picked over

1 medium-size carrot, peeled and diced

1 bay leaf

1 teaspoon dried basil

1/2 teaspoon dried thyme

Freshly ground black pepper to taste

1 large all-purpose potato, peeled and cut into 1/2-inch dice

1 cup canned crushed tomatoes in puree or stewed tomatoes

1. Heat the olive oil in a large saucepan or a small soup pot. Add the onion, celery, and pepper; salt lightly. Cover tightly and sweat over medium-low heat until the vegetables are soft, 8 to 10 minutes.

2. Add the stock, lentils, carrot, bay leaf, and herbs and season with pepper. Bring to a boil, cover partially, and reduce the heat to medium low. Simmer for 15 minutes. Stir in the potato and 1/2 teaspoon salt. Simmer 10 minutes more.

3. Add the tomatoes; cover and simmer, stirring occasionally, another 10 to 15 minutes; check and correct the seasonings as needed.

VARIATION: Add some sliced smoked sausage to the soup when you add the potato.

MAKES 5 TO 6 SERVINGS

Oatmeal Hearth Loaves

If for one reason or another I had to limit my yeast bread baking to a handful of varieties, this would surely be in the mix. It's tasty, attractive, smells wonderful—not that all home-made bread doesn't—and it's excellent for both toasting and sandwiches and just plain eating. How good? Well, there was a time when my children were younger when I was making this bread four loaves at a pop, a couple of times a week, and it *still* wasn't enough. (I'm not quite so ambitious these days; a fellow's gotta have a life, you know.) Unless you work at home, and can fit this in around your work schedule, I suggest saving it for a weekend afternoon. You will need a good 4 hours from the time you start until the time you can slice and serve it.

. . . .

¾ cup rolled (old-fashioned, not instant or quick-cooking) oats

1 cup hot milk

3 tablespoons sugar

1 tablespoon molasses

1¼ cups warm water (105 to 115 degrees F)

2 teaspoons (1 packet) active dry yeast

About 5 cups unbleached all-purpose flour

2½ teaspoons salt

¼ cup vegetable oil

Cornmeal, semolina, or rolled oats, for dusting

1 large egg beaten with 1 tablespoon milk, for glaze

Poppy or sesame seeds, for garnish

. . . .

1. Put the oats in a large bowl. Stir in the hot milk, sugar, and molasses; set aside until mixture cools to about body temperature.

2. Meanwhile, pour ¼ cup of the warm water into a small bowl. Sprinkle on the yeast and stir briefly, to mix. Set aside.

3. When the oat mixture has cooled, stir in the dissolved yeast and the remaining 1 cup warm water. Stir in 3 cups of the flour, 1 cup at a time. After the third cup, beat vigorously with a wooden spoon for 100 strokes. Cover the bowl with plastic wrap and set this sponge aside for 10 minutes.

4. After 10 minutes, stir the salt into the sponge, then stir in the oil. Stir in enough of the remaining flour, about ⅓ cup at a time, to make a fairly firm, kneadable dough.

5. Turn the dough out onto a floured work surface and knead with floured hands for 10 minutes, using additional flour on your work counter when necessary. It makes the dough easier to knead if you take periodic breaks: knead 2 minutes, break 2 minutes, alternating back and forth. (Sorry, but you can't count the break time as kneading time.) Put the dough in an oiled bowl and rotate to coat all surfaces. Cover the bowl with plastic wrap and place in a warm, draft-free spot until doubled in bulk, 45 to 60 minutes.

6. While the dough rises, lightly oil a large baking sheet and dust well with fine cornmeal, semolina, or oats. Set aside.

7. Once the dough has risen, punch it down and turn out onto a floured work surface. Knead briefly, then cut the dough in half. Working with one half at a time, knead the dough into a tight football and place on the prepared sheet. Repeat for the other half of dough. Lightly oil a large piece of plastic wrap and cover the loaves loosely with it. Put the loaves in a warm, draft-free spot and let rise until doubled, 30 to 40 minutes. When nearly doubled, preheat the oven to 400 degrees F.

8. When the loaves have doubled, brush them lightly with the egg glaze. Sprinkle the tops with seeds. Using a sharp, serrated knife, make 3 or 4 lengthwise diagonal slashes about 1/2 inch deep on the top of each loaf. Place the loaves in the oven. Bake on the center rack for 20 minutes, then reduce the temperature to 375 degrees F and bake until dark golden and crusty, another 20 to 25 minutes. When done, the loaves will emit a hollow sound when tapped with a finger. Cool the loaves on a wire rack; you can slice when they've cooled to about lukewarm.

MAKES 2 LOAVES

Pears and Apples Salad with Toasted Walnut Dressing

I sometimes see recipes for salads that use walnut oil in the dressing, walnut oil being expensive and not something I keep around the kitchen. But I love the flavor of walnuts and decided to play around with different ways to make a dressing with a strong walnut taste; here's one way I thought it worked quite well. The bulk of this fruit salad is just pears, apples, and toasted walnuts, some of which are blended with olive oil, vinegar, cider, and brown sugar. This is tossed with the fruit, which is then dressed with a touch of heavy cream, though the cream can be left out if you'd rather not add the calories. You'll still have a great fruit salad.

1 cup walnuts, coarsely chopped

3 tablespoons olive oil

3 tablespoons cider

1½ tablespoons cider vinegar

1 tablespoon firmly packed light brown
   sugar

3 large ripe pears

2 large crisp apples, peeled

Small handful raisins (optional)

2 to 3 tablespoons heavy cream,
   to your taste

1. Preheat the oven to 350 degrees F. Put the walnuts on a baking sheet and toast them in the oven until fragrant and lightly browned, about 10 minutes. Remove from the oven and tilt them off the sheet and onto a plate or your work counter (they'll keep toasting if you leave them on the sheet).

2. Put ⅓ cup of the still-warm nuts in a blender or mini chopper. Add the olive oil, cider, vinegar, and brown sugar and process the mixture until smooth, then set it aside.

3. Quarter and core the pears. Cut them into bite-size chunks and put them in a medium-size bowl. Do the same for the apples. Toss in the remaining ⅔ cup chopped nuts and the raisins, if you're using them.

4. Pour the dressing over the fruit and toss well to coat evenly. Add the cream and toss again to coat evenly. Serve the salad at once, or cover with plastic wrap and refrigerate until needed, up to a few hours.

MAKES 5 TO 6 SERVINGS

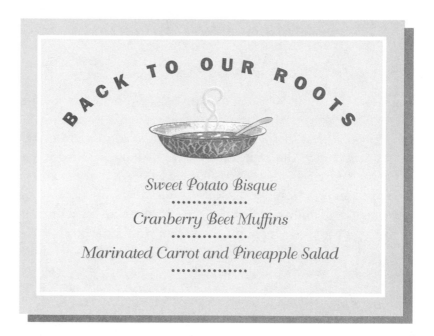

BACK TO OUR ROOTS

Sweet Potato Bisque

....

Cranberry Beet Muffins

....

Marinated Carrot and Pineapple Salad

....

Before there was broccoflower, before anyone had heard of jicama, chayote, or tomatillos, there were your basic root vegetables: sweet potatoes, beets, and carrots. Eating was simpler back then. You could pronounce your vegetables without the help of phonetic prompters in the produce aisle. You knew how to fix them just by going to your tattered copy of *The Joy of Cooking*. And everyone liked them and expected little more than the basics.

Am I nostalgic for those days? Sure I am. Do I want to go back and live in the past? Certainly not. I do, however, want to pay my respects to this colorful threesome in this menu that takes us back to our roots.

I've mentioned elsewhere that I love to incorporate fresh vegetables into my baking, which I do a lot of. Though even I, I must tell you, had reservations about working beets into a muffin, and with cranberries no less. But fiddle with the notion I did, and was delighted. I think you will be, too. I'll bet you've never seen a muffin this color before.

Most baby boomers will find something familiar about this marinated carrot salad. Many of us grew up on some version of this. I've kept the spirit of those old renditions and simply given it a few fresh touches. Some of the early versions dressed this in gobs of mayonnaise. I've replaced that with a refreshing apple cider vinegar dressing.

Lover of maple syrup that I am, I couldn't resist sneaking a little of it into this sweet potato bisque, one of the prettiest orange-as-the-harvest-moon soups you'll ever eat. I've balanced the sweetness of the soup with the smoky-salty flavor of bacon and given it a savory touch of sage. Like the rest of the menu, it's a feast for the senses, grounded in solid roots.

Sweet Potato Bisque

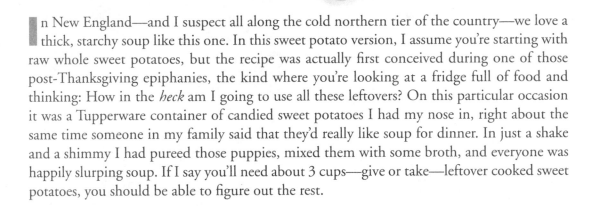

In New England—and I suspect all along the cold northern tier of the country—we love a thick, starchy soup like this one. In this sweet potato version, I assume you're starting with raw whole sweet potatoes, but the recipe was actually first conceived during one of those post-Thanksgiving epiphanies, the kind where you're looking at a fridge full of food and thinking: How in the *heck* am I going to use all these leftovers? On this particular occasion it was a Tupperware container of candied sweet potatoes I had my nose in, right about the same time someone in my family said that they'd really like soup for dinner. In just a shake and a shimmy I had pureed those puppies, mixed them with some broth, and everyone was happily slurping soup. If I say you'll need about 3 cups—give or take—leftover cooked sweet potatoes, you should be able to figure out the rest.

4 cups peeled sweet potato chunks
 (about 3 large)
5 cups chicken or vegetable stock
Salt to taste
4 slices bacon
1 large onion, finely chopped
1 tablespoon unbleached all-purpose
 flour

½ cup light cream or milk
2 tablespoons pure maple syrup
½ teaspoon crumbled dried sage or
 ¼ teaspoon powdered sage
Freshly ground black pepper to taste

1. Put the sweet potatoes and stock in a large saucepan or medium-size soup pot. Season with salt, the amount depending on the saltiness of the stock. Bring to a boil. Cover tightly, reduce the heat to moderately low, and cook at a low boil until the potatoes are tender, about 20 minutes. Remove from the heat.

2. While the potatoes are cooking, fry the bacon in a skillet until crisp. Remove the bacon to paper towels and blot dry; set aside. Add the onion to the bacon fat and cook, stirring, over moderate heat until translucent, about 8 minutes. Stir in the flour, cook for 1 minute, then remove from the heat.

3. Using a large slotted spoon, transfer the sweet potatoes to a food processor, adding a ladle full of the stock as well. Process to a smooth puree, adding a little more stock, if necessary, to facilitate the processing.

4. Scrape the sautéed onions into the stock in the saucepan; whisk well. Stir in the puree, cream or milk, maple syrup, and sage and season with pepper. Bring to a near boil, then reduce the heat to moderately low, and simmer for 10 minutes, adjusting the seasoning. Serve piping hot, crumbling some of the bacon over each serving.

VARIATION: If you want, you can ham this soup up by adding diced ham at any point. Also, if you have any leftover corn, that tastes wonderful in here as well.

MAKES 6 SERVINGS

When Serving Soup, Bowl 'em Over

As any chef will tell you, presentation counts. An attractive presentation can't improve the flavor of a soup, but it can elevate good soup to a higher level of appreciation from everyone at your table.

A soup bowl should be a personal thing. In my family, each of us has preferences. I like my soup very, very hot. Thus, my favorite soup bowl is a tall mug; the depth and limited surface area keep the soup hot longer. My kids like wider bowls so their soup cools off more quickly. On occasion we will use matching bowls for a more formal feel. But more often than not we like the eclectic mix of bowls we've adopted over the years.

Given the seasonal nature of soup, it's nice to have bowls to fit the occasion. Summer soups, especially cold ones, feel more at home in smaller, less hefty vessels, perhaps ramekins or custard cups. My younger son loves his snowman mega-mug for cold-weather soups. And my older son-on-the-go is likely to eat his soup from his coffee travel mug. Yard sales are great places to pick up pottery and find inexpensive bowls for every occasion.

Sometimes the best bowl isn't even really a bowl. Pumpkin and other fall soups can be presented in a pumpkin "tureen." Simply cut a lid from the pumpkin, remove it, and scoop out the seeds and goop. Salt the interior lightly and brush with melted butter. Then bake in a preheated 400 degree F oven for 15 minutes, long enough to heat it through but not so long that the walls soften and collapse. Ladle in the hot soup and bring to the table. Small pumpkins can be treated the same way and used for individual bowls.

Another option is to make individual bread bowls from round loaves of bread. A couple of cautionary notes: when you hollow the insides, leave very thick walls to prevent seepage. And stick with thick, creamy soups; brothy soups tend to leak through. Also, make sure the loaves are stable. If not, take off a thin slice to make a flat bottom.

Cranberry Beet Muffins

These muffins are the embodiment of the phrase "beet red." For most, that might not be a particularly endearing quality in a muffin, but try not to let the color influence you because these are really excellent. I've seen many people who had initial reservations about trying one of these, but none whose hesitation didn't evaporate after just one bite. How do you get the beets in there? Simple: you boil some up, then throw them in the food processor to make a rough puree, which in turn is processed with some of the other ingredients. I haven't, in fact, ever made these with canned, already-cooked beets, but I can't see any reason why that wouldn't work fine. This muffin has two seasons for me: in the summer, when I can get good locally grown beets (and when I sometimes add small blueberries instead of dried cranberries), and the winter, when I cook with a lot of root vegetables.

1 cup dried cranberries	$^1/_2$ teaspoon ground cinnamon
4 medium-size beets, tops discarded and scrubbed	$^3/_4$ cup sugar, plus extra to sprinkle on top
2$^1/_4$ cups unbleached all-purpose flour	1 large egg
1 tablespoon baking powder	1 cup milk
$^3/_4$ teaspoon salt	$^1/_3$ cup vegetable oil

1. Put the cranberries in a small bowl and cover with warm water to rehydrate for 30 minutes. Drain and set aside.

2. Put the beets in a saucepan with enough cold water to cover by an inch. Bring to a boil, then reduce the heat to moderately low and simmer, partially covered, until tender, for 30 to 40 minutes; drain. When cool enough to handle, rub off the skins. Cut into large chunks and set aside.

3. Preheat oven to 375 degrees F and butter 12 muffin cups.

4. Sift the flour, baking powder, salt, and cinnamon into a large bowl; set aside.

5. Put the beets in a food processor and process to a rough puree. Measure out $^3/_4$ cup (leftovers can be added to soup or salad dressing). Return the measured puree to the processor. Add the sugar and egg and process until smooth. Add the milk and oil and process again, briefly.

6. Make a well in the center of the dry ingredients. Add the liquid and stir with a

wooden spoon just until a batter forms; stir in the reserved cranberries. Divide the batter evenly between the muffin cups. Sprinkle the tops with sugar.

7. Bake the muffins for 23 to 25 minutes. When done, the tops will be springy to the touch and sugar-crusty. Let cool briefly in the pan, then transfer the muffins to a wire rack or cloth-lined basket if serving right away.

MAKES 12 MUFFINS

Marinated Carrot and Pineapple Salad

A few gratings of raw carrot on top of a salad are one thing; a lot of them all together need some tenderizing, lest they feel like a mouthful of hay. That explains the preliminary step here of marinating the grated carrots in vinegar, orange juice, and sugar. After an hour, the juice is drained off and the carrots are mixed with the rest of the ingredients. This is a colorful salad that's good throughout the cooler months. If you came of age in the 1950s and '60s, like I did, you probably ate something like this as a child; this is my updated version.

1/4 cup cider vinegar

2 tablespoons orange juice, preferably fresh

1 1/2 tablespoons sugar

1/2 teaspoon peeled and minced fresh ginger

3 cups peeled and grated carrots (about 3 medium-size carrots)

1/2 small red onion, thinly sliced

Salt

1 tablespoon vegetable or olive oil

1 cup drained pineapple chunks (fresh or canned)

1/2 cup peeled mango chunks

2 tablespoons chopped fresh cilantro or parsley leaves

1/4 cup chopped walnuts

1. Whisk the vinegar, orange juice, sugar, and ginger together in a medium-size bowl. Add the carrots and onion, salt lightly, and toss well, to mix. Cover with plastic wrap and refrigerate 1 hour, tossing with a fork every 15 minutes.

2. Drain the carrots, discarding the juice. Return to the bowl and toss with the oil. Add the pineapple, mango, and cilantro or parsley; toss to mix. Transfer to a serving dish and garnish with the walnuts just before serving.

MAKES 5 TO 6 SERVINGS

SAUSAGE SOUP AND SLIPPER BREAD

Swiss Chard and Sausage Soup

· · · · · · · · · · · · ·

Ciabatta

· · · · · · · · · · · · ·

*Cold Cauliflower, Olive, and
Sun-Dried Tomato Salad*

· · · · · · · · · · · · ·

For a former almost vegetarian, I eat an awful lot of sausage. I just can't help myself. Of course, I realize that sausage is too rich and too fatty and may even shorten my life by several weeks. That's hardly news. But I already eat plenty of things that are really good for me. And what fun is life if we can't stray from the path of virtue occasionally and mix it up with the likes of fast coffees, seductive wines, and indulgent desserts?

Sausage takes center stage in the soup on this menu, without apologies; it's the whole point of the soup, not an afterthought. You've probably seen versions of this soup made with kale. They're great, but I sometimes prefer the buttery softness of chard in my soup, as opposed to the chewiness of kale. Maybe it's my imagination, but I think chard does a better job of absorbing the wonderful flavors that the sausage releases.

Rustic soup, rustic bread—this one called *ciabatta* in Italian, or "slipper." I don't know the history of ciabatta, but its free-form manner of shaping suggests it might have been invented by a lazy or inept baker with a devil-may-care attitude toward his work. You don't so much shape the dough as you do gently stretch it out into a big slipper before you bake it. Served with the cold Italian-style cauliflower salad, it adds up to quite a feast.

Swiss Chard and Sausage Soup

I make this same soup with kale but sometimes I prefer it this way, with Swiss chard, which is less fussy to handle. Gently simmer the soup for as long as you can after you add the sausage so the flavor has time to leach into the broth.

1 pound hot Italian sausage

3 tablespoons olive oil

2 large onions, halved and thinly sliced into half moons

2 or 3 cloves garlic, to your taste, minced

1 good-size bunch green or red Swiss chard, rinsed, stems discarded, and leaves chopped

5¹/₂ cups chicken stock

1 large carrot, peeled and diced

1 tablespoon tomato paste

¹/₂ teaspoon salt, plus more to taste

Freshly ground black pepper to taste

1. Bring a large saucepan of water to a boil. Prick the sausage several times with a fork, so it can let off fat, and drop it into the boiling water. Boil the sausage for 8 minutes. Drain and set aside in a bowl to cool. Cover with plastic wrap and refrigerate if not using shortly.

2. Heat the olive oil in a large saucepan or medium-size soup pot over moderate heat. Stir in the onions and garlic and cook, stirring, until the onions are quite soft, 12 to 15 minutes.

3. Stir the chard into the pot and heat, stirring occasionally, until it wilts. Stir in the stock, carrot, tomato paste, salt, and pepper, then bring the soup to a lively simmer.

4. As the soup heats, cut the sausage into ¹/₂-inch-thick slices. Add the sausage to the soup. Cover, reduce the heat to moderately low, and simmer the soup gently for 20 to 30 minutes. Taste just before serving to see if it needs any more salt and pepper. Serve piping hot.

MAKES 5 TO 6 SERVINGS

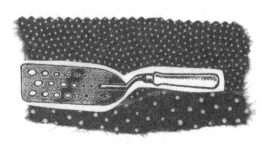

Ciabatta

A year or so ago, I think it was *Bon Appétit* magazine that voted *ciabatta* Bread of the Year. Or maybe it was Bread of the New Millennium. In any case, it amounted to much deserved praise for what has to be one of the most delicious, charming breads to catch the public eye in some time. A lot of cooks shy away from making yeast bread because shaping it is tricky; not so *ciabatta*. You simply knead the dough—you will need a heavy duty mixer, because the dough is so wet—let it rise, then stretch it out on a baking sheet and let rise again. It puffs, then bakes up looking something like the literal translation: a slipper. Only this one tastes unlike any slipper you may have eaten before, crusty, with an uncomplicated, earthy, amber-fields-of-grain flavor. Don't be shy about this one because you can't really mess it up. And don't even bother to cut it either. Just tear off chunks, in the manner of a rustic feasting among close friends. You'll need to start this a day before you plan to serve it.

STARTER
1¹/₂ cups lukewarm water
¹/₈ teaspoon active dry yeast
1¹/₂ cups unbleached all-purpose flour
¹/₂ cup whole wheat flour

**FINISHED DOUGH
AND ASSEMBLY**
³/₄ cup lukewarm milk
2 teaspoons (1 packet) active dry yeast
1 tablespoon olive oil
2 teaspoons salt
2³/₄ cups unbleached all-purpose
    flour, plus more for kneading
Cornmeal or semolina, for dusting

1. To make the starter, put the water in a medium-size bowl. Sprinkle the yeast over it and set aside for 5 minutes. Stir in the flours and beat well with a wooden spoon for 100 strokes. Cover and leave at room temperature for 12 to 24 hours.

2. Stir down the starter. Cover and refrigerate for 1 hour.

3. Pour the milk into a small bowl and sprinkle the yeast over it. Whisk to blend, then set aside for 10 minutes. Scrape the starter into the bowl of a heavy-duty mixer. Stir in the dissolved yeast, olive oil, and salt. Add the all-purpose flour and mix with the flat beater on low speed for 6 minutes. Let the dough rest in the bowl for 10 minutes. It will be very sticky.

4. Scrape the dough onto a well-floured work surface. Using a dough scraper, fold the sides of the dough up onto the dough, then knead it gently with floured hands for 2 minutes, using more flour if necessary to prevent sticking. The dough will feel very smooth, soft, and satiny. Place the dough in an oiled bowl, turning it to coat the dough with oil. Cover the bowl with plastic wrap and set it aside in a warm, draft-free spot until doubled in bulk, 1 to 2 hours.

Finding Flavors in All the Right Places

In the recipe for Cold Cauliflower, Olive, and Sun-Dried Tomato Salad (page 168) I mention that the sun-dried tomato soaking water can be saved and added to soup broth. That's a particularly good example of recycling flavor to put in soups. There are other good places to find extra flavor, too. You just have to know where to find them.

In sauté pans: When you sear a piece of meat, bits of cooked skin and flesh often stick to the pan. If you pour off the fat, add some wine to the pan, then quickly reduce the liquid, you end up with a wonderful essence that can be added to a soup in progress.

In shellfish: If you're steaming mussels or clams, they yield lots of good briny broth for fish soups and stews. Refrigerate whatever you don't slurp with your shellfish, but use it within a day.

In spuds: Mashed potato making yields many cupfuls of flavorful water, good enough to slurp on its own. Don't salt the water heavily if you plan to use it for soups.

In dried beans: You throw away the soaking water, but do save any cooking water that remains. Use within two days.

In dried mushrooms: When you soak dried mushrooms for a recipe, always save the liquid; it has more flavor than the mushrooms do. Use it in beefy onion soup and other meat and vegetable soups where the strong flavor won't overpower the broth.

---

5. Punch the dough down and turn it out onto a floured work surface. Knead the dough for 1 minute. Divide the dough in half and let the halves rest for 5 minutes on a floured surface.

6. Roll each half of the dough into a very loose log. Flour the logs and let them rest on a floured surface for 5 minutes.

7. Very lightly oil 2 large baking sheets and dust them with cornmeal or semolina.

8. Gently stretch each half of the dough into a rectangle roughly 6 inches wide and 14 inches long. As you do so, let the dough rest periodically if it is too elastic. Dust the tops of the loaves with flour, then place them on the prepared sheets. Cover loosely with lightly oiled plastic wrap and let rise in a warm, draft-free spot for 30 minutes.

9. Using your fingertips, "dimple" the dough by making deep indentations here and there on the surface. Lightly dust with flour again and cover with the plastic wrap. Set aside for 20 minutes. Preheat the oven to 425 degrees F.

10. After 20 minutes, remove the plastic wrap and bake the loaves until golden and crusty, about 25 minutes. They'll brown more evenly if you switch the positions of the loaves midway through the baking. Let cool briefly on a wire rack but serve as soon as possible.

MAKES 2 LOAVES

Cold Cauliflower, Olive, and Sun-Dried Tomato Salad

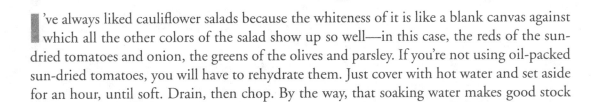

I've always liked cauliflower salads because the whiteness of it is like a blank canvas against which all the other colors of the salad show up so well—in this case, the reds of the sun-dried tomatoes and onion, the greens of the olives and parsley. If you're not using oil-packed sun-dried tomatoes, you will have to rehydrate them. Just cover with hot water and set aside for an hour, until soft. Drain, then chop. By the way, that soaking water makes good stock material (see page 167).

1 small head cauliflower, cut into bite-size florets

1 medium-size red onion, halved and thinly sliced into half moons

1 cup good-quality sliced pitted green olives

6 to 8 sun-dried tomatoes (see head-note), to your taste, chopped

1 clove garlic, minced

¼ cup olive oil

2 tablespoons red wine vinegar

2 tablespoons chopped fresh parsley leaves

Salt and freshly ground black pepper to taste

½ to 1 cup crumbled feta cheese (optional), to your taste, for garnish

1. Bring a large saucepan of salted water to a boil. Add the cauliflower, return to a boil, then cook for 2 minutes. Drain, then briefly run the cauliflower under cold running water to stop the cooking. Spread it out on a large plate to finish cooling.

2. Put the cooled cauliflower in a large bowl with the remaining ingredients, except the feta cheese. Toss well. Transfer the salad to a serving bowl and garnish with the feta cheese if you are using it. Refrigerate if not serving right away.

MAKES 5 TO 6 SERVINGS

A BOWLFUL OF BEEF AND POTATOES

Robust Beef and Potato Soup

· · · · · · · · · · · · ·

Pumpkin Pecan Bread

· · · · · · · · · · · · ·

Red Cabbage and Apple Slaw

· · · · · · · · · · · · ·

Vegetarians may blanch when they hear me say this, but we are still a meat and potatoes nation. You're reminded just how much when you go to a place like Texas, as I did recently, where you can't walk a block without running into a barbecue joint or steakhouse. The smells issuing from some of these places are downright heady, especially when they have the smokers right out back and the smell is wafting through the parking lot and down the street. Makes a fellow's mouth water.

In the spirit of this American tradition, our menu features its own mouth-watering meat dish, an aromatic soup with a rich broth, lots of potatoes, and tasty little bits of this and that. I don't, frankly, make too many beefy soups but, when I do, I want something that really says beef and doesn't merely allude to it. This one obliges. And it's easily expandable: if you're expecting more people for dinner, just buy a little extra beef and toss in another potato. Pretty soon you'll have a stew.

A rich, dark soup goes best with a side of something bright, crisp, and light; this red cabbage slaw is just the thing. I learned a little trick I think elevates red slaw immensely: giving it a preliminary dressing with hot cider, vinegar, and sugar. The liquid absorbs and reduces the insistent chewiness that often plagues raw red cabbage. Served with a sweet pumpkin pecan bread, you have the makings of a true American feast.

Robust Beef and Potato Soup

This one is for the meat and potato lovers of the world. It has all the flavor and aroma of your favorite beef stew and, like stew, it tastes better on the second day. To make this even more stew-like, you might include some green beans or frozen lima beans.

1¼ pounds beef stew meat, trimmed of fat

1½ tablespoons vegetable oil

1 large onion, chopped

1 rib celery, chopped

8 ounces mushrooms, thinly sliced

1 carrot, peeled and diced

1 clove garlic, minced

6 cups beef stock

¾ cup canned crushed tomatoes in puree

⅓ cup dry red wine

¾ teaspoon salt, plus more to taste

Freshly ground black pepper to taste

½ teaspoon dried thyme

1 to 1½ teaspoons Worcestershire sauce, to your taste

2 large all-purpose potatoes, peeled and cut into large dice

1. Cut the stew meat into bite-size chunks. Heat the oil in a large soup pot over moderately high heat. Add the meat and brown it on all sides; it doesn't have to cook through.

2. Transfer the meat to a bowl, then stir the onion and celery into the pot, adding a little more oil to the pot if needed. Cook, stirring, over moderate heat for 5 minutes, then stir in the mushrooms, carrot, and garlic and cook, stirring, for 3 more minutes. Add the remaining ingredients, except for the potatoes, and add the beef.

3. Bring the soup to a simmer, partially cover, and simmer, stirring occasionally, for 20 minutes. Taste the soup, adding more salt and pepper if necessary. Add the potatoes and return the soup to a simmer. Cover the soup partially and simmer until potatoes are tender, an additional 20 minutes. Serve piping hot.

MAKES 8 SERVINGS

Pumpkin Pecan Bread

Not only is this a wonderful dinner bread—sweet though it be—it's pumpkin-pretty enough to give as a little holiday gift to a party hostess, even more so if you include a jar of the Cranberry Orange Preserves (recipe follows). This slices best if made 8 to 12 hours ahead, so try to take that into consideration.

2 cups unbleached all-purpose flour	¾ cup sugar, plus some to sprinkle on top
1 teaspoon baking soda	2 large eggs, at room temperature
1 teaspoon baking powder	1 teaspoon pure vanilla extract
1 teaspoon salt	Finely grated zest of 1 lemon
½ teaspoon ground cinnamon	1 cup canned pumpkin puree
½ teaspoon ground cloves	½ cup sour cream
½ teaspoon ground ginger	½ cup milk
½ cup (1 stick) unsalted butter, softened	1½ cups chopped pecans, preferably toasted (page 218)

1. Preheat the oven to 325 degrees F. Grease a 5 x 9-inch loaf pan; set aside.

2. Sift the flour, baking soda, baking powder, salt, and spices together into a medium-size bowl; set aside.

3. Using an electric mixer, in a large bowl cream the butter on high speed, gradually adding the sugar. Beat in the eggs, one at a time, beating well after each addition. Blend in the vanilla, lemon zest, and pumpkin.

4. Whisk the sour cream and milk together in a small bowl. Blend half of it into the creamed mixture. Blend half of the dry mixture into the creamed mixture, then the last half of the liquid, then the rest of the dry, blending just until smooth after each addition. Fold in the pecans.

5. Scrape the batter into the prepared pan and smooth the top with a spoon. Sprinkle the top generously with sugar.

6. Bake the bread on the center rack of the oven until a tester inserted deep into the center comes out clean, about 70 minutes. Let cool in the pan, on a wire rack, for 10 to 15 minutes. Run a knife around the edges, then turn the bread out onto the rack. Let cool before slicing. Wrap the bread as soon as it has cooled.

MAKES 10 TO 12 SERVINGS

Cranberry Orange Preserves

Though this tastes great with many breads, it makes an especially good match with the Pumpkin Pecan Bread. Refrigerate overnight before using so the flavors can mingle, mellow, and get acquainted with one another.

1 thin-skinned orange	²/₃ cup sugar
1³/₄ cups fresh cranberries (may be frozen), picked over for stems	1 cup water
	1 tablespoon fresh lemon juice

1. Halve and seed the orange (if it has seeds). Cut each half into 4 sections and place in a food processor. Add 1 cup of the cranberries and the sugar. Process to a coarse puree, until the orange peels are reduced to very small dice.

2. Transfer the fruit to a medium-size, nonreactive saucepan and add the water and remaining ³/₄ cup cranberries. Bring to a boil, stirring occasionally. Reduce the heat to moderately low and cook at a low boil, stirring occasionally, for 5 minutes. Remove from the heat, transfer to a small bowl, and let cool to room temperature (don't refrigerate at this point or it may not set properly).

3. Stir the lemon juice into the cooled fruit. Cover with plastic wrap and refrigerate, or transfer to a small jar and screw on the lid. This will keep at least a week in the refrigerator.

MAKES 2 CUPS

Red Cabbage and Apple Slaw

I like red cabbage, but have always thought that more than just a token amount was too intrusive in coleslaw because of its chewy texture. Then I learned to tone it down with the sort of treatment I give here, pre-dressing it with cider, vinegar, and sugar. This dressing is drained off, but the flavor remains and is bolstered by a second, lighter dressing. Use good crisp and flavorful apples here; a mealy apple can really ruin this great dish.

4 to 5 cups cored and very thinly sliced red cabbage	2 tablespoons granulated sugar
1 cup cored and very thinly sliced green cabbage	Salt to taste
	1 tablespoon olive oil
1 medium-size carrot, peeled and grated	1 tablespoon firmly packed light brown sugar
$^1/_2$ cup raisins	$1^1/_2$ cups peeled, cored, and diced apples
$^1/_2$ cup cider	
$^1/_4$ cup plus 1 tablespoon cider vinegar	

1. Mix the cabbages, carrot, and raisins together in a large bowl.

2. Heat the cider, $^1/_4$ cup of the vinegar, and the sugar in a small nonreactive saucepan until the sugar dissolves. Pour the liquid over the cabbage and toss well to coat evenly. Lightly salt the mixture and set aside for 20 minutes, tossing often.

3. After 20 minutes, drain the cabbage thoroughly. Transfer the cabbage back to the bowl and mix in the olive oil, brown sugar, remaining 1 tablespoon vinegar, and the apples. Cover with plastic wrap and refrigerate if not serving shortly. It will keep overnight, but drain it before serving.

MAKES 6 SERVINGS

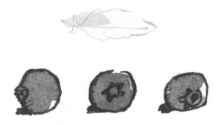

A THANKSGIVING ENCORE

Mexican Turkey Soup (Caldo de Guajolote)

....

Steamed Pumpkin Date-Nut Bread

....

Mixed Green Salad with
Pears, Pecans, and Cranberry Vinaigrette

....

So you've eaten nearly all the turkey, overdosed on football, and now you're getting antsy and you're looking for something constructive to do. Well, you could always make supper and glean some inspiration here.

What I've done is take some of those leftovers that are just hogging valuable room in the fridge and found a few ways to put them to good use. I know you have leftover turkey and corn. They go in the soup. It's a Mexican soup; you've had enough rich American food this weekend.

Those cans of pumpkin that will probably sit in the pantry till next Thanksgiving? You can put some of that in the bread, a *steamed* bread, something you might find rather fun to make. And the cranberry sauce goes in the salad dressing. Of course, you could always serve this meal for Thanksgiving instead of the usual one. And that would certainly be a break from tradition, but not nearly as much as one as I heard about recently: tofu turkey.

Mexican Turkey Soup
(Caldo de Guajolote)

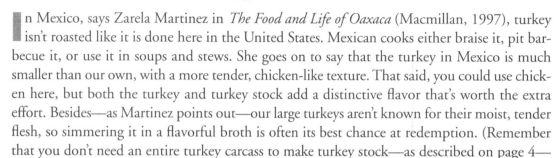

In Mexico, says Zarela Martinez in *The Food and Life of Oaxaca* (Macmillan, 1997), turkey isn't roasted like it is done here in the United States. Mexican cooks either braise it, pit barbecue it, or use it in soups and stews. She goes on to say that the turkey in Mexico is much smaller than our own, with a more tender, chicken-like texture. That said, you could use chicken here, but both the turkey and turkey stock add a distinctive flavor that's worth the extra effort. Besides—as Martinez points out—our large turkeys aren't known for their moist, tender flesh, so simmering it in a flavorful broth is often its best chance at redemption. (Remember that you don't need an entire turkey carcass to make turkey stock—as described on page 4— you can simply throw some turkey parts in a pot of water with some aromatic vegetables, and an hour later you have great stock.) The seasonings in this soup will be familiar to you, with that sort of throat-clearing, south-of-the-border *zing!* you need at the first sign of a cold.

2 tablespoons vegetable oil	1 teaspoon chili powder
1 large onion, chopped	1/2 teaspoon sweet paprika
1 rib celery, thinly sliced	5 cups turkey stock
1 small red bell pepper, seeded and cut into small dice	2 cups chopped cooked turkey meat
	1 cup corn kernels, fresh or frozen
1 medium-size carrot, peeled and cut into small dice	2 teaspoons tomato paste
	Freshly ground black pepper to taste
Salt to taste	2 tablespoons chopped fresh cilantro or parsley leaves
2 cloves garlic, minced	
1 teaspoon ground cumin	

1. Heat the oil in a large saucepan or medium-size soup pot over moderate heat. Add the onion and cook, stirring, for 5 minutes. Add the celery, bell pepper, and carrot, salt lightly, cover, reduce the heat slightly, and sweat the vegetables for 5 minutes. Stir in the garlic and spices and cook, stirring, for 1 minute.

2. Add the stock, turkey meat, corn, and tomato paste and season with salt and pepper. Bring to a near boil, cover, and reduce the heat to moderately low. Gently simmer for 15 minutes, then turn off the heat and let the soup sit for at least 15 minutes. Reheat and serve, stirring in the fresh herbs just before serving.

MAKES 6 SERVINGS

Steamed Pumpkin Date-Nut Bread

I love to make steamed breads, a habit I fell into years ago when I started heating my house with wood. The first kind I made, and the only one most people know about, is Boston brown bread, which I ate tons of as a kid. But there's another steamed bread far fewer people have ever heard of—this one—mainly because I only made the recipe up a few months ago. You don't need a woodstove to make steamed bread. All you need is a retired coffee can, a stove, and a pot large enough to hold the can sitting on a trivet or small rack of some sort. In the old days I used to secure the foil lid with twine to hold it fast. But more often than not that just made things worse because pressure would build in the can and the lid would eventually blow off. You'd take the lid off the pot to investigate the cause of all this commotion and what you'd see was something like a bizarre bid by someone to make Dumpling Can Soup. Anyway, the reason you steam a bread is because it makes for an uncommonly moist loaf you can't duplicate in the dry air of an oven. Probably the most important thing you need to know about making this is not to attempt it on Thanksgiving day, like I always used to, when burner space is already hard to find. Wait until there's no competition on top of the stove, and then make it.

1/2 cup unbleached all-purpose flour	1/4 cup chopped walnuts
1/2 cup whole wheat flour	2/3 cup buttermilk
1/2 cup fine-ground yellow cornmeal	1/2 cup canned pumpkin puree
1 teaspoon baking soda	1/2 cup honey
1/2 teaspoon salt	1 large egg yolk
1/4 cup chopped dates	

1. Butter a clean 13- or 14-ounce coffee can, including the inside of the lid. Put a trivet inside a large, deep pot. Add enough water to cover the trivet by about 2 inches, then put the pot on the stove and bring the water to a boil.

2. Mix the dry ingredients together in a large bowl; mix in the dates and walnuts. Whisk the buttermilk, pumpkin, honey, and egg yolk together in a medium-size bowl. Make a well in the center of the dry ingredients, add the liquid, and stir with a wooden spoon just until evenly blended. Scrape the batter into the buttered can and put on the lid. Poke 2 steam vents in the lid with the tip of a paring knife, then cover the top of the can securely with aluminum foil. Put the can on the trivet. Cover the pot with the lid or a foil tent.

3. Reduce the heat to moderately low and simmer for about 1 1/2 hours. Check the water level midway through and replenish with boiling water if it gets low. To check for doneness, insert a tester down into the center of the bread; it should come out clean. Transfer the can to a wire rack and let cool for 10 minutes, then invert the can and let the bread slide out. Let cool thoroughly—on end—on a rack. Store overnight in a plastic bag before slicing.

MAKES 1 LOAF

Mixed Green Salad with
Pears, Pecans, and Cranberry Vinaigrette

Use any combination of greens here—romaine hearts, Boston lettuce, baby spinach, or mesclun mix. A few bitter greens would be fine, too, because the sweetness of the cranberry vinaigrette will soften their bite.

CRANBERRY VINAIGRETTE
2/3 cup canned whole-berry cranberry
   sauce
2 tablespoons cider vinegar
2 tablespoons fresh orange juice
1 tablespoons pure maple syrup
3 tablespoons olive oil
Pinch of salt

SALAD AND ASSEMBLY
Enough greens to make 6 servings
1 ripe pear, peeled, cored, and thinly
   sliced
1/2 small red onion, very thinly sliced
1/2 cup pecans halves, toasted (page
   218) and coarsely chopped
1/2 cup crumbled blue cheese
Freshly ground black pepper to taste

1. To prepare the vinaigrette, put half of the cranberry sauce in a blender with the vinegar and process until smooth. Scrape into a salad bowl and whisk in the rest of the cranberry sauce and the remaining dressing ingredients. Set aside.

2. Rinse the salad greens and pat dry between paper towels. When ready to serve, put the greens in the bowl with dressing. Add the sliced pear and onion. Toss well to coat evenly with the dressing. Sprinkle the pecans and cheese over the salad. Grind fresh pepper over the top and serve.

MAKES 6 SERVINGS

A Guide to Greens

If your salads are sometimes met with a chorus of yawns rather than a round of cheers, you might need to spice things up with a little variety. Here's a brief rundown on some of your options.

ARUGULA: Also known as rocket, and rightly so since it adds a peppery-mustardy boost to any salad. Some describe the flavor as smoky.

BOSTON AND BIBB LETTUCE: Mild tasting, with a soft, buttery texture. Wash the leaves well as they tend to hide grit and dirt in their folds.

CABBAGE: A little green or red cabbage adds crunch to mixed green salads. Slice very thinly, as thick slices are intrusive and off-putting.

ENDIVE AND ESCAROLE: Both are a type of chicory. Curly endive—sometimes called frisée when young—has thin, wispy leaves that tickle the mouth. Escarole has broad, smooth, sharply cut leaves. The flavor is strong enough that it should be used somewhat sparingly in salads. Belgian endive is expensive but its crunchy, spear-like leaves look and taste good in salads.

ICEBERG LETTUCE: Much maligned, but faithfully crisp and it stores well. I use it for chef's salads and when I'm feeling too lazy to wash a head of leaf lettuce.

LEAF LETTUCES: Red or green, it is the workhorse of many a salad bowl. The flavor is mild, the quality generally good, the price right compared to many fancier greens available today.

MESCLUN: The word means mixture in Latin. Traditionally, it is a combination of wild young field greens, including edible flowers and herbs. What you'll generally find in the market is somewhat more ordinary: a basic blend of leaf lettuces, romaine, radicchio, endive, baby spinach, and perhaps a few others. Try to find a mix of young, whole leaves as opposed to larger, cut leaves, which would indicate it is made from larger, less tender plants.

RADICCHIO: Prized by the ancient Romans, radicchio is a member of the chicory family. It looks like a small head of red cabbage and has a flavor that runs from mildly bittersweet to quite bitter. The leaves can be torn into small pieces or cut into thin strips.

ROMAINE LETTUCE: Reliably crunchy, the inner leaves are the real prize. The outer leaves are often too tough or tasteless for salads, but they can be sliced and added to vegetable soups.

SPINACH: Now that baby spinach greens are widely available, I tend to buy them instead of leaf spinach, which is less tender and a pain to wash.

WINTER HEARTY AND WHOLESOME

When Only Serious Soup Will Do

MINESTRONE FOR MANY

White Bean and Kale Minestrone
....
Savory Pull-Apart Party Bread
....
Roasted Pepper, Potato, and Greens Salad
....

A soup menu is a great way to feed a crowd. Soup is humble and it often has an osmotic humbling influence over a table full of hungry souls. I've seen it happen time and time again. When soup is served, people's pretensions just get up and walk away. They relax. Nobody talks about what stocks they bought today when you serve them soup. They tell you how their kids are doing, and ask about yours. Then they pet the dog and offer to help with the dishes. By all means, let them.

Every so often we need a soup menu to feed a crowd. Here's one I think you'll like, and, more to the point, it's a soup menu for a *hungry* crowd. This is not a summer menu for dainty appetites. It's a menu you might serve after a day of yard work and getting the place ready for winter. Or a menu for the cobbled-together crew of neighbors and friends helping you put the new addition on the house. Or a crowd of teenagers who haven't eaten in 20 minutes (I have four of them, so trust me on this).

The main event is a minestrone with everything in it but the kitchen sink, a real carnival of beans, vegetables, and herbs. It's got lots of kale, my favorite green vegetable, and, if your crowd doesn't go for meat, you can easily make this into a vegetarian soup using vegetable stock instead of chicken stock.

You can't have a carnival soup without a party bread to go with it, and this savory pull-apart bread is just right. Instead of shaping the dough into a loaf, you arrange balls of it in a shallow dish. It bakes up into a pretty panful of little convex segments, like a cobblestone street. Everyone gets to pull off their own piece of bread and it won't be long before said bread starts to play bobbing for minestrone.

You could, of course, just serve a big mixed green salad, but then you'd miss the pleasure of watching your guests enjoy this hearty salad of roasted peppers, potatoes, and crisp greens. Roasted peppers are an indulgence of mine; I keep a jarful of them around as often as I can and now that I use the simple roasting technique I describe in the recipe headnote, I have them around more often than not.

White Bean and Kale Minestrone

If there is such a thing as the Kale Promotion Board, I should be its spokesperson, so often do I sing its praises. It is, without question, my favorite green vegetable, an affinity all of my kids seem to have inherited; we can sit there and eat great bowls of the stuff, steamed and sautéed with onions, garlic, and vinegar. Here it is in a favorite minestrone, along with many of the usual suspects. Substitute canned beans for the dried at your peril; as I've said before, the flavor of that bean cooking water is irreplaceable. This is a very colorful, convivial soup, nearly substantial enough to be considered a stew.

³/₄ cup dried small white beans, picked over and rinsed

3 tablespoons olive oil

1 large onion, coarsely chopped

1 small green bell pepper, seeded and coarsely chopped

2 cloves garlic, minced

3 quarts water

1 large all-purpose potato, peeled and finely diced

1 cup seeded and finely diced winter squash

2 ribs celery, chopped

1 bay leaf

¹/₂ pound kale

1 cup coarsely chopped canned tomatoes, with their juices

2 tablespoons tomato paste

1 teaspoon dried basil

¹/₂ teaspoon dried rosemary

1¹/₂ teaspoons salt

1¹/₂ teaspoons freshly ground black pepper

¹/₂ cup packed fresh parsley leaves, chopped

1. Put the beans in a large saucepan and cover with plenty of water. Bring to a boil, continue to boil for 2 minutes, then remove from the heat. Cover and set aside to soak for 1 hour.

2. Heat the olive oil in a large soup pot over moderate heat. Add the onion and bell pepper and cook, stirring, until the onion is translucent, about 8 minutes. Stir in the garlic, cook 1 minute, then add the water, potato, squash, celery, and bay leaf. Drain, then add the beans. Bring the soup to a boil, then reduce the heat to moderately low and cook at a very gentle boil until the beans are tender, about 1 hour.

3. Strip the kale leaves from their stems, ripping the leaves into bite-size pieces; discard the stems. Rinse the leaves by dunking them in a bowl of cool water. Add the kale, tomatoes, tomato paste, and herbs to the soup. Add the salt and pepper. Simmer for 15 minutes, then correct the seasonings. Stir in the parsley just before serving.

MAKES 6 TO 8 SERVINGS

Savory Pull-Apart Party Bread

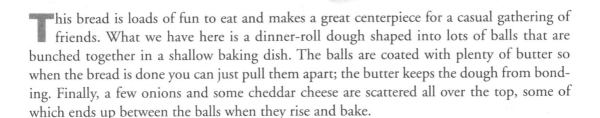

This bread is loads of fun to eat and makes a great centerpiece for a casual gathering of friends. What we have here is a dinner-roll dough shaped into lots of balls that are bunched together in a shallow baking dish. The balls are coated with plenty of butter so when the bread is done you can just pull them apart; the butter keeps the dough from bonding. Finally, a few onions and some cheddar cheese are scattered all over the top, some of which ends up between the balls when they rise and bake.

1 recipe Wheaten Parker House Rolls
   dough (page 39)
¼ cup (½ stick) unsalted butter

1 medium-size onion, finely chopped
1 cup grated sharp cheddar cheese

1. Prepare the dough and let it rise, as directed. While the dough rises, butter a large, shallow baking dish. A 2½-quart rectangular or oval gratin will do nicely.

2. When the dough is nearing the end of its rise, melt the butter in a medium-size skillet over very low heat. Add the onion and cook, stirring, for 5 minutes. Remove from the heat and let cool.

3. When the dough has doubled, punch it down and turn it out onto a floured work surface. Knead the dough for 1 minute.

4. Divide the dough into 16 to 20 pieces of roughly equal size. Shape each piece into a ball. As you do so, roll the dough around in the melted butter in the pan. Transfer the balls to the prepared baking dish, arranging them somewhat randomly though evenly spaced. When all of the dough is in the pan, spoon the remaining butter and the onion over and between the balls. Strew the cheese over the top.

5. Cover the dough with tented aluminum foil and set aside in a warm, draft-free spot until doubled in bulk, 30 to 45 minutes. As the dough approaches that point, preheat the oven to 400 degrees F.

6. When the dough has doubled and the balls are nicely swollen, remove the foil and put the rolls on the center rack of the oven. Reduce the oven temperature to 375 degrees F and bake until golden brown, about 45 minutes.

7. Transfer the pan to a wire rack and let cool off for at least 10 minutes before serving directly from the pan.

MAKES 10 OR MORE SERVINGS

Roasted Pepper, Potato, and Greens Salad

I used to roast my peppers on the stovetop over an open flame, or on the grill. And for many years it was a lot of fun, and primal, and a neat way to get in touch with my inner caveman and all that. When I finally got to the point where I just wanted to get the blessed things roasted, I started doing it under the broiler in my oven, which I discovered is much simpler because you just tuck them under there and check back every few minutes, instead of every few seconds. That said, since it's now so little trouble to roast peppers, I do it much more often. I especially like them in this big party salad, with lots of tomatoes, potatoes, and greens. I dress everything simply, with a tomato vinaigrette, the tomato in this case being tomato paste and chopped fresh tomato. For a deeper tomato flavor, you could also put thick-sliced tomatoes on the baking sheet when you roast the peppers, then chop this roasted tomato and add it to the vinaigrette. I've done that before and it's quite good.

SALAD

3 large green bell peppers

1½ pounds small red-skinned potatoes

Salt to taste

4 medium-size ripe tomatoes, cored and cut into eighths

2 to 3 tablespoons chopped fresh parsley leaves, to your taste

2 tablespoons chopped fresh basil leaves

Freshly ground black pepper to taste

1 small head romaine lettuce, heart only, rinsed, dried, and torn into pieces

TOMATO VINAIGRETTE

¼ cup olive oil

1½ tablespoons red wine vinegar

2 teaspoons balsamic vinegar

1 medium-size ripe tomato, cored, seeded, and finely chopped

1 teaspoon tomato paste

1 teaspoon Dijon mustard

1 clove garlic, minced

¼ to ½ teaspoon sugar, to your taste

Salt and freshly ground black pepper to taste

1. Preheat your oven's broiler and place the peppers on a jelly-roll pan. Or put them on a sheet of aluminum foil if the broiler is too small to hold a pan. Slide the peppers under the broiler and roast them for as long as it takes to get all the sides charred and blistered, turning them as needed.

2. Transfer the peppers to a medium-size bowl, cover with plastic wrap, and let steam for 10 minutes. After 10 minutes, peel or scrape off the skins and cut out the stems, seeds, and ribs. Cut the peppers into strips about ¼ inch wide and transfer to a small bowl. Cover with plastic wrap and refrigerate.

3. Put the potatoes in a medium-size saucepan and add enough lightly salted water to cover. Bring to a boil, then boil until the potatoes are just tender, 15 to 20 minutes. Pierce with a knife or cake tester to check them. Drain, let cool briefly, then peel off the skins and cut them into large pieces.

4. When the potatoes have cooled slightly, mix them with the peppers, tomatoes, herbs, and black pepper in a large serving bowl. Put the greens on top.

5. Make the vinaigrette by blending the dressing ingredients together in a small bowl. Pour the dressing over the salad and toss well, seasoning with salt and pepper.

MAKES 6 SERVINGS

GETTING CHEESY WITH CHOWDER

Cheesy Potato and Cauliflower Chowder

....

Swedish Limpa Soda Bread

....

Radish, Celery, and Apple Salad

....

I don't mean to sound too proud or highfalutin about it, but this menu is a study in balance and the carefully considered juxtaposition of contrasting courses. In other words, it all works together quite nicely and—while I'm generally the first to encourage personal departures and menu flights of fancy—I'd hate to see you make substitutions here that might yield a less satisfying meal.

We start with a robust Jarlsberg cheese chowder that may remind you of your favorite fondue. Indeed, this meal often takes on a fondue-like party atmosphere because all gathered tend to start dunking slices of this dark, grainy soda bread into their bowls with rather careless abandon. (Bear in mind that I live in the sticks of New Hampshire and, especially in the depths of winter, we look for a party atmosphere wherever we can find it.) If you're familiar with traditional Swedish limpa, you're going to make fast friends with this quick bread version, of that I'm quite certain. It has much of the flavor and whole grain charm of the yeasted version, but you can have it on the table in less than half the time.

So, creamy white, rich chowder, dark grainy bread—what this menu clearly cries out for is a salad that's light and slightly sweet-sharp to provide some snap and sparkle. Thus, the radish, celery, and apple salad. You don't even have to mix a dressing for this one; just throw everything into a bowl and toss well. Grate a little lemon peel right over the whole salad, if you like; the summery aroma can go a long way in the dead of winter.

Cheesy Potato and Cauliflower Chowder

I love rich, cheesy soups. They're something you seldom find in restaurants, among other reasons, because a good one gets its body from lots of good cheese, instead of lots of flour, and good cheese is a lot more expensive than flour. Here's one I make with Jarlsberg cheese—a lot of it—which accounts for the intensely nutty-buttery flavor of the soup (the 5 tablespoons of butter helps, too). I've seen soups like this made with a beer base, but I prefer the flavor and smoothness that comes with the combination of chicken stock and half-and-half. If there's a soup that's better suited to a cold winter night, I'm not aware of it.

5 tablespoons unsalted butter

1 large onion, chopped

4 cups chicken stock

2 cups peeled and diced all-purpose potatoes

2 1/2 cups small cauliflower florets

Salt and freshly ground black pepper to taste

2 tablespoons unbleached all-purpose flour

2 cups half-and-half or whole milk

3/4 pound Jarlsberg cheese, grated

2 teaspoons chopped fresh thyme or parsley leaves, for garnish

1. Melt 2 tablespoons of the butter in a large, heavy, enameled soup pot over moderate heat. Add the onion and cook, stirring, until light golden, about 12 minutes. Add the stock, potatoes, and half of the cauliflower. Bring to a boil, reduce the heat to medium low, and cover.

2. Simmer gently until the vegetables are very tender, 10 to 12 minutes. Taste after several minutes, seasoning with salt and pepper. Using a large slotted spoon, remove the solids from the soup. Put them through a ricer or food mill and add them back to the soup along with the remaining raw cauliflower. Hold at a bare simmer for 7 to 8 minutes.

3. While the stock simmers, melt the remaining 3 tablespoons butter in a medium-size saucepan over moderate heat. Stir in the flour and cook, stirring, for 2 minutes; do not allow it to brown. Add the half-and-half or milk. Whisk, stirring, gradually bringing it to a boil. Reduce the heat to medium low and simmer gently for 1 minute. Remove from the heat and whisk in the cheese, a handful at a time, until melted.

4. Scrape the cheese mixture into the broth and stir well until heated through; do not boil. Serve hot, with some of the fresh thyme or parsley sprinkled over each portion.

MAKES 6 SERVINGS

Swedish Limpa Soda Bread

If you like to make yeast bread, there's a good chance you've made Swedish limpa, recipes for which you'll find in most comprehensive bread books. Indeed, it was one of the first yeast breads I ever made, from James Beard's classic *Beard on Bread*. Over the years, as my yeast bread output decreased, I found myself missing limpa's unique flavor combination of beer, anise seeds, orange zest, and whole grains. So I got smart and adapted it to a quick soda bread. I still make the yeast version from time to time, but now I can enjoy this new version on a much more regular schedule. Also, it freezes well, up to a month. Just thaw and rewarm in the oven wrapped in aluminum foil.

Cornmeal or semolina, for dusting
3 cups unbleached all-purpose flour
1/2 cup whole wheat flour
1/2 cup rye flour
1 1/2 teaspoons baking powder
1 teaspoon baking soda
1 1/4 teaspoons salt
1 teaspoon anise seeds
2 tablespoons cold unsalted butter,
  cut into 1/4-inch pieces

3/4 cup buttermilk
3/4 cup dark beer or stout
1/4 cup honey
2 tablespoons molasses
1 tablespoon vegetable oil
Finely grated zest of 1 orange
Milk, for brushing on loaves

1. Preheat the oven to 375 degrees F. Lightly grease a large baking sheet and dust with cornmeal or semolina; set aside.

2. Sift the flours, baking powder, baking soda, and salt together into a large bowl. Mix in the anise seeds. Add the butter and cut it into the dry ingredients with a pastry blender or your fingertips until it is broken into fine bits.

3. Whisk the remaining ingredients—except the milk for brushing—together in a medium-size bowl to blend. Make a well in the dry ingredients, add the liquid, and stir briskly with a wooden spoon until the dough pulls together in a shaggy mass. Set aside for 3 minutes.

4. Lightly flour your hands and a work surface. Cut the dough in half, right in the bowl, and transfer half to your work area. Knead gently for 45 seconds, shaping into a stubby football. Place the loaf on the prepared sheet; repeat with the other half of the dough, leaving a fair amount of space between the loaves. Using a serrated knife, make a long, lengthwise slash 3/4 inch deep down the center of each loaf. Lightly brush the loaves with milk.

5. Bake for 30 minutes, then turn the sheet 180 degrees. Reduce the oven temperature to 350 degrees F and bake another 15 minutes. When done, the loaves will be golden and crusty and the bottoms will sound hollow when tapped. Cool the loaves on a wire rack. Do not slice until nearly completely cool.

MAKES 2 MEDIUM-SIZE LOAVES

Radish, Celery, and Apple Salad

Giving the vegetables a quick ice water bath accentuates their crispness, but you can skip this step if you like. Use a good crisp-tart apple, like a Granny Smith.

....

1 bunch (8 to 10) good-size radishes,
   tops discarded and scrubbed
3 ribs celery, cut crosswise into thin
   slices
1/2 red or green bell pepper, seeded and
   diced

1 1/2 teaspoons sugar
1 large apple, peeled, cored, and diced
1 tablespoon olive oil
1 tablespoon cider vinegar
Salt and freshly ground black pepper
   to taste

....

1. Cut the radishes into matchsticks or slices 1/8 inch thick. Place in a medium-size bowl with the celery and bell pepper. Add some ice cubes and just enough cold water to cover. Set aside for 15 minutes.

2. Drain the vegetables and pat dry between paper towels. Transfer to a serving bowl; add the sugar and apple and toss well. Add the olive oil and vinegar and season with salt and pepper. Serve right away, or cover with plastic wrap and refrigerate until serving.

MAKES 6 SERVINGS

A FEAST WITH FRENCH ACCENTS

French Onion Soup

· · · · · · · · · · · · · ·

Prune and Port Bread

· · · · · · · · · · · · · ·

Streamlined Salade Niçoise

· · · · · · · · · · · · · ·

It's probably professional suicide to admit this, but I have never been to France. Well, that's not entirely true, because I was there once back in the early 1970s when I was in the Navy. At the time, I was making a beeline for the Oktoberfest in Munich, by train, and few things gastronomic, at my tender age, could hold a candle to the thought of winsome young German lovelies hoisting steins of beer my way.

I didn't stop in Paris then and I haven't been back since. But that hasn't kept me from developing a fondness for good French cooking, which I've learned about through cookbooks, articles, stories about chefs—all the different ways we cooks educate ourselves.

This menu includes a couple of French dishes most of us have heard of: onion soup and salade niçoise. I'm not sure about the prune bread. It doesn't feel as French as I would like it to; it would probably help if I provided a French translation. But I have an intuitive sense that the French are big on their prunes, maybe even more so than we are. I know they eat it with pork and I've seen other French recipes for prune cakes, breads, tarts, and the like, so I don't think I'm too far off track. But French or not, any way you slice it, it's a very good bread.

French Onion Soup

Indulge me here for just a moment. I think I've said this elsewhere, but I'm an inveterate recipe comparer. I've never taken an official poll, but whatever traits those of us in the cookbook and food writing business share, an eagerness to compare and contrast recipes has to be foremost. It has been, in large part, the basis of my own self-education as a cook. Take a recipe like this, for instance. You'll find recipes for French onion soup in all of the general purpose cookbooks, and the more specialized ones, too. And they will be similar up to a point. That's where the interesting part begins. Why does one cook use beef stock, and another use chicken? Why does this recipe, which yields the same as that one, call for a pound fewer onions? Here's one with dry sherry, another with red wine, still another with brandy. How does each ingredient affect the flavor? What makes a given recipe authentic, and does it even matter as long as the finished soup tastes good? Which is perhaps a rather roundabout way of saying that I've cooked countless variations of French onion soup over the years, and this one is my favorite, a synthesis of many good recipes and possible permutations.

3 tablespoons unsalted butter

1 tablespoon vegetable oil

2½ pounds (about 5 large) yellow onions, halved and thinly sliced into half moons

About 1 teaspoon salt

1 teaspoon sugar

2 tablespoons unbleached all-purpose flour

7 cups beef stock

⅓ cup dry sherry

1 teaspoon finely chopped fresh thyme leaves or ½ teaspoon dried

Freshly ground black pepper to taste

1 loaf French bread, cut into ½-inch-thick slices

10 to 12 ounces Jarlsberg or Gruyère cheese, grated, to your taste

1. Melt 2 tablespoons of the butter with the oil in a large, heavy soup pot over moderate heat. Stir in the onions, ½ teaspoon of the salt, and the sugar. Heat for 1 minute, stirring, then cover tightly and cook for 10 minutes. Remove the lid and continue to cook over moderate heat (or slightly hotter) until the onions are caramelized and very soft, about 25 minutes—adding the last tablespoon of butter to the pan about midway through.

2. Reduce the heat slightly, add the flour to the onions, and cook, stirring, for 3 to 4 minutes. Stir in the stock, sherry, thyme, pepper, and another ¼ teaspoon of the salt. Cover the soup and simmer gently for 15 minutes, adding more salt if needed.

3. When ready to serve, toast the bread and preheat your broiler. Ladle the soup into ovenproof soup bowls and place them on a baking sheet. Put enough bread on top—cutting and fitting if necessary—to pretty much cover the soup. Arrange a thick layer of grated cheese over the top, then slide the bowls under the broiler until the cheese is bubbly and golden. Remember to tell everyone that the bowls are very hot!

MAKES 6 TO 7 SERVINGS

Prune and Port Bread

Port-soaked prunes make for a densely fruited quick bread that tastes just right against the meaty-salty flavor of French onion soup. This makes an excellent tea bread around the holidays.

2 cups chopped pitted prunes

1³/₄ cups ruby port

1¹/₂ cups unbleached all-purpose flour

¹/₂ cup whole wheat flour

2¹/₂ teaspoons baking powder

¹/₂ teaspoon salt

¹/₂ teaspoon ground cinnamon

³/₄ cup firmly packed light brown sugar

¹/₄ cup (¹/₂ stick) cold, unsalted butter, cut into ¹/₄-inch pieces

2 large eggs

¹/₄ cup plain yogurt or sour cream

1 teaspoon pure vanilla extract

Finely grated zest of 1 lemon

¹/₂ cup finely chopped walnuts

1 tablespoon granulated sugar, to sprinkle on top

1. Put the prunes and port in a medium-size, nonreactive saucepan. Bring to a near boil and remove from the heat. Set aside for 1 hour. Meanwhile, grease a 5 x 9-inch loaf pan and preheat the oven to 350 degrees F.

2. Put the flours, baking powder, salt, cinnamon, and brown sugar in a large mixing bowl. Rub with your fingers to mix well. Add the butter and rub it into the dry mixture—or cut it in with a pastry blender—until the mixture resembles fine meal. Transfer to a large bowl.

3. Whisk the eggs in a medium-size bowl. Whisk in the yogurt or sour cream, vanilla, and lemon zest. Drain the soaked prunes, reserving ³/₄ cup of the port. Whisk the port into the egg mixture. Make a well in the center of the dry mixture and add the liquid all at once, stirring with a wooden spoon until partially blended. Add the drained prunes and walnuts and continue to stir until evenly blended.

4. Scrape the batter into the prepared pan and smooth the top. Sprinkle the top with the granulated sugar. Bake until a tester inserted deep into the center of the loaf comes out clean, 55 to 60 minutes. Let the bread cool in the pan, on a wire rack, for 15 minutes. Run a knife around the outside of the bread and invert the pan onto a rack, right side up. Let cool thoroughly before slicing.

MAKES 10 TO 12 SERVINGS

Streamlined Salade Niçoise

The main difference between this and other artfully composed salades niçoise is the art-fully composed part. All the usual suspects are here—olives, mustardy vinaigrette, potatoes, green beans, eggs, tuna—so the flavor is right on target. I just don't go to the trouble of arranging it prettily.

2 cups trimmed green beans broken into
    large pieces

1½ pounds very small red-skinned
    potatoes (or cut into chunks, if not
    very small)

¼ cup olive oil

2 tablespoons red wine vinegar

1½ tablespoons Dijon mustard

½ teaspoon sugar

One 6-ounce can tuna, preferably Italian
    oil-packed, drained and flaked

2 medium-size ripe tomatoes, cored and
    cut into wedges

½ cup pitted sliced olives

2 to 3 tablespoons capers, to your
    taste, drained

2 tablespoons chopped fresh parsley
    leaves

Salt and freshly ground black pepper
    to taste

1 head Boston lettuce, leaves rinsed
    and dried

3 or 4 hard-cooked eggs, peeled and
    quartered

1. Bring a large saucepan of salted water to a boil. Add the green beans and potatoes and boil until the vegetables are tender, about 10 minutes. Drain and spread the vegetables on a platter to cool. When they're cool enough to handle, halve the potatoes if they're whole small ones.

2. Meanwhile, whisk the olive oil, vinegar, mustard, and sugar together in a large bowl. Add the vegetables—it's fine if they're still a little warm—and toss well to coat evenly. Add the tuna, tomatoes, olives, capers, and parsley, season with salt and pepper, and toss well.

3. Arrange several lettuce leaves on individual salad plates. Put several egg sections on each plate, then spoon some of the salad over the lettuce and serve.

MAKES 4 TO 5 SERVINGS

APRÈS SKI ITALIAN

Garlicky White Bean Soup

• • • • • • • • • • • • •

Bruschetta of Blue Cheese, Tomatoes, and Pecans

• • • • • • • • • • • • •

Grilled Zucchini and Tortellini Salad

• • • • • • • • • • • • •

I'm not a big skier myself, but I know quite a few people who are, and it seems like there are more than a few weekends every winter when I'm feeding all of them at once. Of course, this doesn't include my four teenagers and all of their friends, who wouldn't be caught dead on skis since snowboarding became *the* way to fly down the slopes.

If there's anything a skier or snowboarder loves more than six inches of fresh powder and free lift tickets, it's a hearty meal—like this one—at the end of the day. Skiers have tremendous appetites. I've seen them arrive, pack away salad, lasagna, garlic bread, apple pie, and ice cream and *then* ask me when dinner will be ready.

Not just skiers, but anybody who whips up a winter appetite, will appreciate stoking it with a hearty cold-weather menu like this. There's lots of heft here to replenish calories, and lots of gutsy flavors to enjoy doing it—garlicky bean soup, toast topped with blue cheese and other good stuff, a grilled zucchini and pasta salad. And if you've a less than gargantuan appetite, one or two of these together will do quite nicely.

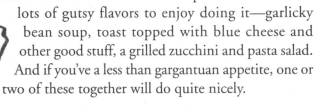

Garlicky White Bean Soup

I like the little white navy beans for this simple soup. You can't put too much garlic in here; I call for six big cloves but twice that amount would be fine. The most important thing to remember with bean soups is this: don't undercook the beans. A little overcooked is better than a little undercooked.

1 cup dried white navy beans
1 teaspoon chopped fresh rosemary
　leaves or ¹/₂ teaspoon dried
¹/₄ cup olive oil
1 large onion, chopped
6 big cloves garlic, or more to your
　taste, minced

1 large ripe tomato, cored, seeded,
　and chopped
3 to 4 chicken or vegetable bouillon
　cubes, to your taste
Salt and freshly ground black pepper
　to taste

1. Put the beans in a colander and pick over them to remove any dirt and debris. Rinse well, then put them in a large saucepan with plenty of water to cover. Bring the water to a boil, boil for 1 minute, then remove from the heat. Cover and set aside to soak for 1 hour.

2. Drain the beans, then put them back in the pan with 5¹/₂ cups fresh water. Bring to a boil, reduce the heat to moderately low, and simmer, partially covered, until they are tender, about an hour.

3. While the beans are cooking, heat the olive oil in a separate large saucepan over low heat. Add the onion and garlic and cook, stirring occasionally, about 20 minutes; there should be enough oil in the pan so the onion essentially stews in it. After 20 minutes, stir in the tomato, increase the heat somewhat, and stew another 8 to 10 minutes.

4. When the beans are tender, carefully pour the beans and their cooking water into the onion and tomato mixture. Add the bouillon cubes. Bring the soup to a simmer, stirring occasionally. Taste the soup, seasoning with salt and pepper.

5. As the soup comes to a simmer, remove about 1 cup of the beans with a slotted spoon. Put them, and a little of the broth, into a blender and process until smooth. Stir the puree back into the soup. Simmer the soup for about 10 minutes, partially covered, before serving.

MAKES ABOUT 5 SERVINGS

Bruschetta of Blue Cheese, Tomatoes, and Pecans

This is a step or two beyond basic bruschetta—just toasted bread with olive oil and garlic—but I sometimes like the added richness of the cheese on a winter day. Note that I call for cherry tomatoes here; out of habit I prefer them in the off-tomato season as the quality tends to be better than for the larger tomatoes. Use a good rustic store-bought bread or Cuban Bread (page 24) or Ciabatta (page 166).

½ cup crumbled blue cheese

2 ounces cream cheese

2 tablespoons chopped pecans

Four to six ¾-inch-thick slices crusty, firm-textured bread

2 cloves garlic, halved

1 cup cherry tomatoes, halved or quartered

Freshly ground black pepper to taste

Chopped fresh basil leaves, for garnish

1. In a small bowl, mash the cheeses together with a fork, leaving the mixture somewhat chunky. Mix in the pecans.

2. Toast the bread in the oven, toaster oven, or under the broiler until golden on both sides.

3. Rub one side of each bread slice with garlic then spread some of the cheese mixture on the same side. Arrange some tomato pieces on top of the cheese. Dust with pepper and basil, then serve.

MAKES 4 TO 6 SERVINGS

Grilled Zucchini and Tortellini Salad

I call this a grilled zucchini salad, but just as often—like in the middle of winter, when it's just not convenient to fire up the grill—I simply panfry zucchini rounds in a little oil rather than grilling strips of them. The trick is to get the pan good and hot first, so the slices char in the pan. It usually takes under 2 minutes per side to cook them this way. In any case, the zucchini slices are spread out on a platter and the tortellini salad mix is just spooned over the top.

3 medium-size zucchini

1/3 to 1/2 cup olive oil, as needed

Salt and freshly ground black pepper to taste

One 7- or 8-ounce package cheese tortellini

1 large, ripe tomato, cored, sliced, and finely chopped

1 tablespoon balsamic vinegar

1 clove garlic, minced

1 tablespoon chopped fresh basil leaves

1 tablespoon chopped fresh parsley leaves

Freshly grated Parmesan cheese, for garnish

1. To grill the zucchini, cut them into lengthwise slices about 1/3 inch thick. Brush with olive oil and grill them until tender, turning once or twice; salt and pepper the slices as they grill, and don't worry if they char a little bit; they're supposed to. Transfer the slices to a serving platter.

2. Bring a large saucepan of salted water to a boil. Add the tortellini and cook according to the package instructions. Drain, transfer to a bowl, and toss well with 3 tablespoons of the olive oil, the tomato, vinegar, garlic, and herbs. Season with salt and pepper. Set aside for 15 minutes.

3. Spread the tortellini mixture over the grilled zucchini. Cover with plastic wrap and refrigerate if not serving right away. Garnish with the cheese just before serving.

VARIATION: Use other grilled vegetables in addition to the zucchini: peppers, tomatoes, and eggplant are great.

MAKES 6 SERVINGS

A SIMPLE CHRISTMAS EVE CELEBRATION

Choucroute Soup

....

Stollen Soda Bread

....

Raw Vegetable Salad with Blue Cheese Dip

....

There are a couple of ways of looking at a Christmas Eve menu: you can knock yourself out by preparing a bona fide feast, or, you can relax and do something a bit more low key. I've done both, and enjoyed doing both, but I have to tell you that the older I get, the more I prefer the latter approach.

Soup, salad, and bread fit nicely into the relaxed atmosphere I like to cultivate on Christmas Eve. By the time this evening rolls around, I've about had as much celebrating and festivity as I can handle. I like to start winding down so I can enjoy the next few days off, not catch up on the dishes.

There are all sorts of festive soup menus you *could* serve tonight—I just happen to like this one. These aren't recipes my mom used to make or treasured family recipes that came over on the *Mayflower*. They're just good recipes that I've enjoyed in recent years and thought you would, too: a hearty sauerkraut soup; a quick version of stollen that's as good as any yeast version I've eaten; and a platter of healthy raw vegetables and blue cheese dip. I do like to eat as many healthy foods as I can over the holidays, to balance out all the sweet, rich foods we tend to eat this time of year. The entire meal, incidentally, can be made ahead, then rewarmed—or pulled from the fridge—shortly before serving. On Christmas Eve, that amounts to a bonus of a gift for the cook.

Choucroute Soup

Seems that everywhere you turn these days you read about choucroute, that rib-sticking Alsatian casserole made with sauerkraut, pork, wine, and root vegetables. I'm crazy about it myself, and I especially love the authentic version Alsatian chef/owner Raymond Ost makes at his restaurant, Sandrine's, in Cambridge, Massachusetts. Making choucroute takes several hours; this soup, which is like a brothy version of it, takes only about an hour and is nearly as good as the genuine article. Though I've never seen tomatoes in any choucroute recipe, I've taken the liberty of using tomato paste here; it adds a little sweetness to balance out the acidity of the sauerkraut. Which explains the addition of the sugar as well.

3 tablespoons flavorless vegetable oil

2 large onions, halved and thinly sliced into half moons

1 clove garlic, bruised

5 cups chicken stock

1/3 cup dry white wine (see note)

1 large carrot, peeled and grated

1 large all-purpose potato, peeled and grated

1 pound sauerkraut

1 bay leaf

1/4 to 1/2 teaspoon salt, to your taste

3/4 pound kielbasa or other fully cooked smoked sausage

1 tablespoon tomato paste

1 to 2 teaspoons sugar, to your taste

Freshly ground black pepper to taste

1. Heat the oil in a good-size heavy enameled soup pot over moderately low heat. Add the onions and garlic and cook, stirring, until very soft, 12 to 15 minutes. Stir in the stock, wine, carrot, and potato, cover, and simmer gently for 15 minutes.

2. Drain the sauerkraut and squeeze it between your palms to express nearly all of the liquid. Add to the soup with the bay leaf and 1/4 teaspoon of the salt. Cover and simmer gently for another 15 minutes.

3. Slice the sausage into 1/2-inch-thick rounds and cut the rounds in half. Add the sausage to the soup, then stir in the tomato paste and 1 teaspoon of the sugar. Cover and simmer gently 15 minutes more, seasoning with pepper and adding more salt and sugar if necessary before serving.

NOTE: If you'd rather, you can skip the wine. Just add stock in its place.

MAKES 6 SERVINGS

Stollen Soda Bread

This is an amazing little bread, and one that's virtually gotten me out of the business of making yeasted stollen anymore. The dough is sticky; don't be intimidated by it, simply keep your kneading surface well covered with flour. It has the most wonderful crunchy crust you've ever had on a bread.

³/₄ cup raisins	1 teaspoon baking soda
³/₄ cup chopped pitted dates	¹/₂ teaspoon ground cinnamon
³/₄ cup diced dried figs or apricots	¹/₄ teaspoon ground cardamom
Orange juice	3 tablespoons cold unsalted butter,
Cornmeal or semolina, for dusting	cut into ¹/₄-inch pieces
4 cups unbleached all-purpose flour	1 large egg
¹/₂ cup sugar, plus a little to sprinkle on	1¹/₂ cups buttermilk
loaves	Finely grated zest of 1 orange
1¹/₂ teaspoons salt	Finely grated zest of 1 lemon
2 teaspoons baking powder	Milk, for brushing on loaves

1. Put the dried fruit in a medium-size bowl and add enough orange juice to just cover. Set aside to soak for 30 to 60 minutes. Lightly oil a large baking sheet and dust with cornmeal or semolina. Preheat the oven to 375 degrees F when the fruit is done soaking.

2. Sift the flour, sugar, salt, baking powder, baking soda, and spices together into a large bowl. Add the butter and cut it into the dry ingredients with a pastry blender or your fingers until the mixture resembles fine crumbs. Set aside. Whisk the egg in a small bowl. Whisk in the buttermilk and citrus zests.

3. Drain the fruit; discard the orange juice (or drink it, for that matter; there's nothing wrong with it). Add the fruit to the dry ingredients and toss well, to coat. Make a well in the center of the dry mixture, add the buttermilk mixture, and stir briskly with a wooden spoon, just until the dough pulls together in a shaggy mass. Let sit for 3 minutes.

4. Dust your hands and work surface with flour. Cut the dough in half right in the bowl, then place half on the floured surface. Knead very gently for 30 to 45 seconds. Either shape into a stubby football, or shape like a stollen: pat into a disk about 1 inch thick, then fold half of it over the other half, but don't cover the bottom half entirely; it should look almost like a pair of pouting lips, the bottom one stuck out further than the other. Before you make the fold, brush any flour off the surface, so it makes a good seal. Repeat for other half of the dough. Place on the prepared baking sheet with some space in between them. Lightly brush the loaves with milk and sprinkle generously with sugar.

5. Bake the loaves on the center rack for 30 minutes. Turn the sheet 180 degrees. Reduce the oven temperature to 350 degrees F and bake another 20 minutes. When done, the loaves will be a very dark golden color and very crusty. Let cool on a wire rack; they should be at least lukewarm before slicing.

MAKES 2 LOAVES

Raw Vegetable Salad with Blue Cheese Dip

There's an art to serving raw vegetables with dip. First, the vegetables must be agreeably bite sized. I cringe when I see veggies the size of redwoods on a raw vegetable platter. Someone will go dip the offending broccoli or whatever into the dip, take a bite, and stick the same piece in for more dip. Yuck. So, I suggest making everything of the one-bite size to prevent double dipping. Provide toothpicks on the side. Next, of course, the vegetables should be in very good shape, as they are going to be served raw. Only the pick of the crop, or produce section, as the case may be. Broccoli, cauliflower, celery, and carrots are generally safe bets. Unless it is summer and you can get tender young ones, don't bother with green beans, as they tend to be stringy. Cukes are pretty safe. Summer squash can be okay, texturewise, but winter specimens have so little taste it's hardly worth it. Finally, the dip must have the right texture: too thin and it will dribble all over the place onto your pretty holiday clothes; too thick and it won't coat the vegetable when you dip it, but rather cling in big lumps. Keep that in mind when you're adjusting the blue cheese dip here.

BLUE CHEESE DIP
1 cup crumbled blue cheese
2 ounces cream cheese
Small handful fresh parsley leaves
3 tablespoons chopped onion
1 clove garlic, coarsely chopped
2/3 cup sour cream
1/3 cup mayonnaise

2 to 3 teaspoons prepared
   horseradish, to your taste
2 to 3 teaspoons fresh lemon juice,
   to your taste
2 teaspoons tarragon vinegar or wine
   vinegar
Salt and freshly ground black pepper
   to taste

THE VEGETABLES

2 cups small broccoli florets

2 cups small cauliflower florets

1 cucumber, thinly sliced

2 ribs celery, cut into smallish sticks

1 carrot, cut into smallish sticks

Chopped fresh parsley leaves
(optional), for garnish

1. To prepare the dip, put the blue cheese, cream cheese, parsley, onion, and garlic in a food processor. Pulse several times, to blend.

2. Add the remaining dip ingredients and process again, until smooth, adding salt and pepper and more lemon juice and vinegar, if needed. If the mixture seems too thick, add water 1 teaspoon at a time. Transfer the mixture to a serving bowl, then cover with plastic wrap and refrigerate until needed. You can prepare this up to a day ahead.

3. To serve, put dip in the middle of a serving platter and arrange the vegetables around it. Garnish the dip with parsley, if desired.

MAKES 5 TO 6 SERVINGS

Some Thoughts on Parsley

When using parsley anywhere as a garnish, use the Italian flat-leaf parsley as opposed to the sort with curly leaves. Why? Because unless they're meticulously minced, those curly leaves have a nasty way of catching in the throat on the way down—harmless enough, but not a very pleasant experience either. You won't have that problem with flat-leaf parsley. Don't forget that those parsley stems have a lot of flavor and should go into your stocks and soups whenever possible. I often just cut off the stems wholesale, a handful at a time, tie some kitchen twine around them, and toss them into the simmering soup. Then it's an easy matter to retrieve them before the soup is served.

DIPPING FOR DUMPLINGS

Cabbage Soup with Parmesan Potato Gnocchi

· · · · · · · · · · · · · · ·

Parmesan Potato Gnocchi

· · · · · · · · · · · · · · ·

Radicchio "Slaw" with
Raspberry Balsamic Dressing

· · · · · · · · · · · · · · ·

I fell in love with the word *gnocchi* before I knew what they were, or how to pronounce it—imagine a hard *G* sound followed by a KNOCK and you'll have some idea how badly I butchered it—and well before I knew how to make them. None of that mattered. They just sounded exotic from the get go. Then I learned how to make them and I was really hooked.

If you've yet to be initiated, gnocchi are little Italian dumplings. The Italian word *gnocco*—according to Marcella Hazan—means "a little lump," of the sort you might get on your head if you walked into a door jamb. (And these do look something like little lumps.) Mrs. Hazan is, of course, one of the foremost authorities in this country on Italian cooking. She says that Italian cooks usually don't put eggs in their gnocchi, thinking that it makes for too rubbery a dumpling. But—with apologies to Mrs. Hazan—I've always made them that way and I think the result is wonderful and not at all rubbery. And when you try them in this peasant-like cabbage soup—which I like to serve with a multicolored bitter and sweet radicchio salad—I think you'll agree.

Cabbage Soup with Parmesan Potato Gnocchi

I'm quite fond of cabbage soup, in part because it's bulky, has great flavor when cooked, and is inexpensive. What more could you ask for? Here it is featured with few competing elements, save for the gnocchi. Since there's not much in the soup to boost the flavor of the broth, be sure to use a strong-tasting beef stock.

2 tablespoons olive oil

6 cups cored and thinly sliced green cabbage (¹/₂ small head)

1 large onion, halved and thinly sliced into half moons

Salt to taste

1 clove garlic, chopped

6 cups beef stock

¹/₂ cup canned tomato puree or crushed tomatoes in puree

1 bay leaf

Freshly ground black pepper to taste

1 recipe Parmesan Potato Gnocchi (recipe follows)

Freshly grated Parmesan cheese, for garnish

1. Heat the olive oil in a good-size soup pot over moderately high heat. Add the cabbage and onion and cook, stirring occasionally, for 5 minutes; it's fine if it browns a little. Sprinkle about ¹/₄ teaspoon salt over the cabbage. Cover, reduce the heat to moderately low, and cook, stirring occasionally, for 15 minutes. Stir in the garlic during the last minute of cooking.

2. Stir the beef stock, tomato puree, and bay leaf into the soup and season with pepper. Bring to a gentle simmer and cook for 10 minutes, adding more salt, if necessary.

3. Gently drop the gnocchi into the soup; push them down so they're beneath the surface. Increase the heat and bring the soup to a low boil. When it reaches a low boil, cook the gnocchi for about 6 minutes. When they're done, they'll rise to the top of the liquid and look swollen. Serve the soup with some of the dumplings in each portion. Pass the cheese at the table, for garnish.

MAKES 6 TO 7 SERVINGS

Another Way to Cook Gnocchi

You might like these gnocchi enough to think about other ways to serve them. The most common way is to drop them into a pan of simmering water or chicken or beef stock. When they rise to the surface—as they do in the soup—simmer them for 5 to 6 minutes. As you would with any dumpling, keep the water at a lively simmer but not a rolling boil or they'll start to fall apart. Pluck them out of the pan with a slotted spoon and transfer to a buttered baking dish. Top with a little bit of tomato sauce and some Parmesan cheese, then bake about 15 minutes in a preheated 400 degree F oven. They're wonderful as a side dish with all sorts of Italian foods.

Parmesan Potato Gnocchi

Whenever I make these, I'm reminded how easy they are to prepare. And fun. I enjoy the handwork of rolling and cutting the dough, then rolling it again into little torpedo shapes, which are not quite the traditional shape but make up in simplicity what they lack in authenticity. It keeps things all the simpler, and makes the dumplings easier to handle as well, if you prepare these ahead of time and refrigerate them while you make the soup and salad.

1 pound all-purpose potatoes (3 medium-size), scrubbed
³/4 cup unbleached all-purpose flour
¹/2 cup freshly grated Parmesan cheese

¹/2 teaspoon salt
Freshly ground black pepper to taste
1 large egg

1. Put the unpeeled potatoes in a medium-size saucepan and cover with plenty of salted water. Bring to a boil, then adjust the heat and gently boil the potatoes until they're tender at the center, 30 to 40 minutes; poke them with a cake tester to check. Drain.

2. Let the potatoes cool briefly. As soon as you can, peel off the potato skins, then put the potatoes through a ricer or food mill, letting the flesh fall into a large bowl. Add the flour, cheese, salt, and a good measure of pepper, tossing gently to mix.

3. Make a well in the center of the potatoes. Add the egg to the well, whisk briefly, then mix the dough with your hands until it pulls together into a uniform mass. Shake a little flour onto your work surface and knead the dough 5 or 6 times.

4. With floured hands, roll the dough into a rope about 1½ inches in diameter. (It might be easiest to do this part in sections.) Cut the dough into 1-inch segments, then roll each one gently on the counter—crosswise, not the same direction you've just rolled it—into little torpedos about 2 inches long. Transfer to a baking sheet as you cut them. Cover with plastic wrap and refrigerate until using, no longer than 1 hour.

MAKES ABOUT 30 GNOCCHI

Radicchio "Slaw"
with
Raspberry Balsamic Dressing

I was never a big admirer of bitter radicchio in salads until I discovered the trick to serving it: you need to balance the bitterness with something fairly sweet. It might be a sweet dressing or fruit in the salad, anything to take off the bitter edge. Here I do that with a raspberry balsamic dressing, and I keep it simple by using plain old raspberry preserves. It works like a charm and makes this "slaw" one of those salads the kids might go for. Assemble this right before serving so it stays good and crisp.

SLAW
1 small head radicchio, quartered, cored, and thinly sliced crosswise
1 smallish head romaine lettuce, heart only, sliced crosswise 1/4 inch thick
1 small red onion, halved and thinly sliced into half moons
1 carrot, peeled and grated
1 crisp apple, cored and diced
Small handful fresh parsley leaves
1 lemon

RASPBERRY BALSAMIC DRESSING AND ASSEMBLY
1 1/2 tablespoons balsamic vinegar
2 teaspoons honey
2 tablespoons raspberry preserves
2 tablespoons olive oil
Freshly ground black pepper to taste
Handful chopped walnuts

1. Put the radicchio, lettuce, onion, carrot, apple, and parsley in a large bowl. Finely grate the lemon right over the salad, using about half of the zest.

2. To make the dressing, heat the vinegar and honey together in a small saucepan until the honey dissolves. Transfer to a small bowl and whisk in the preserves and olive oil.

3. Pour the dressing over the salad and toss well, seasoning with pepper. Mix in the walnuts and serve right away.

MAKES 5 TO 6 SERVINGS

VEGETARIAN FRIENDS' FARE

No Bones About It Split Pea Soup

....

Oat and Cornmeal Raisin Bread

....

Salad-Bowl Salad with Tahini Dressing

....

It can be a cruel world. I mean, think about all of the vegetarians who must go to bed at night feeling like second-class citizens because nearly every split pea soup recipe in the world begins, "First, find a meaty ham bone." What's a vegetarian to do? Well, as a former almost vegetarian myself, here's what I do: simply stir in some good barbecue sauce when the soup is just about done. Serious vegetarians will take me to task and point out that barbecue sauce traditionally has Worcestershire sauce in it, which is made with anchovies, and is therefore not strictly vegetarian. Whereupon I will note that most health food stores do indeed carry barbecue sauces that are free of all animal products. So there.

With our meatless pea soup as the focal point of this menu, we round things out with a bread and salad that will sound as salubrious and satisfying as they truly are: a grainy oat and corn bread spiked with raisins and a big salad-bowl salad that gets to the heart of healthy eating without standing on any precious or pretentious ground. The salad is served with tahini dressing. All told, a wonderful menu for anyone who likes wholesome, hearty vegetarian fare.

No Bones About It
Split Pea Soup

Vegetarian or not, you may want to try this split pea soup, which I rank among the best I've ever tried. And if you just can't stand the thought of pea soup without the ham, use the bone or throw in some diced ham at the end, if you want.

2¹/₂ tablespoons olive oil or vegetable oil

1 large onion, chopped

2 ribs celery, chopped

2 cloves garlic, minced

7 cups water

1¹/₂ cups dried green split peas, picked over and rinsed

1¹/₄ teaspoons salt, plus more to taste

1 large all-purpose potato, peeled and diced

¹/₄ to ¹/₃ cup smoky-style barbecue sauce, to your taste

Freshly ground black pepper to taste

1. Heat the oil in a large soup pot over moderate heat. Add the onion and celery and cook, stirring, until the onion is translucent, 8 to 9 minutes, adding the garlic during the last minute. Stir in the water and split peas, bring to a boil, stirring occasionally, turn off the heat, and cover. Set aside, undisturbed, for 1 hour.

2. After an hour, bring the water to a simmer. Simmer gently for 1 hour, partially covered. Add the potato, then continue to simmer, partially covered, until the peas are soft, about another 30 minutes. When they are almost soft, add the salt.

3. Remove from the heat. Working in about 4 batches—to keep the soup from flying out of your food processor (see page 34)—puree the soup in the processor, transferring each portion to another pan that you can reheat the soup in. When all the soup is pureed, stir in ¹/₄ cup of the barbecue sauce. Taste, adding more salt and pepper as needed. If it seems to need a little more barbecue sauce, add a bit more. Serve piping hot.

MAKES 8 SERVINGS

Oat and Cornmeal Raisin Bread

When I start mixing grains in breads, these two—corn and oats—often end up in the mix together. It's become almost an unconscious move on my part, reflecting long-standing experience that the two never fail to strike a harmonious note. I use a little honey to sweeten this bread, which is baked in an ordinary cake pan (though a warmed skillet would do nicely). Then I add a good handful of raisins, which effectively does for this bread what raisins do to your morning bowl of oatmeal: makes it all the more fun, fruity, and tasty. Note that this has whole wheat flour, oats, and cornmeal—whole grains all—so don't expect an ethereal bread. It has a somewhat compact, chewy texture.

½ cup rolled (old-fashioned, not instant or quick-cooking) oats

2 cups plus 2 tablespoons buttermilk

1 large egg, lightly beaten

2 tablespoons honey

¼ cup vegetable oil

1 cup fine-ground yellow cornmeal

1 cup whole wheat flour

1 teaspoon baking powder

¾ teaspoon baking soda

½ teaspoon salt

¾ cup raisins

1. Preheat the oven to 400 degrees F and grease a 9-inch cake pan. Set aside.

2. Stir the oats, buttermilk, egg, honey, and oil together in a medium-size bowl.

3. Sift the cornmeal, flour, baking powder, baking soda, and salt together into a large bowl. Make a well in the center of the dry ingredients and add the liquid. Stir the batter just until blended, taking care to stir out any dry streaks. Stir in the raisins, then scrape the batter into the prepared pan.

4. Bake the bread for about 30 minutes. When done, the top will be golden brown and springy to the touch. Transfer the pan to a wire rack and let the bread cool at least 10 minutes before slicing into wedges.

MAKES 10 SERVINGS

Salad-Bowl Salad with Tahini Dressing

This is the best sort of old-school salad-bowl salad, where everything is put in your best-looking bowl, tossed, then served—no fancy presentation, just good healthy salad fixings with a creamy, good-for-you garlicky dressing served on the side.

SALAD

1 head green or red leaf lettuce, leaves rinsed and dried

1 cucumber, peeled and thinly sliced

Large handful cherry tomatoes, halved

1 small green bell pepper, seeded and thinly sliced

1 carrot, peeled and grated

1 cup very thinly sliced green or red cabbage

1 cup grated sharp cheddar cheese (optional)

TAHINI DRESSING

½ cup tahini (available in health food stores)

½ cup water

3 tablespoons red wine vinegar

2 teaspoons Dijon mustard

1 teaspoon tamari or regular soy sauce

2 cloves garlic, minced

2 tablespoons chopped fresh parsley leaves

¼ to ⅓ cup plain yogurt, to your taste

Salt and freshly ground black pepper to taste

1. To prepare the salad, tear the lettuce into pieces and drop them into a large salad bowl. Add the remaining salad ingredients and toss to mix.

2. To make the dressing, put all of the dressing ingredients in a small bowl and whisk well, to blend. Taste and correct the seasoning; it might even need a pinch of sugar, to take off the edge. Serve the salad with the dressing on the side.

MAKES 6 SERVINGS

Salad Savvy, Kid Style

Kids and salad are often thought to be on less than easy terms, but it doesn't have to be that way. In fact, my own kids have always eaten their salad with gusto. I've actually seen waitresses slack-jawed at the sight of my four kids wolfing down their salads at one restaurant or another. My trick? It's simple, really: I've never made salad an issue. If they like it, great; they won't need any encouragement from me. If not, that's fine, too. I don't bribe or cajole. I do, however, listen to what they tell me about salad, what they like and what turns them off. No use serving it if they're not interested. If I want to introduce something new to the family salad bowl, I'll always try to tip them off so there are no surprises. Kids don't like to feel like you're trying to sneak one past them.

If your own kids suffer from salad phobia, one way to thaw the chill is by getting them involved. Asking them to join in—handling and washing raw ingredients, cutting them up—just may change their attitude. They'll take pride in their contributions and be more motivated to dig in. Here are a few suggestions for working with your young salad recruit.

• Kids like to wash lettuce. Even a young child can fill a bowl with cold water, dunk the leaves, and place them in a colander. Show them how to stand the leaves up so the water drips off.

• Explain to your child how watery lettuce can dilute a dressing and ruin a salad, so it has to be dried well. Have them spread the greens in a single layer on heavy-duty paper towels and blot them dry.

• Better yet, get your child a salad spinner; kids love these gadgets. The push-plunger type with a nonskid bottom is easier for a child to operate than a pull-cord spinner.

• Show them how to tear the lettuce into bite-size pieces, and how to tear it away from discardable center stems when the stems are too big (the exception being iceberg lettuce, which is durable enough to slice).

• Kids like decorative touches, so demonstrate how to run a lemon zester along the surface of a cucumber to make a striped edge.

• Finally, offer them the job of mixing the dressing, kid style. The ingredients for small batch dressings, especially vinaigrettes, can be made right in the jar. Cover tightly, wrap a tea towel around the jar for a good grip, then let 'em shake like mad.

ROASTED SOUP AND SILVER DOLLARS

Roasted Potato, Onion, and Garlic Soup

• • • • • • • • • • • • •

Blue Cheese and Walnut Silver Dollars

• • • • • • • • • • • • •

Salad of Fennel, Grapes, and Endive

• • • • • • • • • • • • •

Things matter when you make soup. That's why, even when we use the same recipe, my soup is going to taste a little different from yours. In fact, my soup might even taste a little different from mine if—say—I use a different brand of crushed tomatoes tomorrow than I used yesterday. Taste is beholden to so many factors. How ripe are the tomatoes you're using? What about your soup pot? Is it tall, narrow, and nonstick? Or wide and thin stainless steel? The latter is more likely to make your sautés darker and that will influence the flavor of the broth. If you make a lot of soup, you become attuned to such things.

Roasting is one thing that has a profound effect on flavor, and the soup on this menu is a good example. Roasting concentrates flavors, emboldens them, and makes things sweeter; that comes across clearly in the finished product. But take those same vegetables and simply simmer them in broth and you get something entirely different, a much softer flavor. Both are good; they just have different personalities. Sometimes one suits the mood more than the other. And when the mood calls for bold flavor, try this roasted soup.

Of course, it also matters what you serve with your soup. Bold matches bold with our blue cheese–walnut silver dollars, little crackers that I like to serve with this. You can crumble these and drop them in the soup, put a spot of jam on them, or even smear a little extra blue cheese–cream cheese spread on them. At the holidays, you can give them as gifts. Cut them to fit a little baking powder tin and cover the tin with festive wrapping paper.

All these big flavors get a little respite with the salad. It's crisp, refreshingly fruity, and a snap to toss together.

Roasted Potato, Onion, and Garlic Soup

Roasting vegetables adds a bold flavor dimension to soup. The flavors become crisp and intensified, as if the soup had been grilled, for lack of a better way to describe it. Here's a simple version of a roasted vegetable soup: everything goes on one baking sheet and you pop it in the oven for an hour. Do keep the vegetables in the oven until the onions have become quite crisp, even charred in places, because undercooking them will give the soup a raw taste. If anything, err on the side of overcooking. Since roasting leaves a brown skin on the potatoes, expect the soup to have some texture. Don't be concerned that this calls for an entire bulb of garlic; roasting mellows the flavor nicely. This is a fine winter soup.

2 pounds all-purpose potatoes, peeled

2 good-size yellow onions, halved

2 tablespoons olive oil

Salt and freshly ground black pepper to taste

1 head garlic

2^1/$_2$ tablespoons unsalted butter

2 teaspoons water

6 cups hot chicken stock

1^1/$_2$ tablespoons unbleached all-purpose flour

^{1}/$_2$ cup milk, half-and-half, or light cream

1. Preheat the oven to 400 degrees F and get out a large jelly-roll pan. Cut the potatoes into slightly-larger-than-bite-size chunks and transfer to a large bowl. Snip the root ends off the onions and cut each half into quarter sections. Add the onions to the potatoes, breaking the onions up with your fingers so some of the layers separate. Drizzle with the olive oil, toss well, then spread the vegetables over the pan. Lightly salt and pepper them.

2. Slice the top third off the head of garlic and place it on top of a sheet of aluminum foil. Put ^{1}/$_2$ tablespoon of the butter on top of the garlic and dribble the water onto the foil. Fold up the sides of the foil to enclose the garlic. Place the foil packet on the pan with the vegetables. Roast the vegetables in the oven for 45 minutes, then remove the garlic. Continue to roast until done, another 10 to 15 minutes.

3. Working with no more than half the vegetables at a time, transfer them to a food processor and add a small ladle full of the stock. Process until almost smooth, then transfer to a medium-size bowl. Repeat for the remaining vegetables, squeezing the garlic cloves into the last batch. Stir the puree back into the stock.

4. Melt the remaining 2 tablespoons butter in a small saucepan over moderately low heat. Add the flour and cook, stirring, until it turns a light golden color, 1¹/2 to 2 minutes. Stir in the milk, half-and-half, or cream and cook until thickened. Stir in a ladle full or two of the soup and continue to cook, stirring, another minute.

5. Stir this mixture back into the soup. Heat for 10 minutes, stirring, until the soup is heated through. (Whisk briskly if the thickening mixture forms little lumps; that should break them up.) Serve piping hot.

MAKES 6 TO 8 SERVINGS

Blue Cheese and Walnut Silver Dollars

These thin, crusty-crisp rounds are somewhere between a cracker and a biscuit: the thinner you slice them, the more cracker-like they become. I like to eat them plain and just dunk them in my soup—or break off chunks and drop them in. But the sharp, salty flavor of the blue cheese also goes well with just a dab of jam; peach is nice. Note that you will have to make the dough 3 to 4 hours ahead, so it has time to firm in the fridge. People like the charmingly cute, small size of them.

1¹/2 cups unbleached all-purpose flour

1 teaspoon baking powder

¹/4 teaspoon salt

¹/4 teaspoon freshly ground black pepper

¹/2 cup coarsely chopped walnuts,
    toasted (page 218)

¹/2 cup crumbled blue cheese

2 tablespoons cold unsalted butter,
    cut into 4 or 5 pieces

Scant ¹/2 cup milk

1. Put the flour, baking powder, salt, and pepper in a food processor and pulse to mix. Add the walnuts, blue cheese, and butter and pulse again, several times, until everything is broken into small pieces.

2. Remove the lid and add the milk to the processor. Pulse—in short bursts—until the dough pulls together in large clumps; don't let it make one big ball.

3. Turn the dough out onto the counter and knead once or twice. On a piece of plastic wrap, shape the dough into a log about 7¹/2 inches long and about 1³/4 inches in diameter. Wrap snugly in the plastic and refrigerate for at least 3 hours or overnight.

Nuts: To Toast or Not To Toast

Toasting is to nuts what roasting is to vegetables: a way to bring out and concentrate the essential flavors. The gain in flavor is significant, the effort minimal. When you toast nuts before adding them to quick breads, you can nearly always tell with the first bite. Nonetheless, I don't always toast nuts if I'm in a rush to get a bread in the oven: you still have to wait ten minutes for the oven to preheat, another ten to toast them. That's twenty minutes I sometimes don't have.

One good solution is to toast nuts ahead, so you have them when you need them. Once they're cooled, they can be bagged and frozen, ready to add to muffins or scones on a moment's notice. The procedure is pretty much the same for most nuts: just spread them on a large baking sheet, without crowding, and place them in a preheated 325 degree F oven. Set the timer for 10 minutes because if you forget them, they will quickly go from pleasantly toasted to unpleasantly burned. After 10 to 12 minutes, the fragrance of toasting nuts will start to fill the kitchen; that first evidence of aroma is usually an indication that they're done. Check the color: the nuts will have darkened by several shades. If they look like they could use a minute or two more, take them out anyway and cool them right on the sheet; the residual heat will finish them off. But if they seem to be toasted enough, immediately tilt them off the sheet and onto a plate or another baking sheet because the lingering heat in the pan can overcook the nuts. Let cool thoroughly, then bag and freeze. They will keep in the freezer for 2 to 3 months.

4. When ready to bake, preheat the oven to 375 degrees F. Very lightly grease a large baking sheet.

5. Remove the dough from the plastic wrap and slice into rounds ¹/₄ to ¹/₃ inch thick. Lay them on the prepared sheet, leaving a little space between them; they won't really spread. Bake for 15 minutes; they'll rise and get good and crusty and dark brown on the bottom. Either serve at once or transfer to a wire rack to cool.

MAKES ABOUT 2 DOZEN, GIVE OR TAKE

Salad of Fennel, Grapes, and Endive

I love this simple salad, just a few basics and no more dressing than a splash of this and a squeeze of that. If you want to get a little fancier, add a few thin slices of ripe pear and garnish the salad with crumbled blue cheese. Instead of endive, you can substitute the tender interior leaves of escarole.

1 bulb fennel	**Salt and freshly ground black pepper**
Handful of green or red grapes, halved lengthwise	**Few thin slices red onion**
	Fresh mint or parsley leaves
Juice of ¹/₂ small lemon	**1 small head curly endive, rinsed and**
Olive oil	**dried**
¹/₂ teaspoon honey	

1. Remove the tough outer leaves from the fennel bulb and cut the bulb in half, down through the root end. Slice the fennel thinly crosswise and transfer to a salad bowl. Add the grapes.

2. Pour the lemon juice over the fennel then dress very lightly with olive oil. Add the honey, salt and pepper, onion, and herbs. Toss well. Tear the greens into large bite-size pieces, add to the salad, and toss again; taste and correct the seasonings and dressing. Serve at once.

MAKES 4 TO 6 SERVINGS

SPICY BLACK BEAN CUISINE

Spicy Black Bean Soup
....
Cornmeal Rusks
....
Guacamole Dip with Jicama Strips
....

It never ceases to amaze me how many ingredients I can put into black bean soup. I mean, just count them—there are twenty-three. To be fair, I have tried making this with fewer ingredients, but as soon as I start subtracting, I can taste a very subtle change in the broth. Seasonings can be like that, almost like a stone wall at times. You leave out one or two key ones, and the whole thing comes tumbling down.

So: My apologies for the long ingredient list, but I hope it doesn't scare you away because this is a very good soup—and if a fellow can't make a good soup in twenty-three ingredients, he had better find other work, and fast.

This soup goes so well with corn-type breads I had a hard time picking just the right one. I finally came up with these rusks, very thin, crunchy biscuits with a seafaring past. Rusks used to be, more commonly, rock-hard biscuits that sailors would take to sea on long voyages. They would last forever, often longer than the sailors themselves. Our cornmeal rusks have little in common with those and I guarantee they won't last long after you pull them out of the oven.

If you've only heard of jicama, or gazed at it in the supermarket wondering whatever on earth one does with it, here's your answer: you use it for scooping up guacamole dip. It actually has a very crisp, radish-type texture, though I can't say the flavor is arresting. It's more subtle, so it's good with this dip since it doesn't compete with it. And if the kids just aren't buying, you can always whip out the celery.

Spicy Black Bean Soup

I make exceptions, but I think most bean soups taste best when you start with dried beans—instead of canned—and use some of the bean cooking water for the broth: the soup has a richer, fuller flavor. Make sure you pick over the beans before rinsing to remove any foreign objects. If there's time, this tastes best if allowed to sit for several hours—in a cool place or overnight in the fridge—before serving. This is a big batch, but if you're going to go to the trouble of cooking the dried beans, you might as well have leftovers because it freezes quite nicely.

1 pound dried black beans, picked over and rinsed

2 tablespoons ground cumin

1½ tablespoons mild chili powder

1 tablespoon ground coriander

⅛ to ¼ teaspoon cayenne pepper, to your taste

2 teaspoons unsweetened cocoa powder

1 tablespoon unbleached all-purpose flour

⅓ cup flavorless vegetable oil

2 large onions, chopped

1 large green bell pepper, seeded and chopped

2 to 3 cloves garlic, to your taste, minced

1 cup chopped canned tomatoes or tomato puree

2 cups V-8 or other tomato juice

1 teaspoon salt, plus more to taste

1 cup fresh or canned chopped green chiles

2 tablespoons tomato paste

1½ teaspoons dried oregano

1½ teaspoons dried basil

1 bay leaf

2 tablespoons firmly packed light brown sugar

Juice of 1 orange

1 tablespoon cider vinegar

3 tablespoons chopped fresh parsley leaves

1. Put the beans in a large pot and cover with plenty of cold water. Bring to a boil, then let boil for 2 minutes. Turn off the heat, cover, and let sit for 1 hour. Drain the beans and put them back in the pot with 4 quarts fresh cold water. Bring to a boil, then continue to cook at a low boil, partially covered, until tender, about 1 hour; do not undercook. Remove from the heat but don't drain.

2. Mix the spices, cocoa, and flour together in a small bowl and set aside.

3. Heat about half of the oil in a very large skillet over moderate heat. Add the onions and bell pepper and cook, stirring, about 8 minutes. Add the remaining oil to the skillet, then stir in the garlic and spice mixture. Lower the heat slightly and cook for 2 minutes, stirring often. Remove from the heat.

4. Ladle a cup or so of the bean water into the skillet, then scrape the contents of the skillet back into the beans. Stir in the tomatoes, tomato juice, salt, chiles, tomato paste, oregano, basil, bay leaf, and brown sugar.

5. Bring the soup to a simmer, then simmer, partially covered, stirring occasionally, for 30 minutes. Taste, adding more salt if needed. Add the orange juice and vinegar and simmer 10 minutes more. The soup should be soupy but thick. Serve hot, garnished with the fresh parsley.

MAKES 10 SERVINGS

Cornmeal Rusks

Rusks are the biscotti of breads, a twice-baked biscuit that's all about crust and a distant second about crumb, or interior. We accomplish this crusty trick quite simply; by baking them longer than seems right for a thin biscuit, about 20 minutes. There's a second way of doing this that's even more authentic, and that is rolling the biscuits a little thicker—say ¹/₂ inch—then baking them for 12 minutes; quickly splitting them with a fork; and continuing to bake another 10 or 12 minutes, until they're good and golden. It's your choice. This dough is quickly made in the food processor; just be sure not to overprocess.

1¹/₂ cups unbleached all-purpose flour

¹/₂ cup fine-ground yellow cornmeal

1 tablespoon sugar

2 teaspoons baking powder

³/₄ teaspoon salt

¹/₄ cup (¹/₂ stick) cold unsalted
   butter, cut into ¹/₄-inch pieces

Scant ²/₃ cup milk

---

1. Put the flour, cornmeal, sugar, baking powder, and salt in a food processor. Pulse the machine several times, to mix.

2. Remove the lid and scatter the butter over the dry ingredients. Replace the lid and pulse again repeatedly until the mixture resembles fine crumbs.

3. With the machine running, add the milk through the feed tube in one continuous 3- to 4-second stream. Stop the machine as soon as the dough starts to gather around the blade in big clumps.

4. Turn the dough out onto a large piece of floured plastic wrap. Knead gently 2 or 3 times. Slide the dough and plastic onto a baking sheet and place a second piece of plastic wrap on top. Using a rolling pin, carefully roll the dough out about ¹/₃ inch thick. Refrigerate the dough for 20 minutes. Preheat the oven to 400 degrees F.

5. Slide the refrigerated dough off the baking sheet but keep the sheet handy. Using any size biscuit cutter, cut the dough into rounds, placing the rounds on the ungreased baking sheet, leaving about 1 inch between them.

6. Bake the rusks until dark golden and crusty, 20 to 22 minutes. Transfer the rusks to a wire rack if not serving them right away. Alternatively, use the method described in the headnote for rolling and baking. These reheat beautifully.

MAKES 12 TO 16 RUSKS

Guacamole Dip
with Jicama Strips

The quality of any guacamole or guacamole dip rests squarely on the quality of the avocados: use unripe ones and you end up with a bland, watery mess. Use good ripe avocados, and you get the real deal—rich, full-flavored, and buttery. If you haven't tried jicama yet, this is your chance. And the kids might like it this way, too, teamed up with something familiar. Try not to mix this too much; it has a better texture and appearance if you don't.

- 4 perfectly ripe avocados
- 1/4 teaspoon salt, plus more to taste
- Fresh lemon juice to taste
- 1/2 cup chopped red onion
- 1 large ripe tomato, cored, seeded, and chopped
- 2 to 3 tablespoons chopped pickled jalapeño chiles, to your taste, drained
- 1/2 cup sour cream or plain yogurt
- 3 to 4 tablespoons chopped fresh parsley or cilantro leaves, to your taste
- Freshly ground black pepper to taste
- 1 large jicama

1. Halve and pit the avocados. Score the avocado flesh in a crisscross pattern, then scoop out the chunks and transfer them to a large bowl. Add the salt and 2 to 3 teaspoons of lemon juice. Mash gently to mix. Set aside.

2. In a medium-size bowl, blend the onion, tomato, jalapeños, sour cream or yogurt, parsley or cilantro, and pepper. Add to the avocado and mix briefly. Taste and see if the dip needs more salt or lemon juice. Transfer the dip to a smallish serving bowl.

3. Peel the jicama and cut it into 1/4-inch-thick slabs. Lay the slabs down and cut them into strips 1/2 inch wide. Arrange the jicama strips and guacamole dip on a serving platter. Cover with plastic wrap and refrigerate if not serving right away; remember, though, that guacamole will start to discolor the longer it is held.

MAKES 5 TO 6 SERVINGS

POP OVER FOR AN OLD-FASHIONED SOUP

Cream of Chicken and Mushroom Soup

....

Popovers

....

Roasted Beet and Onion Salad

....

Popovers always remind me of political campaigns: lots of hot air and drama, but very little substance. Still, there's a place for political campaigns and there's a place for popovers, too, on a menu like this where both the soup and the salad are pretty filling.

If you've never made them before, popovers are—literally—full of hot air. You pour a thin, unleavened crepe-like batter into muffin cups. It builds up steam in the oven and essentially inflates the popover. You end up with a very firm crust, a thin wall of bread just under it, and a hollow inside that, if deftly handled, can serve as a handy spoon until it falls apart or is eaten. I like to put butter and peach jam inside my popovers. There are, by the way, special popover pans, which I describe in the headnote to the recipe. They really do a superior job and if you're at all enamored of popovers I hope you'll get one.

Since popovers are an old-fashioned bread, I thought they'd go nicely with an old-fashioned soup such as this one, with chicken thighs simmered in a wine and mushroom broth. It's delicious and reminds me of something you might find at an inn in the French countryside. Even before you start the soup, get the beets roasting. It takes longer to cook beets this way, but the beauty is you don't have to tend them. The flavor and sugars concentrate rather than leaking out into the boiling water.

Cream of Chicken and Mushroom Soup

This is pretty much a variation of a favorite chicken and noodle dish I do, only this one has lots more broth and far fewer noodles. It's not a dish for the lite of appetite: it is hearty and rich and derives more than a little of its flavor from chicken fat and butter—in short, the sort of delicious soup that's become far too rare in these days of dietary correctness. After the chicken simmers in the winey broth, the meat is pulled from the bones and added back to the broth with a roux thickener. As the soup finishes simmering, you'll cook up some noodles—I like lemon-pepper linguine, but flat egg noodles are nice, too—and stir them into the soup for the last few minutes.

1/4 cup (1/2 stick) unsalted butter
4 skinless chicken thighs, rinsed and
    patted dry
Salt and freshly ground black pepper to
    taste
1 large onion, chopped
2 cups thinly sliced mushrooms
2 cloves garlic, minced
2 bay leaves

4 cups chicken stock
1 1/2 cups dry white wine
Several sprigs fresh thyme or
    1/2 teaspoon dried
1/4 cup unbleached all-purpose flour
3/4 cup milk, light cream, or half-and-
    half
2 ounces noodles (see headnote)

1. Melt 1 tablespoon of the butter in a heavy covered Dutch oven or casserole over medium-high heat. When the pan is hot, add the chicken and brown about 3 minutes on each side, lightly salting and peppering when the chicken goes in the pan. Remove the chicken to a platter.

2. Pour off all but about 2 tablespoons of the fat. Add the onion, mushrooms, and garlic and cook over moderate heat, stirring, for 5 minutes. Return the chicken to the pan. Add the bay leaves, stock, wine, thyme, and 1/2 teaspoon salt. Bring to a boil. Reduce the heat to moderately low, cover, then simmer gently for 30 minutes. Transfer the chicken to a plate. When the meat is cool enough to handle, tear off bite-size pieces and add them to the soup.

3. Bring a small pot of water to a boil for the noodles. Melt the remaining 3 tablespoons butter in a medium-size saucepan and stir in the flour. Cook over moderate heat, stirring, for 1 minute, then stir in the milk, cream, or half-and-half. When it thickens, gradually whisk in a couple of cups of the broth and stir until it thickens. Stir this mixture back into the soup pot. Taste the soup, adding salt and pepper as needed. Simmer, stirring over moderately low heat.

4. When the water boils, add the noodles and cook according to the package instructions. Drain and add the noodles to the soup. Simmer several more minutes, then serve.

MAKES 6 SERVINGS

Popovers

You get the best-looking popovers with lovely domed tops if you have a special popover pan with deep cups and nearly straight sides; if you like the way these come out, you might consider buying one. I've got a glazed pottery one that works beautifully. Custard cups work well, too, as does a muffin pan. These popovers are excellent with butter and jam or honey.

2 large eggs

1 cup milk

1 tablespoon vegetable oil

1 cup unbleached all-purpose flour

¼ teaspoon salt

1. Lightly oil 6 popover cups or custard cups, or about 8 muffin cups; set aside.

2. Whisk the eggs in a medium-size bowl until frothy. Whisk in the milk and oil. Sift the flour and salt over the liquid, then whisk rapidly to form a smooth batter. Let the batter rest for 10 minutes while you preheat the oven to 425 degrees F.

3. Whisk the batter again, then divide it evenly between the custard cups, filling each one about two thirds full.

4. Bake the popovers for 35 minutes—without opening the oven door—until they are tall and dark golden brown. After 35 minutes, you can open the door and check them. Immediately remove them from the oven and poke a hole in the top of each one with a knife, to let off some of the steam. Serve immediately.

CHEESE POPOVERS: Sprinkle 1 tablespoon grated cheddar cheese into each cup after you add the batter.

MAKES 6 TO 8 POPOVERS

Roasted Beet and Onion Salad

Roasting beets—or any vegetable, for that matter—produces a different result than boiling or steaming them. The flavors concentrate and become sweeter. And if you do it right, you get that crispy-charred flavor that everyone loves. Here we roast the beets and onions differently, for different effect: the beets wrapped in foil, which traps needed moisture, and the onions on a baking sheet, to get that crispy flavor I just mentioned. Combine the two, and you have one great salad. One nice surprise here is the brown sugar and balsamic vinaigrette, which gives the salad a pretty mahogany sheen. Another is a sugar–brown sugar mixture that gets sprinkled on top of the salad. If you're inclined, this sweetness tastes great with some crumbled crisp-cooked bacon for garnish.

SALAD

6 medium-size beets, scrubbed

2 large onions, halved

1 1/2 tablespoons olive oil

Salt and freshly ground black pepper
  to taste

BROWN SUGAR VINAIGRETTE

2 1/2 tablespoons balsamic vinegar

1 tablespoon firmly packed light
  brown sugar

1 1/2 tablespoons olive oil or
  vegetable oil

ASSEMBLY

4 to 6 ounces baby spinach or other
  greens (some bitter greens are fine),
  washed well and patted dry

2 teaspoons firmly packed light brown
  sugar mixed with 2 teaspoons
  granulated sugar, for garnish

4 to 6 slices bacon (optional), to
  your taste, crisp-cooked, drained
  on paper towels, and crumbled

1. Preheat the oven to 375 degrees F. Tear off a large sheet of aluminum foil and wrap the beets in it, tightly sealed. Place in the oven and roast until tender, about 1 1/2 hours. (Leave room in the oven; the onions will join the beets shortly.)

2. Cut each half onion into 4 or 5 sections, cutting from the outer surface toward the center of the onion. Place the onions in a medium-size bowl. Add the olive oil and toss well to coat with the oil. Spread the onions on a lightly oiled baking sheet; salt and pepper lightly. Bake until they're tender and some of them are crispy-charred, 45 to 50 minutes. Transfer the onions to a large salad bowl.

3. When the beets are done, remove the packet from the oven and open to let heat escape. When cool enough to handle, rub off the skins and slice the beets thinly. Add the beets to the onions.

4. To make the vinaigrette, heat the vinegar and brown sugar in a small saucepan just long enough to melt the sugar. Whisk in the oil. Pour the dressing over the vegetables and toss well to coat evenly. Set aside for 10 minutes.

5. Add the greens to the salad bowl and toss again to coat with the dressing. Arrange the salad on individual salad plates, sprinkling a little of the sugar mixture over each one. Sprinkle with bacon, if desired.

MAKES 5 TO 6 SERVINGS

A BISQUE BUILT FOR TWO

Crab and Scallop Bisque
....
Quick Parmesan Bread Sticks
....
Baby Spinach and Fennel Salad
....

Of course it might be any two, but what I had in mind was an intimate dinner for just you and the one you love most, or perhaps the one you're hoping to some day love most. There are, after all, less effective ways to woo your lover than through his or her stomach. Aren't the connections between food, love, and the romantic arts well established? When Valentine's Day rolls around, you bring your love a box of chocolates, don't you? And isn't the language of food the language of love? You're his little pumpkin; he's your dumpling. Or maybe even your studmuffin. When French chefs make crepes and they heat up the pan and rub melted butter in it, they say they're "getting the pan in the mood."

Indeed, the right food eaten in the right circumstances can go a long way in setting the mood for a little romance. I can't do much about the circumstances, but I can help you with the menu, a little something you'd serve, perhaps, on Valentine's Day. It won't take you half the day to put it together. And the portions are couple size, so you won't be eating leftovers for the next three weeks.

To start things off we have crab and scallop bisque. The coast has always felt like a very romantic place to me, so it's no surprise I would feature a seafood soup. If you don't live near the seashore, perhaps the aroma will remind you of a trip there with your beloved, when you walked the beach in bare feet, watched a glorious sunset, and kissed under the rising moon.

The soup is perfect with the delicately crunchy bread sticks, which—because they're so long—are in turn perfect for sharing across the dinner table: you give him a bite of yours, and he reciprocates. And when you send him home at the end of the evening—*if* you send him home at the end of the evening—they'll be a few extras to send along to remind him of you the next day.

The salad is light. Too much heavy food dulls our appetite for romance, so we end with a few crisp greens tossed in the lightest of dressings, just olive oil and lemon juice. There's a little fennel, too, to keep your breath fresh, sweet, and kissable.

Crab and Scallop Bisque

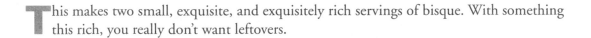

This makes two small, exquisite, and exquisitely rich servings of bisque. With something this rich, you really don't want leftovers.

2 tablespoons unsalted butter

1 shallot, minced

3/4 cup diced fresh tomato

1/3 pound large (sea) scallops

2 1/2 tablespoons dry sherry

1/2 cup bottled clam juice

Scant 1/4 teaspoon salt

2/3 cup heavy cream

3 ounces lump crabmeat, picked over
    for cartilage and shells

Freshly ground black pepper to taste

1. Melt the butter in a small saucepan over low heat. Stir in the shallot, cover the pan, and sweat for 3 to 4 minutes. Add the tomato, increase the heat slightly, and cook briefly, uncovered, until it starts to get saucy.

2. Stir the scallops, sherry, clam juice, and salt into the pan. Cover tightly and stew the scallops over moderate heat until they're done—they should turn from opaque to white all the way through—5 to 7 minutes. Stir in the cream, heating it briefly.

3. Transfer the scallops and a little of the broth to a food processor. Process until fairly smooth, leaving just a little texture. Add the puree back to the soup, stir in the crabmeat, and season with pepper. Heat the soup almost to the boiling point, then serve right away.

MAKES 2 SERVINGS

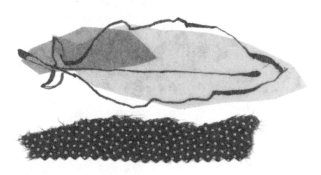

Quick Parmesan Bread Sticks

Most bread sticks are made with a yeast dough, but you can relax because this one isn't. Instead, I use a modified biscuit dough that's mixed entirely in the food processor so you can breeze through these and get on with your life. In your preparations, figure in an extra hour so the dough has time to chill. Actually, it's great if you make these earlier in the day and just leave them out on a rack, unwrapped; they get crunchier that way.

1¼ cups unbleached all-purpose flour

2 tablespoons semolina flour or fine-
  ground yellow cornmeal

½ cup finely grated Parmesan cheese

1½ teaspoons baking powder

¼ teaspoon salt

½ teaspoon dried basil

⅛ teaspoon freshly ground black
  pepper

2 tablespoons cold unsalted butter,
  cut into ¼-inch pieces

1 tablespoon olive oil

⅓ cup milk

1 tablespoon water

1. Put the flour, semolina or cornmeal, cheese, baking powder, salt, basil, and pepper in a food processor. Pulse the machine several times, to mix.

2. Remove the lid and add the butter and olive oil; replace the lid. Pulse the machine several times, until the butter is broken into fine bits.

3. Put the milk and water in a measuring cup. With the machine running, pour the liquid through the feed tube in a continuous 3- to 4-second stream. When all the liquid is added, start pulsing the machine just until the dough forms large clumps without any traces of flour; you don't want the dough to ball up around the blade.

4. Empty the dough onto your work counter. Pack it together and knead it twice. On a large piece of plastic wrap, pat the dough into a rectangle a little more than ½ inch thick. Wrap the dough in the plastic and refrigerate for 1 hour.

5. Preheat the oven to 425 degrees F and get out a large baking sheet.

6. On a sheet of wax paper, roll the dough out with a floured rolling pin into a rectangle about ⅓ inch thick, 12 inches long, and 5 inches wide. Using a sharp knife or pizza cutter, cut the dough into narrow strips not quite ½ inch wide. Put one of the strips in front of you on the counter and roll the ends under your fingers in opposite directions. Or simply twist the ends in opposite directions. Transfer these twisted sticks to the ungreased baking sheet, leaving about 1 inch between them.

7. Bake the bread sticks until they're a rich golden color, 15 to 16 minutes. Carefully transfer them to a wire rack—they're a little fragile—and let cool.

MAKES 10 TO 12 BREAD STICKS

A Gift of Food

These bread sticks would make a particularly nice gift for someone at the holidays or anytime. They're great to serve at parties, and what host or hostess wouldn't appreciate getting a cellophane bag of them with a neat bow tied around the middle? Do be careful, though, and handle them gently so they don't break. For gift giving, you might consider making them half as long so they're not as prone to breakage.

While we're on the subject, why not consider giving an entire meal of soup, bread, and salad to a family member or friend? You can prepare the entire meal, putting the soup in a handsome jar, the bread in clear cellophane bags; salads are a little trickier because they need to be kept fresh. The marinated vegetables (page 41) are one good choice. Or, instead of giving the actual meal on the spot, you can present a certificate for one, to be redeemed later: the recipient picks the day, you deliver the goods. Who wouldn't want such a thoughtful gift?

Baby Spinach and
Fennel Salad

Y ou will have to judge the exact amount of greens you'll need for the two of you. You can use either baby spinach or mesclun mix, whichever looks better, or some combination of specialty greens. If you want to add a splash of color, a small amount of thinly sliced radicchio would look good in the salad, too.

1 fennel bulb

About 4 ounces baby spinach or other
    greens (see headnote)

Small handful fresh mint leaves

2 to 3 teaspoons olive oil, to your taste

1 to 1½ teaspoons lemon juice,
    to your taste

Small block Parmesan cheese

Freshly ground black pepper to taste

1. Slice off the upper stalks of the fennel just below where they meet the bulb. Trim the bottom of the bulb, peel off the tough outer layers, and halve the bulb lengthwise. Cut one half of the bulb crosswise into very thin slices and set them aside.

2. Put the greens in a salad bowl. Tear the mint leaves into pieces and scatter them and the sliced fennel over the top. Drizzle the olive oil and lemon juice over the greens and toss well to coat evenly.

3. Divide the salad on individual salad plates. Using a vegetable peeler, shave thin strips of Parmesan over each salad and serve at once, passing the pepper at the table.

MAKES 2 SERVINGS

A SALUTE TO TEXAS

Cream of Jalapeño Soup

....

Double Corn Bread

....

Leftover Steak Salad with
Parmesan Peppercorn Ranch Dressing

....

If you've ever been to Texas, or have the good fortune to live there, then you know that Texans don't believe in understatement. Everything they do in Texas is big, bold, and grand. The steaks you buy aren't the size of a credit card and they don't come served in the middle of fancy greens. They hang off the side of the plate, and you get a fist-size baked potato on the side, mounded with sour cream and butter. Nor has anyone ever described native Texas cuisine as subtle. The flavors all but jump off your plate and into your mouth. Even Texas cooks are bigger than life. One of my good chef friends is Grady Spears, formerly chef at Fort Worth's Reata restaurant. He's about 6 foot 5 and that's not counting with his cowboy hat on.

Actually, it was Grady who inspired the cream of jalapeño soup on this menu. A while back, I was in Grady's restaurant kitchen, when I removed the lid from this incredibly thick, creamy, and good-smelling stuff that at first looked like a sauce. I immediately grabbed a spoon and whisked some into my mouth. It was sensational. He told me this was the restaurant's favorite soup recipe by a long shot and that he got dozens of requests for the recipe every week. My version is not quite so rich as Grady's and I've added a little cheese to mine.

What do you put on salad in Texas? *Ranch* dressing, of course. It's cool, creamy, and a refreshing balance to some of the big flavors you're often up against in the same meal. Since this is serious steak country, I thought it only appropriate to add some leftover steak to the salad. It might be worth grilling an extra one next time you're at it, so you have it for the salad. Then there's the cornbread that has a double dose of corn by way of the added kernels. Cut it into Texas-size slabs, dust off your cowboy boots, kick back, and enjoy the meal.

Cream of Jalapeño Soup

This is a lot less rich than the way my friend Grady makes it: his version calls for *eight* cups of heavy cream, to my two cups. Still, this is rich enough. Small portions are appropriate.

2 tablespoons unsalted butter

4 jalapeño chiles, seeded and finely chopped

1 large red onion, finely chopped

3 to 4 cloves garlic, to your taste, minced

2 large ripe tomatoes, cored and well chopped

1 ripe avocado

2 cups heavy cream

1 cup strong chicken stock

Large handful fresh parsley or cilantro leaves

1/2 to 3/4 teaspoon salt, or more to taste

Freshly ground black pepper to taste

1 cup grated sharp cheddar cheese

1. Melt the butter in a large saucepan or medium-size soup pot over moderate heat. Add the jalapeños, onion, and garlic and cook, stirring, for 8 to 9 minutes. Stir in the tomatoes and continue to cook, stirring occasionally, until it starts to form a sauce, about 7 minutes.

2. While the vegetables cook, cut the avocado in half, remove the pit, and score the flesh of the avocado down to the skin, then scoop the flesh out and into a small bowl. Break it up coarsely with a fork and add it to the vegetables. Heat briefly, then stir in the heavy cream, chicken stock, parsley or cilantro, salt, and pepper.

3. Simmer—do not boil—the soup for about 5 minutes, stirring occasionally, until heated through, stirring in the cheese at the very end, off the heat. Taste once before serving, adjusting the salt and pepper as needed.

MAKES 5 SERVINGS

Double Corn Bread

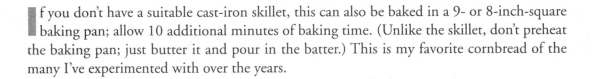

If you don't have a suitable cast-iron skillet, this can also be baked in a 9- or 8-inch-square baking pan; allow 10 additional minutes of baking time. (Unlike the skillet, don't preheat the baking pan; just butter it and pour in the batter.) This is my favorite cornbread of the many I've experimented with over the years.

¼ cup (½ stick) unsalted butter	1 teaspoon salt
1½ cups unbleached all-purpose flour	2 large eggs, lightly beaten
1 cup fine-ground yellow cornmeal	1 cup buttermilk
2 tablespoons sugar	1 cup milk
1½ teaspoons baking powder	1 cup corn kernels, fresh or frozen
½ teaspoon baking soda	and thawed

1. Preheat the oven to 400 degrees F. Put the butter in a 10-inch cast-iron skillet and place it in the preheating oven until the butter has melted. Swirl the pan to coat the bottom and sides (remember, the handle is *hot*), pouring all but a little of the butter into a medium-size bowl.

2. Sift the dry ingredients into a large bowl. In the medium-size bowl, whisk the eggs into the buttermilk, milk, and melted butter. Make a well in the center of the dry ingredients, add the liquid, and stir with a wooden spoon just until the batter is evenly blended. Stir in the corn kernels.

3. Scrape the batter into the hot pan and bake until the top is golden and springy to the touch, about 30 minutes. Let cool in the pan for about 10 minutes before slicing.

MAKES 8 SERVINGS

Leftover Steak Salad with Parmesan Peppercorn Ranch Dressing

Here's a novel use for leftover steak: slicing it very thin and serving it in this Texas-style chef's salad.

SALAD

8 to 10 ounces leftover steak, trimmed
   of fat and very thinly sliced

Chili powder to taste

1 head iceberg lettuce

2 large ripe tomatoes, cored and cut into
   thin wedges

1 or 2 ripe avocados, to your taste,
   halved and pitted

**PARMESAN PEPPERCORN
RANCH DRESSING**

2/3 cup buttermilk

2/3 cup sour cream

2/3 cup mayonnaise

1 medium-size red onion, finely chopped

1/2 cup finely grated Parmesan cheese

3 cloves garlic, minced

2 to 3 tablespoons chopped fresh
   parsley leaves, to your taste

Freshly ground black pepper, preferably
   coarsely ground, to taste

1. Put the steak in a small bowl and dust it with a little bit of chili powder—several good-size pinches will do; set aside.

2. To assemble the salad, core the lettuce and cut into a number of thin wedges. Arrange 3 wedges in a fan-shaped pattern on each individual salad plate, leaving a little room between the wedges. Place a few tomato wedges in one of the spaces.

3. Score the flesh of the avocado down to the skin. Scoop out the flesh and scatter the avocado dice in the other space between the wedges.

4. Make the dressing by blending all of the dressing ingredients together in a medium-size bowl. Either spoon dressing over each salad, or pass the dressing at the table.

MAKES 5 TO 6 SERVINGS

FLATBREAD AND CURRIED SOUP

Curried Vegetable Soup

....

Chapatis

....

Papaya and Cucumber Chutney Salad

....

Baker sorts will immediately be drawn to the fun and challenge of making these chapatis, the flatbreads that are so common to Indian feasts. As a baker sort myself, I think I can say with some certainty that most of us love a good rolling challenge. There's something primal and satisfying about taking a lump of dough and rolling it thin—paper thin if necessary. It doesn't matter if it's a pie crust, cracker, tortilla, or chapati. Each has its little quirks and knowing how to work with them is half of the fun.

And if you aren't a bread maker? Should you pass this menu by? Hardly. There's a fine curry soup here and you'd miss it if you did. If you want, just choose another bread from this book or substitute flour tortillas, heated and brushed with melted butter. Not to mention there's a sweet-tart and refreshing cucumber fruit salad that provides a cooling counterpart to the warm and spicy curry soup.

Curried Vegetable Soup

This is one of those soups I never seem to make the same way twice, probably because there's no reason to, since it tastes great with almost any mix of vegetables. I might use more cauliflower, more potatoes, or more carrots in place of something else. Or add some broccoli or a little dish of leftover vegetables from the fridge. The broth has good body and, unlike some soups made with sour cream, you don't have to worry about it curdling if it comes to a low boil: mixing the flour with the sour cream before blending it into the soup keeps the sour cream from breaking. Just don't bring the soup to a rolling boil.

2 tablespoons vegetable oil

1 large onion, chopped

1 clove garlic, minced

4 teaspoons curry powder

3 to 4 cups small cauliflower florets, to your taste

1 large all-purpose potato, peeled and cut into 1/2-inch dice

1 cup frozen peas

4 cups chicken or vegetable stock

1/2 cup canned crushed tomatoes or tomato puree

3/4 teaspoon salt

1/2 cup sour cream

3 tablespoons unbleached all-purpose flour

1. Heat the oil in a medium-size soup pot over moderate heat. Add the onion and cook, stirring, until translucent, 8 to 9 minutes. Stir in the garlic and curry powder and cook over low heat, stirring, for 1 minute.

2. Add the vegetables, stock, tomatoes, and salt, bring to a boil, reduce the heat to moderately low, and cover. Simmer just until the vegetables are tender, 10 to 12 minutes.

3. While the vegetables cook, whisk the sour cream and flour together in a small bowl. Add a ladleful of the broth to the mixture and whisk again. When the vegetables are tender, stir the sour cream mixture into the soup. Simmer, stirring often, for 8 to 10 minutes; don't worry if there are small lumps of flour in the soup—they should cook out. Briefly whisking the broth might help. Taste the soup before serving, adding a bit more salt if necessary.

MAKES 5 TO 6 SERVINGS

Chapatis

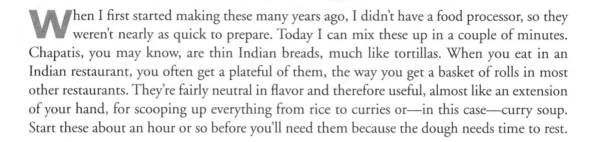

When I first started making these many years ago, I didn't have a food processor, so they weren't nearly as quick to prepare. Today I can mix these up in a couple of minutes. Chapatis, you may know, are thin Indian breads, much like tortillas. When you eat in an Indian restaurant, you often get a plateful of them, the way you get a basket of rolls in most other restaurants. They're fairly neutral in flavor and therefore useful, almost like an extension of your hand, for scooping up everything from rice to curries or—in this case—curry soup. Start these about an hour or so before you'll need them because the dough needs time to rest.

---

2 cups fine-ground whole wheat flour
    (not coarsely ground)
½ cup unbleached all-purpose flour
¼ teaspoon salt

¾ cup plus 2 tablespoons lukewarm
    water
Melted butter, for brushing on the
    chapatis

---

1. Put the flours and salt in a food processor and pulse, to mix. With the machine running, add the water in a stream, continuing to run the processor until the dough is no longer dry looking and starts to ball up around the blade.

2. Dump the dough onto a lightly floured work surface and knead it for about 2 minutes into a soft ball. Wrap the dough in plastic wrap and leave at room temperature for 1 to 2 hours.

3. Divide the dough into 12 pieces, shaping each one into a little ball. Cover and let rest for 10 minutes. Put a heavy, preferably cast-iron, skillet on the burner.

4. Keeping the rest of the balls covered, flatten one of them into a pancake, then roll it, on a lightly floured work surface, into a circle 7 inches in diameter. Since the dough is likely to be a little springy, it works best to be rolling 2 or 3 of them simultaneously, switching from one to the other to minimize the springiness.

5. Get the skillet quite hot, then lay one of the chapatis in it. Within 30 to 45 seconds it will start to blister and puff. Let it puff somewhat, but occasionally push it back down with a metal spatula. Cook on the first side for no more than about 45 seconds—there will be little burn marks here and there underneath—then flip and cook on the other side for a little less time. As soon as they come off the heat, brush with a little melted butter.

6. Serve the chapatis at once, or stack them on an ovenproof plate, cover with aluminum foil, and keep warm in a low oven until ready to serve.

MAKES 12 BREADS, ABOUT 6 SERVINGS

Papaya and
Cucumber Chutney Salad

This is like a chutney, only there's more of it and everything is cut bigger. You can use fresh papaya, but, for simplicity's sake, quality, and ease of handling, I like both the papaya and mango slices you can now find, in jars, in the produce section of most supermarkets.

2 large cucumbers, peeled, halved,
  seeded, and diced
2 cups peeled and seeded papaya cut
  into large dice
1 small, just ripe banana, peeled and cut
  into large dice
1¹/₂ tablespoons sugar
1¹/₂ tablespoons fresh lemon juice

1¹/₂ tablespoons fresh lime juice
1 to 2 teaspoons peeled and minced
  fresh ginger, to your taste
1 to 2 tablespoons chopped fresh
  cilantro or parsley leaves, to your
  taste
Pinch of salt

Combine all of the ingredients in a medium-size bowl and toss gently, to mix. Cover with plastic wrap and refrigerate for 15 minutes before serving, stirring once or twice.

MAKES 6 SERVINGS

SQUARE MEAL, ROUND PLEASURES

American Meatball Soup

. . . .

Sesame-Onion Crescent Rolls

. . . .

Buttermilk Slaw

. . . .

I've never looked into the matter of meatballs, at least not enough to know whether they are truly an Italian creation, an American invention, or just where they might have come from. Even if they are Italian in origin, so assimilated have meatballs become in American culture and cuisine that they certainly *feel* like American food. We sure eat enough of them: on spaghetti, of course; on subs; at weddings and parties, impaled on the ends of toothpicks. Meatballs, as the younger set might put it, rule.

They rule on this menu, too, supported by two other very important players: coleslaw and dinner rolls. I enjoy coleslaw with my meat and I think it makes a cool and refreshing balance to the heartiness of the beef. I also like the contrast between the comforting softness of the soup and the crunch of the slaw.

For those with the inclination, these sesame dinner rolls are perfect. You can dunk them in the broth, tuck butter between the swirls, and pull them apart to scoop up the last bits of soup. If you'd rather not make a yeast bread, I'd suggest one of the biscuits in this book. Just don't skip the meatball soup; it brings whole new meaning to the phrase "global warming."

American Meatball Soup

I love this soup. It's brothy, meaty, and just about as soul-satisfying as soup gets. And it's not that involved, either: a bit of chopping and mixing for the meatballs, but the broth couldn't be simpler to assemble. The only fiddling I ever do with this recipe, to give it a little more substance, is to cook a little pasta on the side; small shells are nice—about $1/2$ cup dried would be plenty—and add them to the soup for the last couple of minutes.

MEATBALLS

$3/4$ cup fine fresh bread crumbs

$1/2$ cup freshly grated Parmesan cheese

$1/4$ cup finely chopped onion

2 tablespoons chopped fresh parsley
   leaves

2 cloves garlic, finely chopped

1 teaspoon dried basil

$1/2$ teaspoon dried oregano

1 large egg, lightly beaten

$3/4$ pound lean ground beef

$1/4$ teaspoon salt

$1/4$ teaspoon freshly ground black pepper

BROTH AND ASSEMBLY

2 tablespoons olive oil

1 medium-size onion, chopped

1 rib celery, chopped

1 small green bell pepper, seeded and
   chopped

2 cloves garlic, minced

4 cups beef stock

$1^1/2$ cups canned crushed tomatoes in
   puree

$1/4$ teaspoon salt

Freshly ground black pepper to taste

Freshly grated Parmesan cheese, for
   garnish

1. To make the meatballs, mix the bread crumbs, Parmesan, onion, parsley, garlic, and herbs together in a large bowl. Pour the egg over the mixture and mix it together lightly with a fork. Add the ground beef, salt, and pepper and mix together with your hands to blend. Form into meatballs 1 to $1^1/4$ inches in diameter and place them on a plate. Cover with plastic wrap and refrigerate until needed.

2. Heat the olive oil in a medium-size soup pot or large saucepan over moderate heat. Add the vegetables and cook, stirring, until the onion is translucent, about 9 minutes. Stir in the garlic and cook, stirring, for 30 seconds. Stir in the remaining ingredients and bring to a simmer.

3. Drop the meatballs into the simmering broth. Cook at a gentle simmer until there's no pink meat at the center of the meatballs, about 10 to 13 minutes. Serve piping hot, passing Parmesan cheese at the table.

MAKES 6 SERVINGS

Sesame-Onion Crescent Rolls

The fun of making rolls is in the handwork. You don't make a recipe like this to get dinner on the table quickly; you make it for the sheer tactile pleasures associated with kneading, shaping, cutting, folding, or stacking—whatever the particular handwork the rolls require. In this case, it's a little knead-and-roll action: first, you roll the dough out into a circle and cover it with sautéed onions; next, cut the dough into wedges; then, roll up those wedges and shape them into crescents. Let rise, sprinkle with sesame seeds, and into the oven they go. Have plenty of soft butter on the table because you can't serve good ol' American dinner rolls with a crock of olive oil.

1 cup warm water (105 to 115 degrees F)

2 teaspoons (1 packet) active dry yeast

1 cup lukewarm milk

1 large egg

1 tablespoon sugar

About 5 cups unbleached all-purpose flour

2 tablespoons olive or vegetable oil

2½ teaspoons salt

3 tablespoons unsalted butter

3 cups finely chopped onions

Fine-ground yellow cornmeal or semolina, for dusting

1 large egg beaten with 1 tablespoon milk, for glaze

2 tablespoons sesame seeds

1. Pour ¼ cup of the warm water into a small bowl. Sprinkle the yeast over it and stir to blend. Let stand for 5 minutes. In a large bowl, whisk the remaining ¾ cup water, milk, egg, and sugar together. Stir in the dissolved yeast. Add 3 cups of the flour and stir vigorously with a wooden spoon for 100 strokes. Cover the bowl with plastic wrap and let rest for 15 minutes.

2. Stir the oil and salt into the batter. Using a wooden spoon, mix in enough of the remaining flour, ½ cup at a time, to make a firm, fairly smooth dough. Turn the dough out onto a floured work surface and knead with floured hands until smooth and elastic, about 10 minutes, adding more flour as necessary to keep the dough from sticking. Place the dough in an oiled bowl, turning the dough to coat the entire surface with oil. Cover with plastic wrap and set aside in a warm, draft-free spot until doubled in bulk, about 1½ hours.

3. While the dough rises, melt the butter in a large skillet over moderate heat. Add the onions and cook, stirring, until golden, about 15 minutes. Set aside.

4. Punch the dough down. Turn it out onto a floured work surface and cut in half. Knead each half into a ball, then loosely cover with plastic wrap; let rest for 10 minutes. Lightly oil 2 large baking sheets and dust them with cornmeal or semolina. Set aside.

5. Using a floured rolling pin, roll 1 ball of dough out into a 14-inch round. Spread half of the onions over the dough circle, leaving a 1-inch border. Cut the dough into 8 pieces as you would a pie. Starting at the wide end of the wedge, roll it toward the point. Place the roll on the prepared baking sheet, seam (or point) facing down; turn the ends downward, shaping into an exaggerated crescent shape. Repeat for the remaining rolls and the other half of the dough. Cover very loosely with plastic wrap, then let the rolls rise in a warm, draft-free spot until nearly doubled in bulk, about 30 minutes.

6. Meanwhile, position 1 rack in the center and 1 rack in the top third of the oven. Preheat the oven to 375 degrees F.

7. Brush the rolls with the egg glaze. Sprinkle with the sesame seeds. Bake until the rolls are golden and sound hollow when tapped on the bottom, 25 to 30 minutes, changing the position of the sheets after 15 minutes. Serve at once or transfer the rolls to a wire rack and let cool.

MAKES 16 ROLLS

Buttermilk Slaw

There's so much you can do with a good slaw. I like it on top of burgers and with sandwiches, roast chicken, and other meat dishes. It's great for potlucks, of course. I've no doubt you'll get some mileage out of this recipe. Something to remember about buttermilk, especially when you're using it raw in a recipe like this: buy the cultured variety, the kind that's inoculated with a bacterial culture, rather than the acidified variety. The former has a smoother flavor and you can taste the difference. Do slice the cabbages as thinly as possible; it helps to sharpen your knife first. Thick slices of raw cabbage just aren't that much fun to eat.

8 cups cored and thinly sliced green cabbage
2 cups cored and thinly sliced red cabbage
3/4 cup peeled and grated carrots
1/4 cup minced red onion
2 tablespoons minced fresh parsley leaves

2/3 cup chilled buttermilk
1/2 cup mayonnaise
1 teaspoon Dijon mustard
1 teaspoon sugar
1/2 teaspoon celery seeds
Salt and freshly ground black pepper to taste

Mix the cabbages, carrots, onion, and parsley together in a large bowl. In a small bowl, whisk the buttermilk, mayonnaise, mustard, sugar, and celery seeds together, to blend. Pour the dressing over the cabbage mixture and toss to blend well. Season with salt and pepper. Cover with plastic wrap and chill at least an hour before serving.

MAKES 6 SERVINGS

I ALMOST FOCACCIA THIS ITALIAN MENU

Italian Spinach Rice Soup

Roasted Tomato Focaccia

Cucumbers Vinaigrette

In addition to his big feet and height, my younger son Sam has something else in common with his father: a corny sense of humor. As you might have gleaned from reading the menu heading, some of it revolves around the featured bread on this menu, focaccia. Sam and I play catch with focaccia puns all the time. I might tell him that I was planning to make this, his favorite bread, on Wednesday "but I focaccia you weren't going to be here." Or he'll smell this baking in the oven and say, "I'll bet you focaccia put extra garlic on mine." And whenever we do this, he and I will erupt in great gales of laughter and my other kids will roll their eyes heavenward and say a little prayer that their father will one day grow up.

Focaccia, you're probably aware by now, is a pizza-like bread, though generally thicker than pizza and not (or barely) sauced. Too, they sometimes have big pieces of cooked vegetables on them. My own version has roasted tomatoes. Roasting does great things to good tomatoes and good things to lesser ones, so this is a bread you can make successfully with less-than-perfectly-ripe tomatoes. Yes, you do have to make a yeast bread. But the good news is you can do it right in the food processor.

There are two other things on this menu that my son Sam is crazy about: the meatless Italian rice soup and the cucumbers vinaigrette. Other than a simple, tossed-together green salad, I think this cucumber dish is the salad we eat most often. It's fast, easy, and nice and light for occasions like this when the rest of the menu is substantial.

Oh, yes. There was one other thing I wanted to tell you about the soup, but I'm afraid I focaccia what it was.

Italian Spinach Rice Soup

This minestrone-like soup packs a lot of flavor; it's one of my favorite meatless soups and all my kids love it. As the soup simmers, the rice releases its starch and adds just the right amount of body to the broth. If you'd rather, substitute Swiss chard for the spinach.

2½ tablespoons olive oil

1 medium-size zucchini, ends trimmed and cut into ½-inch dice

1 rib celery, thinly sliced

2 cloves garlic, minced

Salt to taste

6 cups vegetable stock

2 tablespoons chopped fresh parsley leaves

1 bay leaf

1 teaspoon dried basil

1 large carrot, peeled and grated

¾ cup Arborio rice

Freshly ground black pepper to taste

6 to 8 ounces fresh spinach, to your taste, rinsed well and stems removed

1 cup canned crushed tomatoes in puree

Freshly grated Parmesan cheese, for garnish

1. Heat the olive oil in a large enameled soup pot over moderate heat. Add the zucchini, celery, and garlic; salt lightly and stir to coat with the oil. Cover tightly and steam-sauté the vegetables for 10 minutes.

2. After 10 minutes, add the stock, 1 teaspoon salt, herbs, carrot, and rice and season with pepper. Increase the heat and bring the soup to a boil. Reduce the heat to low, cover tightly, and simmer soup for 10 minutes without disturbing.

3. Chop the spinach coarsely. After 10 minutes, stir the spinach and tomatoes into the soup. Cover tightly and simmer for 12 minutes without disturbing. Serve hot, passing the cheese at the table.

MAKES 6 TO 7 SERVINGS

Roasted Tomato Focaccia

When we're talking about flatbread, the difference between putting a raw tomato on top versus a roasted one is much like the difference between a wimpy handshake and a firm one: it's essentially the same gesture, but the former makes one heck of a better (sweeter, concentrated, more tomatoey) impression. Don't overestimate the difficulty of roasting tomatoes, if it's something you've never tried; it takes all of 3 minutes to get them into the oven. You take them out 75 minutes later. While they're roasting, you can make the dough. That's the push-button food-processor dough that's so easy to do you'll be making it in your sleep. I love this so much I could easily have included it in a dozen of the menus in this book.

1 recipe dough for Push-Button Rosemary Flatbread (page 151)	¼ to ⅓ cup olive oil, to your taste and as needed
5 medium-size ripe tomatoes, cored, seeded, and halved crosswise	1 tablespoon chopped fresh basil leaves
Salt and freshly ground black pepper to taste	¼ cup freshly grated Parmesan cheese (optional)

1. Follow the instructions for making the dough and getting it onto the baking sheet, steps 1 through 4 on page 151.

2. While the dough rises, roast the tomatoes. Preheat the oven to 325 degrees F. Line a large jelly-roll pan with aluminum foil and oil the foil. Put the tomatoes on the sheet, flat sides facing up. Salt and pepper the tomatoes lightly and drizzle them with the olive oil. Roast for 60 to 75 minutes; when done, they should be somewhat shrunken, about half their former size. Remove from the oven and increase the oven temperature to 400 degrees F.

3. By now—or shortly—your dough should be resting on the baking sheet. After the 15-minute rest, with oiled fingers, press and pat the dough into a 10½-inch circle. Roll up the edge just slightly, to create an upstanding rope-like perimeter. Cover the dough and let rest for 20 minutes.

4. Place the tomato halves on top of the dough inside the perimeter. You will probably get one in the center and the rest snugly positioned around it. Brush the edge of the dough with olive oil and drizzle more oil over the tomatoes.

5. Bake the focaccia until nicely browned, 25 to 30 minutes. Transfer to a wire rack and sprinkle on the basil and cheese immediately, if using. Let cool briefly before slicing.

MAKES 6 TO 8 SERVINGS

Cucumbers Vinaigrette

It never ceases to amaze me what a big impression this simple little salad makes. I often make the mistake of trying to dress it up with extras, like halved cherry tomatoes, garlic, or some other perfectly reasonable flourish, but it's never quite the same when I do, so take that under advisement. It's the ideal light and crunchy companion to many pasta meals as well.

3 large cucumbers, peeled

1 medium-size red onion, halved and thinly sliced into half moons

1 teaspoon sugar

Salt and freshly ground black pepper to taste

2 tablespoons vegetable or olive oil

2 tablespoons red wine vinegar

1 tablespoon Dijon mustard

1 to 2 teaspoons chopped fresh dill or parsley leaves, to your taste

1. Quarter the cucumbers lengthwise and scrape out the seeds. Cut the cukes into 1/4-inch-thick slices and place in a large bowl with the sliced onion. Sprinkle with the sugar and salt—don't skimp too much—and pepper as needed. Set aside for 10 minutes.

2. Whisk the oil, vinegar, mustard, and dill or parsley together in a small bowl. Pour the dressing over the cucumbers and onions and toss well to coat evenly. Serve immediately, or cover and refrigerate until serving, up to several hours.

MAKES 6 SERVINGS

Index